Palgrave Studies in Literature, Culture and Economics

This series showcases some of the most intellectually adventurous work being done in the broad field of the economic humanities, putting it in dialogue with developments in heterodox economic theory, economic sociology, critical finance studies and the history of capitalism. It starts from the conviction that literary and cultural studies can provide vital theoretical insights into economics. The series will include historical studies as well as contemporary ones, as a much-needed counterweight to the tendency within economics to concentrate solely on the present and to ignore potential lessons from history. The series also recognizes that the poetics of economics and finance is an increasingly central concern across a wide range of fields of literary study, from Shakespeare to Dickens to the financial thriller. In doing so it builds on the scholarship that has been identified as the 'new economic criticism', but moves beyond it by bringing a more politically and historically sharpened focus to that earlier work.

Harry Pitt Scott

Financial Petroleum Cultures

Narrating Volatile Futures, 1973–2050

palgrave
macmillan

Harry Pitt Scott
University of Glasgow
Glasgow, UK

ISSN 2946-5397 ISSN 2946-5400 (electronic)
Palgrave Studies in Literature, Culture and Economics
ISBN 978-3-031-99660-3 ISBN 978-3-031-99661-0 (eBook)
https://doi.org/10.1007/978-3-031-99661-0

This Palgrave Macmillan imprint is published by the registered company Springer Nature Switzerland AG
The registered company address is: Gewerbestrasse 11, 6330 Cham, Switzerland

Acknowledgements

I completed this book in the first few months of my time as a Leverhulme Early Career Fellow at the University of Glasgow. I'd like to thank the Leverhulme Trust for funding my research. My gratitude also to the Infrastructure Humanities Group—Alex Campbell, Fred Carter, Farai Chipato, Henry Ivry, and Rhys Williams—who helped me get there, welcomed me, and provided valuable insights in the closing stages of this project. I'd also like to extend my appreciation to the editors at Palgrave MacMillan for guiding me through the publication process.

This book began as a doctoral thesis in the English and Comparative Literary Studies department at the University of Warwick. I owe much to the intellectual culture there. Graeme Macdonald is a fount of generosity, humour, and wisdom. From start to finish, he has never wavered in his support, intellectual rigour, and friendship. For reading early drafts of this work and so much more, my thanks to Amul Gyawali, Nora Castle, Arianna Autieri, Mantra Mukim, Giulia Champion, Lúcia Collischonn, Sam Weselowski. Charlotte Spear and Betsy Porritt have been, and continue to be, good friends. Warm thanks to Myka Tucker-Abramson, Stephen Shapiro, Mark Storey, and Nick Lawrence, for being excellent colleagues and comrades. Mike Niblett provided exceptional input at an earlier stage of this project and helped me to stick around when I needed time to get the book done. I also owe thanks to the team at the Institute of Advanced Studies at Warwick, who gave me space to work on the manuscript.

Beyond Warwick, colleagues in English Literature and American Studies at the University of Manchester helped me navigate a tumultuous time and made me feel at home, for which I am very grateful. Ian Scott, David Alderson, Andrew Fearnley, Molly Geidel, Chris Vardy: thank you. Special thanks to Peter Knight, whose innumerable kindnesses and timely action made this book possible, in more ways than one. Thomas Waller, Sean O'Brien, Tomos Hughes, and Harry Warwick inspired me at a crucial moment and provided friendships that continue to be important to me. Thomas and Harry provided constructive comments on the manuscript and many energising conversations. Ben Brown has read carefully and kindly over many years. Sharae Deckard has always been unhesitatingly supportive. Imre Szeman offered excellent criticism of an earlier version of the book and has given much wise counsel since.

My thanks and deep appreciation to my family, my parents Amanda Pitt and Peter Scott and sister Esther, who have been a source of unconditional support and unlimited kindness. I wouldn't have done it without them.

To Lowri, my closest friend: for love, strength, joy, and kindness—thank you for everything.

A section of Chapter 2 has been adapted from 'Offshore Mysteries, Narrative Infrastructure: Oil, Noir, and the World-Ocean', *Humanities* 2020, 9(3): 71. Thanks to the editors for allowing me to reproduce this in expanded form.

Contents

List of Figures

CHAPTER 1

Introduction

1.1 Simple Economics

At the Eighty-sixth Annual Meeting of the American Economic Association conference in December 1973, economist Robert M. Solow gave the prestigious Richard T. Ely Lecture, named for the founder of the scholarly association. Much of the conference proceedings were taken up with the issue of resource economics, which had become an important concern, as the oil crisis by this time was in full swing and the price of a barrel of oil had quadrupled (from about \$3 to about \$12). Referencing a foundational text of the environmental movement, *Limits to Growth* (1972), Solow decided to see what economic theory would say about the genre of "Doomsday forecasts" that described a distant depleted future, and what economic mechanisms were available in his profession for regulating the present usage of non-renewable resources so that doom would be avoided. The principal concern of the lecture is a well-known economic paper by Harold Hotelling, 'The Economics of Exhaustible Resources', from which Solow draws out a condition of stock equilibrium in the asset market: resource deposit values must increase with the interest rate or else they depreciate in the ground. This is because, he told the lecture hall, that a "resource deposit draws its market value, ultimately, from the prospect of extraction and sale" (Solow, 1974, p. 2). But because exhaustible resources such as petroleum are of such importance to the

H. Pitt Scott, *Financial Petroleum Cultures*, Palgrave Studies in Literature, Culture and Economics,
https://doi.org/10.1007/978-3-031-99661-0_1

economies of the twentieth century, this "brings to the fore is the importance of the long view, and the value of reasonable information about reserves, technology, and demand in the fairly far future" (Solow, 1974, p. 13).

Solow describes a shift in temporal register from "spot or flow decisions" to "future or stock decisions"—from the present to the future—to find a way of thinking and managing resource exhaustion (Solow, 1974, p. 13). Solow points to a problem of representation. If "the future brings no endowment of its own to whatever markets actually exist" then the problem that exhaustion poses was how to write the future into existence, to regulate the demand curve of resources like oil that are essential to the long-term functioning of modern societies (Solow, 1974, p. 10).

The expectation that markets can regulate resource consumption rates depends on the belief that depletable energy sources will eventually be replaced by other energy sources, otherwise the price would tend upwards exponentially as resources decreased. Solow references a contemporaneous paper by economist William Nordhaus—2018 winner the Nobel Memorial Prize in Economic Sciences—that saw futures markets as central mechanisms for governing resource consumption. In Nordhaus' argument, to make resource economics fit with the discipline's economic theorems—to make the world look an economic model for the purposes of controlling oil and money flows—required two assumptions: a perfect knowledge of future energy prices through a futures market, and a 'backstop technology': a future limitless energy source. Solow suggests either nuclear fusion or solar energy. For resource economics to work, unproven energy technology was assumed. As cheap oil became more expensive in Nordhaus' energy future, it would be eclipsed by nuclear fusion and solar power, in a natural, market-led energy transition into energy abundance, driven by financial calculation, power, and profit. The purpose of energy markets was to make that vision a reality. Economics met the challenge that there was an external limit to growth by suggesting that this problem could be solved in the representational space of resource markets.

Solow's lecture is of interest because it outlines the historical and conceptual presuppositions of seeing markets as regulators of to the present through an imagined distant future. It articulates an economic response to a historical period in which fossil fuels contoured the economic and the ecological future, as the public became concerned with exhaustion and cartel pricing power. Alongside eliminating the uncertainties of depletion, the market for exhaustible resources "could have the additional purpose of generating a set of consistent expectations about the distant future" (Solow, 1974, p. 14). No doubt this was an appealing idea. Because oil had been cheap and abundant, its replacement receded into a distant future. But the prospect of its ultimate exhaustion meant consistent expectations about resource futures were necessary for a society increasingly saturated by petroleum and vulnerable to its volatility. But as the 1973 crisis brought into view, oil was also a weapon wielded by OPEC against America, puncturing certain national myths about American independence and the infrastructures upon which it rested. Through financial representation, energy markets would write that volatile future into the present, uniting an economic horizon with a resource that increasingly seeped into every aspect of modern life. *Narrating* the future of oil was understood to be central to managing it through markets.

In Sydney Pollack's political thriller *Three Days of the Condor* (1975), a CIA analyst, Joe Turner, produces a report decoding secret messages in a thriller novel, pulling him into a conspiracy that leads to the uncovering of a rogue element in the agency. A scene takes place where Turner confronts the CIA's Deputy Direct of Operations for the Middle East. At this point of the film, the extent and reason for the conspiracy is revealed. Holding the Deputy Director at gunpoint, Turner questions him:

> What the hell does Counterintelligence care about a bunch of goddamn books! A book in Dutch! A book out of Venezuela! Mystery stories in Arabic! What the hell is so important about... Oil... fields. This whole damn thing vas about oil! Wasn't it? ... Wasn't it?

Turner later meets the Director of the CIA New York Office. Here, he threatens to go to the press and reveal the CIA's intention to seize control of oilfields in the Middle East. This Director assures Turner that the public won't care.

> It's simple economics, Turner. There's no argument. Oil now, 10 or 15 years it'll be food, or plutonium. Maybe sooner than that. What do you think the people will want us to do then? Huh-uh. Ask them when they're running out. When it's cold at home and the engines stop and people who aren't used to hunger go hungry! They won't want us to ask. They'll want us to get it for them (Pollack, 1975).

Two years after the oil crisis, Pollack's film expresses a cynical weariness about the strategic necessity of overseas intervention to preserve American oil interests. However, it locates the motive for such action not in the interests of a secretive elite but in the will of the people, which is naturalised as 'simple economics', and which we should understand as the centrality of petroleum to social reproduction.

Less than a decade later, the transformation of the petroleum system by financial markets was in full swing. Energy futures markets were established in London and New York. Oil companies began to act as financial investors and made beholden to shareholders. Markets set the price of gasoline, natural gas, and electricity. By the end of the twentieth century, petroleum saturated the stock market and financial news, it had been integrated into pension funds and portfolios, and it determined currency value, bond prices, and state debts. As economist Scott R. Littlefield notes,

> Energy is a great enabler and the US public regularly sees elements of energy markets: the price of gasoline, natural gas and electricity bills. Nevertheless, the availability and cost of energy is often taken for granted, except during price spikes or shortages. While the public desires energy services the political, economic, and logistical complexities underlying access to a gallon of unleaded gasoline or a kilowatt-hour of electricity are divorced from most people's daily experiences (Littlefield, 2013, p. 782).

Simplifying the socio-political complexities of energy infrastructure to market mechanisms, financialisation reorganised the spatio-temporal form of oil capital and the representational forms that mediated it, framing the primary experience of energy as 'simple economics', which is taken for granted except in moments of price spike or shortage. Finance became crucial to the political, economic, and cultural mediation of oil and energy futures—a primary medium through which people related to and understood the role of energy in their lives.

The topic of this book is a dominant common sense understanding of the relation of finance to energy in a period in which society must transition out of a world built by fossil fuels. Solow and Nordhaus' narrative of that change is comforting. A market-led transition in which a market price destroys fossil-fuel demand at a speed that allows for the development of renewable replacements, switching from one abundant energy source to another—to see that "the current stage of history is a transitory phase between dependence on cheap but scarce resources and dependence on more costly but abundant resources" (Nordhaus, 1973, p. 548). But petroleum is a far more intractable substance than this neoliberal narrative gives credit to. Drills, terminals, refineries, pipelines, tankers, storage facilities, and road systems bind a global system of infrastructure, logistics, and automation to the plastic and synthetic forms that saturate everyday life. Diesel and petrol fuel the container ships, automobiles, and aeroplanes that move commodities and people around the world at speeds and in quantities impossible to imagine before (and likely after) oil. Agriculture is powered by mechanised machinery and synthetically fertilised by natural gas derivatives. Oil is the chemical feedstock of a dizzying array of synthetic materials. When cheap, it powers economic growth and when expensive, slows it. It is the medium of modern means of communication, providing the energy and material for the digital and electrical revolution. It is integral to financial accumulation, from pension funds, state debts, and bond prices to currency markets. It shapes who we are, our sense of autonomy, self-development, and desire. To be modern is to live in a world derived from petroleum, a 'petroculture', made through the wondrous and terrible capacities of this energy dense fuel and malleable material (Szeman & Group, 2016).

Put differently, the transition out of petroculture is a social problem, not (just) a financial or technical one. It will require unmaking and remaking the social relations that are bound together by the material and energetic capacities of petroleum. Yet this is precisely what is missed in the simple economics offered by Solow and Nordhaus and, more recently, in the major institutions driving the energy transition.

While Solow and Nordhaus were initially concerned with the exhaustibility of resources, what motivates discussions of energy transition now is climate change, where the abundance of fossil energy is so great that burning all proven reserves would lead to catastrophic ecological breakdown. Yet this way of thinking in terms of finance is hegemonic in climate discourse. Take the International Energy Agency's (IEA) Net Zero by 2050 flagship scenario as an example.

> There are large reductions in the use of fossil fuels in the NZE. As a share of total energy supply, they fall from 80% to just over 20% in 2050. However, their use does not fall to zero in 2050: significant amounts are still used in producing non-energy goods, in plants with CCUS [carbon

capture, utilisation, and storage], and in sectors where emissions are especially hard to abate such as heavy industry and long-distance transport. All remaining emissions in 2050 are offset by negative emissions elsewhere (IEA, 2021, p. 57).

In this energy future, total energy consumption remains at 2019 levels. Long-distance travel and heavy industry remain fossil-based but offset with carbon sinks. Around 3.5 Gt CO_2 is prevented using CCUS (nearly 10% of CO_2 emitted in 2019), and all other petroleum is used in non-emitting industries such as petrochemicals. Most carbon savings come from clean energy technologies, and nearly half from technologies that are not yet on the market. Global net-zero emissions can be reached by 2050 if $100 trillion of new capital (excluding capital expenditure) is invested in requisite renewable technologies, energy efficiencies increase, CCUS. Supra-national governance enables the world to be suitably 'derisked' so that private investors are assured of *sustainable* profits.

The mechanism for this social transformation is extraordinary levels of private financial investment. Transition is narrated through financial figures, a number of technologies that do not yet exist at industrial scale, and the desire for a global agency that can manage discontent, coordinate inter-state cooperation, and direct finance towards renewable development. In this imagined future, capital markets can only be controlled by a greater political power, which is precisely what a powerful financial system prevents from emerging. My point is not that the IEA think this is likely, this not being the point of scenarios, but it narrates a contradiction: finance both makes and constrains a decarbonised future. There is no other path, but that path is itself premised upon a techno-optimistic and state-centric vision of energy transition. A social problem is given a financial solution.

This book aims to investigate the social and cultural dimensions of energy futures. While energy futures often refer to a type of financial contract whereby traders have the option to purchase a given quantity of an energy commodity, it also describes the horizon of expectations, assumptions, and perspectives that emerge to describe the journey from present to future. In the period after 1973, these two kinds of energy futures delineate one another, as financial representations shape how energy is articulated as a social and cultural problem, far beyond the confines of the economics discipline.

My claim is that the financial horizon of energy futures is also an aesthetic phenomenon. Finance is an economic technology that enframes petroleum, rendering it knowable as an object of simple economics, and integrating it, in that mode, into the daily life of petroculture. This is not the same as saying that finance is only representational, or that representation is the only thing that matters when it comes to the politics and culture of oil. Instead, finance matters to a critical theory of energy precisely because it has the mundane task of describing, evaluating, predicting, and projecting the economy of petroleum, a substance that, to quote petrocritic Jennifer Wenzel, "is everywhere, ubiquitous in our daily life, and yet we so rarely see" (Wenzel, 2014, p. 2). As a study of the cultural representations of petroleum, this book offers an aesthetics and a history of financial petrocultures; how finance gives rise to ways of thinking, framing, and narrating the future of energy.

This study developed in dialogue with the Energy Humanities, the Environmental Humanities, and the Economic Humanities. The theorisation of petroculture grounds the insights into the social and cultural dimension of energy (Wilson et al., 2017). In particular, Imre Szeman's continued attention to the ever-multiplying narratives organising the energy transition has been critical to this book's understanding of energy (e.g., Szeman, 2007, 2024). Jeff Diamanti's important argument about the recursion of energy and finance at the level of material form and narrative after 1973 has been critical to my formulation of a financial petroculture (Diamanti, 2021, pp. 21–41). Graeme Macdonald's continued insistence on thinking the world-systemic scale of petroculture guided my selection of case studies and comparative mode (Macdonald, 2017). Likewise, Jennifer Wenzel's work on the narrative structures mediating the climate crisis has been pivotal to my articulation of financial narrativisations of nature and ecology (Wenzel, 2020). Finally, accounts of financial representation (La Berge, 2015) and economic representation (Crosthwaite et al., 2019) in literary and cultural studies have provided important insights into the form of financial narrative. My intention is interdisciplinary, making use of the concept of energy futures as a bridge between sub-disciplines. These critics (among others) laid the groundwork for my study of the relationship between finance, representation, and energy.

I approach this topic through cultural and economic representations of energy futures in an era in which financial markets, ecological crisis, and the prospect of an energy transition begin to contour their shape.

When finance is imagined as the primary mechanism through which an energy transition is achieved and the threats of climate change prevented, I argue that financial representation is a key terrain in the struggle over what a world after oil will be. If it is often understood as a driver of innovation and change, it is just as often criticised for its self-interest and redistribution of wealth to a financial elite.

This book is a study of financial representations of energy, in two senses. Firstly, I refer to an archive of fictions, images, and discourses about finance and energy, because these engage the assumptions, expectations, and perspectives that render finance as benevolent, progressive expression of human capacities. In doing so, I interrogate a financial petroculture, a modern way of life derived and powered by petroleum, organised and directed by financial imperatives. Secondly, I examine genres of financial writing, including financial reports, scenarios, news, and advertisements, treating them as socio-technical forms of representation by which market actors describe, shape, and produce the energy transition. I am interested in what makes narratives of energy futures credible; what sort of stories a financial petroculture invests in; and what kind of representations appear as durable, realistic futures.

The archive I have selected is intended to be exemplary of important narrative modes in financial petroculture. It would be impossible for this study to be exhaustive. The risk of such a selection is the accusation of arbitrariness: why these objects, not others? The logic guiding my selection is twofold. Firstly, I have attempted to do justice to the world-systemic scale of financial petroculture, gaining in comparison what is lost in granularity. Finance and petroleum are *already* world-systemic, so I pursued my object of analysis across its global infrastructures. Secondly, I departed from a survey of literary texts to study a range of cultural forms (literature, film, architecture, photography, infrastructure, advertisements, and financial reports), because I found this most illustrative of the dominant—and occasionally emergent—financial mediations of petroleum. I am reminded of an observation Diamanti makes that petroleum is "more than one kind of thing in the world, occasioning in turn more than one kind of analytic orientation" (Diamanti, 2021, pp. 83–84). Thinking across different forms of media and mediation brings into focus differing, contradictory, often spatially and temporally dislocated dimensions of energy; a way of seeing how crude materiality is abstracted into and by financial imperatives and so into cultural form.

In moving between these genres of financial petroculture, I elucidate an important ambivalence found consistently across my archive, even as it shifts across moments of rupture and discontinuity. The dominant narrative of energy transition is organised around the assumption that capitalism will persist, and that finance will deliver a future that will be bigger, brighter, and better; a techno-optimistic hope that a market-led energy industry has the capacity to lead an orderly transition to net zero. The objective of a capitalist transition is to govern through organised but dispersed regulations, markets, infrastructures, and technologies that sustain the expanded reproduction of capital after fossil energy. But everywhere this narrative is threatened by volatility, which emerges when projections and predictions begins to lose coherence in the face of unpredictable change. A volatile future is an index of something going amiss in the maintenance of petroculture, a wrongness just as often felt and lived as conceptualised and thought. While much of financial governance is concerned with managing volatility—it is the *raison d'être* of futures markets—I have found that sophisticated meditations on its social dimension are found in cultural constructions of energy futures, which take it as an opportunity to critique the dominant financial representation and foreground alternative relations to energy.

This book demonstrates how finance determines the form and content of energy transition narratives, setting limits and pressures on the kinds of energy futures that are worth investing in, economically and culturally. Financial media has come to dominate the representation of energy futures, and in doing so shape the ecology of a warming world. But this book is equally, if not more concerned with moments in which those narratives break down, when the promise of modernity seems to waver, and other kinds of historical feeling emerge—often crystallising around moments of political upheaval, economic crisis, and ecological breakdown. In tracing this discursive struggle and narrative impasse, I aim to examine financial narrative as a privileged site for a cultural theory of energy. I hope that it will become clear that doing so is of central importance to figuring our relation to the energetic social forms that subtend and sustain the social and ecological crisis of our historical present. Imre Szeman and Dominic Boyer argue that we need to "grasp the full intricacies of our imbrication with energy systems (and with fossil fuels in particular), and second, map out other ways of being, behaving, and belonging in relation to both old and new forms of energy" (Imre Szeman & Boyer, 2017, p. 15). This book is meant to contribute to that project, by making sense of the narratives that finance makes available to petroculture. To that end, this introduction will now provide a discussion of my objects of analysis, method, and periodisation, followed by a chapter summary.

1.2 Narrating Volatility

Financial narratives frame, orient, and direct the future of energy. Yet the conditions of the oil and gas production network often make coherent narrative trajectories impossible. This is partly a result of finance. Assetisation and financialisation (commodity index funds and derivatives markets) introduced new actors to the oil market. Up to sixty per cent of trades in the market are made by speculators, and oil has become a store of financial liquidity, leading to a problem Kent Moors describes as "the increasing inability to determine the genuine value of crude oil based on its market price" and, in consequence, "that inability will erode the ability to predict, plan and compensate" (Moors, 2011). Meant to plan the future, finance as often makes it unpredictable.

This thread runs through my archive: a struggle over the form and meaning of volatility. For those involves in sustaining oil's present future, volatility is a financial risk that might produce dangerous social and political ramifications. It threatens to surface oil, and energy, as an object of political interest, beyond the boundaries of the market. For those who are not invested in the market mediation of oil, volatility—or, the breakdown of narrative—provides a way of contesting how finance claims ownership of future energy infrastructures. What, to an investor, looks like a financial risk, might, to others whose mode of social and political life is constituted by the prospective infrastructures, look like social breakdown, ecological disaster, political domination—a collapse or disappearance of their own future becoming the ground of financial narrative. To reframe other kinds of risk as financial is, in fact, part of the ideological work that finance does. Geographer Michael Watts describes the spatial insertion of oil infrastructures as such: "oil is always 'discovered' in space–time (say, Spindletop, Texas, January 10, 1901), and subsequently inserted into a very specific localised (if more or less globalised) political economy even if the properties of the wider oil assemblage are in some sense generic or normalized" (Watts, 2012, p. 440). This contradiction between the generic and the local provides a zone of friction where conflict, compromise, and violence is keenly felt. Organisations, infrastructures, networks, and actors bring with them narratives that they use to make sense of the infrastructural buildout. Those subjected to the narratives often produce their own, contesting, critiquing, and resisting the imposition. This often makes those for whom financial narratives rings false most valuable as critics, because they see the misalignment of financial promise and infrastructural reality. Thus, for example, the importance I place on Mexican novelist Carlos Fuentes in chapter two, who narrates that feeling of volatilisation as a way of framing the conflict over futurity that emerged in the 1970s Mexican offshore oil boom. Often, in fact, writers and filmmakers provide sustained meditations on these conflicts, offering a multimodal critique—narrative, aesthetic, infrastructural—that is attentive to the financial imperatives making and unmaking modes of life.

As a study of genres and narratives of volatility, my claim is that we can most closely track the financial dimension of petroculture through examining the ways that its narratives are circulated and contested. The following chapters track these narratives in novels, films, architecture, photography, scenarios, and advertisements, seeking to map the articulation of energy infrastructure to financial technologies: petrodollars, insurance, derivatives, project finance, and central banking. Across this archive, this book provides a historical and aesthetic account of financial petrocultures, as well as an investigation into the political and social consequences of finance as representational dominant: how it affects our ideas of transition and agency; how it produces forms of historical time and feeling, from volatility and crisis to delay; how financial media constitutes our relation to energy and infrastructure; and the ways that it frames the future of human life as an expression of the imperatives of value.

What follows from this is a particular mode and scale of analysis. What I have learned from world-systems oriented literary interpretation, is that the scale of the world-system gives you a different perspective when it comes to tracking and unfolding an object of analysis (Deckard et al., 2015). Following the flows of oil and finance between core and periphery requires tracking the metamorphosis of material into value-forms, as hydrocarbons get abstracted into crude, refined into products, and derived into financial contracts. Petroleum itself is transformed in its journey from oil well to stock exchange and petrol station. This transformation is economic and aesthetic—it becomes a commodity and cultural form via refinement into useable and exchangeable forms. A political machinery is established to distribute and control energy flows, performing necessary mediatory functions of relating extraction, refinement, consumption, and financing—while often concealing that relation through infrastructures and financial technologies that abstract from the particularities of a region.

In Joe Sacco's graphic novel *Paying the Land* (2020), a visual history of Canada's Northwest Territories' Indigenous people, documents, among other things, the plight of a small village, Inuvik, living in the aftermath of the unfulfilled promise of a petroleum boom. Members of the community were in favour of a pipeline development, because the jobs it would bring with it would boost the meagre economy currently dependent on trapping. "But the hoped-for benefits of oil and gas extraction", one prominent community member explains to Sacco, "locked as they always will be in a fluctuating market, have not panned out" (Sacco, 2020, p. 225). A generation prior, most of the people there lived on the peripheries of a money-based economy, but after decades of residential schools, the young people have grown up into a world unlike that of their parents and grandparents, only to discover that there is no economy in place to support them. As a result, many communities are only kept alive with welfare.

Paying the Land makes visible how financial trading, the fluctuating market price of oil and gas, sets limits on the kinds of infrastructural promises that can be fulfilled. The region has the resources, but price volatility means that they are not an economic guarantee. A financial narrative about market viability takes precedence over a narrative of development and local renewal. The wealth produced by petroleum will flow around this community, not through it, because the financial risk it poses is too great—a financial risk that is generated out of the structure of market trading. The capacity to avoid this financial risk is infrastructural: the pipeline is a political machine that can cut through, under, and around geographical areas that might cause friction in the flow of oil and money. Imre Szeman notes that "these technologies of energy transport generate indifference not only of a spatial kind, but also of an ethical or political one: extraction zones and networks of transport have little impact on the majority of those who use fossil fuels, for whom the stuff of energy appears, as if by magic, in their furnaces or at gas stations" (Szeman, 2018). To which we might add, in their portfolios.

Narratives of volatility require a multi-scalar analysis attendant to the spatio-temporal dynamics of the petroleum complex in and as a world-system. Petroleum connects small villages with financial centres, regions with metropolises. Financial imperatives determine the form of that connection. Financial narrative, I want to suggest, works on this terrain: forming links if beneficial, concealing connections if not. We will see how mediation—infrastructural, financial, and aesthetic—is crucial to understanding petroculture and the transition. Cultural forms capture and condense this processual, recursive interaction of finance and energy, performing the work of mediation necessary to critically map financial petroculture. In doing so, they often demand a focused attention on the connecting and concealing mediations that determine our relation to energy and its future. They are, by necessity, forward looking, but in terms that are not easily assimilable to the hegemonic narrative of market-led transitions; compelling us to take up infrastructural critique, where we read for the future not as imaginative practice but in prerequisite infrastructures.

1.3 Representing Finance, Reading Infrastructure

In J.C. Chandor's crime film *A Most Violent Year* (2014), set in New York in 1981, the central character, Abel Morales, is seeking to expand his heating oil business by purchasing a fuel oil terminal, for which he needs a substantial loan. Meeting with his banker, who assure him of their financial backing despite current pressures from the mob, his competitors, and a DA investigation, Abel is asked why purchasing the property is so urgent.

> This property gives us many things... firstly direct access to the river. So I can bring in fuel directly from any provider in the world straight to my tanks. Then it has over 10 million gallons of storage capacity, so I can buy in the summers when the price is low and sell to my customers and most importantly some of my competitors when the price is high. I won't just drive trucks anymore... I will control my fate. But the real answer to your question, is that when it feels scary to jump, that is exactly when you must jump, or you risk ending up staying in the same place your whole life. And that I can't do.

The film captures a social promise and an economic horizon that we might understand as generically neoliberal: an entrepreneur ('I cannot stay in the same place my whole life') takes on financial risk to secure the conditions of his own success in a competitive market, ensuring a good life of private wealth and individual freedom ('I will control my fate') for himself and his family. It also frames the importance of an infrastructure, a terminal, as a site where petroleum's materiality is abstracted into the market forms that define quotidian interaction with energy systems (Diamanti, 2021). Storage gives Abel an arbitrage opportunity (taking advantage of a difference in price over time), a competitive edge he intends to use to bankrupt his rivals. The terminal, in other words, enables a market logic and a neoliberal narrative of entrepreneurial spirit.

From the perspective of his creditors, the deal looks different. They must assess whether Abel is creditworthy. They, and by extension the viewer, encounter this scene, which takes place in a restaurant over dinner (somewhere between a client meeting and *The Godfather*), as an assessment of financial risk. They must decide whether his promise to pay is credible, but also whether his calculations about the market are probable. A narrative of arbitrage enabled by a storage infrastructure provides that guarantee.

Finance is necessary to capital accumulation. It reallocates capital, smoothing production and exchange by extending credit to producers or consumers. The concentration of credit accelerates the scale of production by combining smaller capitals, leading to a class of financial capitalists who exert power through the wealth redistributed to financial institutions from the circuit of capital. Financial profits are a share of the profits of capital accumulation, so finance confronts both producers and consumers in an antagonistic relation (Harvey, 2018, pp. 283–329). Definitions of 'finance capital' sometimes refer to a *process* of capital in the credit system and sometimes to a *power bloc* of financial capitalists.

Financial narratives are a way of asserting a claim to, and performatively constituting, the economy they purport to describe (Crosthwaite et al., 2019, p. 661). Financial genres abstract petroleum into representational forms: claims to future value; and the narratives, discourses, and expectations through which that futurity is imagined and lived. To extend credit or commit to a financial trade links the present to an anticipated future through the expectation that certain conditions will be met: production will have reached a certain capacity, stock prices will have risen or fallen a particular amount, and so on. This looping temporality instantiates the future in the present, creating a form, sense, and measure of time. Financial markets and media use representations and narratives to generate expectations about the economy, and when people act in accordance with this expectation, these representations are productive of social reality. For this reason, Leigh Claire La Berge defines finance "as the representational present of that promised future, and, accordingly, an era of financialization is defined by the assumption of finance to a site of representational dominance" (La Berge, 2015, p. 30).

A useful definition, to be sure. What I would add, necessary to the account I give here of petroleum finance, is that these representations need to be secured by real or prospective infrastructures, which ground the claim made on the future. In *A Most Violent Year,* this infrastructure is the terminal, which is already built. But the infrastructure that I focus on in chapter five is prospective one, an oil well that exists only as financial promise.

If infrastructures enable finance, finance often determines the form of infrastructure, even if those financial imperatives can be obscured. It can be hard to see the economic work being done a terminal, a refinery, or a pipeline. It is even harder to do so when infrastructures are in planning stage. Timothy Mitchell describes the strange opacity of finance like this:

> The promoters of new projects justify them to the public by material needs, not financial opportunities. The movements and supplies that will flow faster thanks to new infrastructure are presented as a requirement to be met, a necessity for life, a condition of well-being, an improvement, or, as economists call it, development. Finance—the only element that exists in order to grow, the one factor whose very possibility lies in growth—appears as something secondary. Capital seems to arrive after the fact, to enable needs to be met. In creating the effect of a world divided into the real and the financial, infrastructure projects establish the apparent primacy of the real or the material, of physical needs and human wants, and place finance as the servant, the subservient element existing only to help meet such needs (T. Mitchell, 2020).

In infrastructures built for profit, a certain kind of ideological work is done by foregrounding the dimension of use-value, because financial imperatives are concealed by narratives built around meeting need. Alongside a concern with financial representations of economic futures, I am interested in reading infrastructures as "concrete semiotic and aesthetic vehicles" (Larkin, 2013, p. 329), as modes of conveying and concealing financial imperatives with recourse to narratives of well-being, improvement, and development. A financial expectation is often hidden in the politics and 'promise of infrastructure' (Anand et al., 2018). Such narratives are particularly hard to contest, because they resonate with people's expectations and fears about the things that maintain their life, whether it be transport, water, or energy—and because the material stuff seems more real, more tangible, than the bonds, bank loans, and share certificates that infrastructures move across time. Examining financial narratives is therefore an important dimension of critique concerned with tracing the social and ecological violence of infrastructure.

I understand financial representation in two ways, both necessary to reading financial narratives in texts, images, discourses, and infrastructures. The first I take from Marx, for whom the financial circuit of accumulation, in which money appears to beget more money, is the "the misrepresentation and objectification of the relations of production, in its highest power" (Marx, 1992, p. 516). What distinguishes finance from other forms of capital is their relation to the productive process. According to Marx, capital is reproduced through the exchange of commodities for profit. What makes commodities exchangeable is that each is the product of human labour, and this human labour is reduced to the quantitative expenditure of labour time. Shoes can be measured against coats, cotton against coal, because each commodity is the product of a quantity of abstract labour. Reduced to a commodity, human labour is, nevertheless, unique, because it can produce more value in a day than the value required to maintain it. This is the origin of surplus-value, the basis of the wealth of capital, the secret of the commodity.

To facilitate the exchange of commodities, a universal equivalent, money, is required, which can represent the value of commodities in its own shape. Money is "an object always already given in the form of a representation" (Balibar, 2007, p. 67). It is an object that represents potential or real value, necessary to initiate the productive process by purchasing the means of production and labour. From the perspective of the financier, however, money is loaned on the expectation that it will be returned with interest. To the financier, money has the "capacity to represent and increase value" (Marx, 1992, p. 473), even though its source remains the surplus-value created in the productive process, a share of which is claimed in the form of interest. This is why, for Marx, finance is a misrepresentation that represents. It transforms productive activity, economically and aesthetically, into a financial abstraction, perceptually extinguishing the origin of wealth in labour. But it also sets in motion the circuit of capital, to produce commodities, to once again become money.

Finance sits between circuits of capital, a necessary form for value to take across its metamorphoses.

Financial misrepresentation is the basis of narratives that ascribe an agency to finance. There is a truth to this, since it sets in motion and determines the form of the productive process. But such narratives ensure that "everything that happens in between" lending and paying off the debt "is obliterated" (Marx, 1992, p. 471). It is the capacity to switch between the smooth flow of money and the empirical details of the productive process that makes financial narrative so central to contestation over the future of energy.

The second way in which I understand financial representation is as a performative claim on the future, often taking narrative form. Political economy Martijn Konings argues that claims to value

> work not by creating an external standard but through 'provoking', through activating connections and prompting their reorganization around the validation of the speculative promise. Value is not given before it is signified: the signification of value is performative rather than passively representational, driven by the aim to elicit the generation of the value that it claims to represent (Konings, 2018, pp. 11–12).

Value is by no means given, as a fixed sum, but an anticipated horizon. Applied to finance, we can note that its represented futures are not intended to be an accurate measure of value but rather to provoke a reality in which its claims become true. If this is the case, the future finance represents also must, in some minimal sense, mean something for a reality to be provoked into existence. For example, when then CEO of Shell, Ben van Beurden, said that to adapt to the energy transition, the company must begin by

> developing new types of biofuels and making them commercially viable, for example, or developing hydrogen for heavy-duty road transport in areas where nothing exists yet, not even the business model. We have to invent it, we have to build it, we have to make it happen. In some cases we will have to bring the customers with us as we develop the products, so we can actually sell the products to them (Van Beurden, 2021).

Where nothing exists yet, van Beurden imagines a whole world of biofuels, technologies, infrastructures, and consumer habits built to imagine value after oil.

Jens Beckert calls this capital's 'imagined futures', conceiving it in explicitly narrative terms. In this argument, all capitalist practice must make assumptions about the future and act as if they will come true, to provide a framework for action. "Expectations, Beckert writes, "cannot be predictions of the future: they are mere imaginaries of future states—imaginaries upon which actors base their behaviour "as if" these expectations actually do describe future states and causal relations" (Beckert, 2020, p. 76). The future is structured like a fiction in a performative attempt to shape reality—where biofuels and hydrogen meet the consumer and company needs through technologies and infrastructures not yet built, but which can be, if one imagines that Shell can do so: "Across our businesses, our low-carbon investments will increase significantly over time. In a company as big as Shell, even a strong rate of growth can be hard to notice, but we are accelerating" (Van Beurden, 2021). From the perspective of the investor, the value of narrative lies in producing imagined futures for investment.

In my argument, financial representation grounds the material and discursive struggle over energy after 1973, a date often taken to signal the emergence of a new phase of financial accumulation, or financialisation. Prior to that date, the postwar period had seen astounding productivity growth because of, among other things, cheap energy (Levinson, 2016). The shift to expensive oil, associated with the 1973 crisis, led to falling profit rates and dwindling productivity growth, which drove capital accumulation along financial channels (Jorgenson, 1981). Giovanni Arrighi famously argues that, at the world-historical level, financial expansions are long periods that enact a "fundamental transformation of the agency and structure of world-scale processes of capital accumulation" by laying the technical and infrastructural ground for a new phase of capital accumulation (Arrighi, 2009, p. 87). Amid falling profit rates, capital exits saturated industries and flows into pools of finance capital, where, in search of new returns, it expands outward, to new frontiers. Financialisation occurs when capital cannot get guaranteed returns from productive activity, turning to money-dealing and the extension of credit to resuscitate profitability rates. Curiously, then, financialisation describes a shrinking economic horizon that becomes increasingly saturated by financial claims. A kind of transition is immanent to capitalism's historical trajectory as it enters crisis in 1973, one in which finance, the mechanism whereby the capitalist world-system overcomes its own limits and is transformed, is searching for sites for the productive renewal of capital accumulation.

This is the context that frames the energy transition, where a new sustainable capitalism must provide an adequate infrastructure for profitability, after finance and energy diffracted a stable future of progress and growth into a volatile series of futures. Financial narratives, smooth or volatile, are a social barometer in a warming world.

1.4 1973–2050

When I began the work that culminated this book in the mid-2010s, I had not yet recognised that we were in the middle of a radical shift. The promise of a new kind of energy society was in emergence, unsettling the expectations and assumptions that had calcified into the given in the twentieth century. What had once seemed impossible is slowly becoming the new norm. Renewables, we are now told, will replace fossil fuels as the dominant energy form. Solar, in particular, is cheap, abundant, modular, and scalable. In 2023, global investment in clean energy eclipsed investment in oil, and peak oil will occur in 2030, we are told (IEA, 2023a). Investors had got the message, and the transition is now underway.

A decade prior, this hardly seemed possible. The stock market oozed with oil, with as much as one third of stock market capitalisation directly or indirectly invested in fossil fuels. We were still in the middle of the fracking boom, unleashed by cheap credit in the wake of quantitative easing. Oil was cheap and reliable, while renewables were expensive, inefficient, and intermittent. Financial investment in fossil fuels weighed like a nightmare on the present, holding in place a terrible future through the threat of devaluation, stranded assets, and financial panic. Yet if we no longer inhabit that moment, the transition is not quite the smooth and orderly journey to net zero described by the IEA. It is complex, uneven, prolonged, and subject to delay and reversal, a whole new terrain of discursive and political struggle over the production of the future. Despite the techno-optimism of the solar industry, it remains dogged by low profits, and adding more energy to the energy system does not, in itself, displace fossil fuels, as energy usage continues to rise, while some industries like transport and aspects of industry are hard to electrify. Despite this discursive and infrastructural shift, most financial activity is either directly or indirectly formed by the energetic capacities of fossil fuels, in its investments, institutions, juridical forms, expectations of profitability, the time and space of the global economy, modes of manufacture, transport, and circulation, digital media, the cultural practices of the financial power bloc, and so on. In the words of former central bank governor Mark Carney, what must happen to force a transition is "every financial decision takes climate change into account", which is an oblique way of saying that every financial investment must be disentangled from its current entanglements with fossil fuels (Carney, 2021, p. 8). Unravelling oil from finance is a problem that hangs over the financial elite, as a class, forcing them to deny, delay, avoid, or confront the question, what will power our world after oil, and how should investment build it?

In consequence, I have chosen to frame this book in two ways. First, as a looks backwards at a formative period in petroculture: the era that followed the 1973 oil crisis, neoliberalism, and the global financial crisis until, roughly, the aforementioned shift in the 2010s. 1973 altered the meaning of oil within petroculture, producing a fear of volatility emanating from the global peripheries in the capitalist core, and a new medium of anti-colonial power for oil-producing states. The institutions that mediated oil into its economic and cultural forms changed in the 1970s from a system dominated by private companies to one dominated by OPEC and oil markets, with the transformation of oil into financial products and assets, rewiring its flow to extract financial value (Gkanoutas-Leventis, 2016). But petroleum is not just an external resource shaped into asset classes and financial system. It gives shape to financial forms, processes, and institutions through the physical qualities of hydrocarbons as material inputs, basic commodities, and raw material.

A surging oil price, and the need to invest a surging volume of petrodollars ('petrodollar recycling'), transformed international money markets and increased the financial power of London and New York (Spiro, 1999). Oil markets became a new medium for writing and representing oil's volatile near future, producing a novel sense of historical time. Since then, as much as one third of the stock market is invested in the energy sector, with much of the rest in industrial sectors that would grind to a halt without petroleum energy, materials, and lubricants. Stock market expansions meant widening market participation, through access to information, publishing, and financial news. Oil investments became sources of personal wealth, through pensions, hedge funds, and tracker funds for most citizens of consumer-capitalist democracies, connecting the 'financialization of daily life' to vast hydrocarbon infrastructures across the globe (Martin, 2002). Credit enables the revenues of oil wells, pipelines, refineries, oil tankers, and power stations to circulate in financial markets before they circulate in material forms. Share values may imply decades of combustion, because an oil well or pipeline may, at its outer limit, have a lifetime of thirty years. Oil circulates in stock exchanges and offshore bank accounts before it is mediated by pipelines refineries, oil tankers, and power stations into petroculture's materials and media. This new futurity then came to shape ways of imagining energy as assets, risks, volatilities, and promises. In excavating a history of energy futures, we will discover that many of those futures were actualised in our present.

The second framing I offer is a look at our historical present from that earlier moment, to help better articulate the continuities and the rifts between then and the ongoing now, to put pressure on the claims of novelty that dominate debates around the future of energy. I am interested in the way that cultural forms might provide an aesthetic expression of an affective temporality: how a financial time *feels* as it hardens into the organising temporal structure of a petroleum lifeworld. This dialectical reading of energy futures, I hope to show, grounds the ongoing transition in the forms of world-making that finance makes available to an energy system premised upon, in a useful definition provided by Andreas Malm, "an economy of self-sustaining growth predicated on the growing consumption of fossil fuels, and therefore generating a sustained growth in emissions of carbon dioxide" (Malm, 2016, p. 8). If this is presentist, it is intended to be strategic (Coombs & Coriale, 2016).

If 1973 serves as a periodising break, 2050 is often a historical terminus; the date by which a net-zero society might have arrived, or a time when we are emphatically too late in transitioning beyond fossil fuels. The IEA 2021 scenarios, which might turn out to be the most influential speculative fictions ever written, use the date as a temporal marker, providing "the world's first comprehensive study of how to transition to an energy system at net-zero CO_2 emissions by 2050" (IEA, n.d., p. 5) . What we encounter here is a new kind of temporal orientation that reflects the deliberate, conscious attempt to enact a transition away from the basic materials, energetic inputs, and feedstocks of modernity. But 2050 appears elsewhere too, in the lifecycle of ConocoPhillips' drilling infrastructure in chapter five, the transition goals of bp in chapter six, and the narrative end point of a utopian novel in chapter seven, among others. Its significance, then, is that this mid-century date is often doing political and cultural work in the genres that lay claim to energy futures, as a promise and marker of the end of oil.

The value of narrative, in this instance, is that it represents a way of organising a transition in the making. A transitional society is future-oriented, overlaying a modern narrative of progress with stories of energy, technology, and climate; a meta-narrative develops, trying to provide a causal account what drives that story. Finance is continually called on to play the role of agent in that meta-narrative, writing the future in the terms of its own imperatives. Techno-optimistic visions of renewables promise hope in a discourse darkened by the prospect of exhaustion and ecological collapse. Electricity is proposed to replace fossil fuels, solving the social and ecological harms of a mechanical world by switching internal combustion engines for batteries. A combination of corporations, inventors, and the right kind of visionary investor are imagined to be the agents of this transformation, keeping alive the dream of modernity. As the pressure to transition mounts, the need to narrate and describe the transformation in the primary energy supply—what must change and who will bring that change about—increases. Yet a transition directed by private finance also sets limits on what is possible, organised as it is in service of profit. We will continually return to this financial determination, to see how it produced, negotiated, and contested.

1.5 Chapter Overview

I begin by reading Carlos Fuentes' *The Hydra Head* (1978), a novel set in the middle of the Mexican oil boom. I argue that the conspiracy thriller, situated between the exuberant promise of petroleum wealth and petrodollarisation, provides an important generic mediation of oil crisis. As a rising oil price and a technological revolution in deep-sea drilling reduced the financial risk of offshore oil, it became possible to imagine and narrate, with a relative degree of certainty and consistency, an energy revolution and national transformation for Mexico. The conspiracy, I argue, provides a critical reflection on this promise, reading it instead as the surface expression of privatisation and financialisation. The petrodollar introduced new temporal forms to petroculture, as market abstractions and media speculations began to write energy futures in the language of spot and future price, risk, volatility, and interest rates. The conspiracy narrative I have been reading provides a cognitive map of this moment of discontinuity, because its narrative structure marks out the financial speculations that flow around offshore infrastructures and the juridical blockages that produce its relative hiddenness. It plots a multi-scalar convergence of finance, infrastructure, markets, and media, and a narrative impasse central to the social and political production of petroleum's market future. As a genre capable of making plot out of financial speculation, *The Hydra Head* is suspicious of how information in market media might have begun to reorganise oil into information (or misinformation), making narratives valuable in a new way. It therefore articulates a narrative logic that corresponds to the macroeconomics of oil as its market abstractions become a hegemonic object and condition of representation.

Chapter three continues an investigation into the offshore revolution, this time focalised by Lloyd's of London, an insurance firm based in the City of London instrumental to the formation of financial petroculture. Lloyd's took on its globally significant role because of a convergence of economic, political, infrastructural and architectural shifts. In this chapter, I trace that conjuncture as a prehistory of our volatile present, before finance gets resignified as a driver of climate catastrophe. I am interested in this formation and eventual discontinuity because the story of Lloyd's is of the rise of the offshore to a place of central importance. I have chosen Lloyd's not just because of its historical importance, but due to the fact that architecture has a privileged relation to this new form of financial petroculture: a social practice concerned with producing cultural and economic settings that enable financial accumulation. Tracing this financial offshoring through the development of the Lloyd's Building between 1978 and 1986, I use it to frame the convergence of finance, oil, and neoliberalism in the United Kingdom, as a way of thinking through financial centres as petrocultures.

Chapter four is about how volatility is recomposed in form, setting, and representation by the globalisation and financialisation of oil. It focuses on the derivative, a financial contract used to trade expectations about the future price of oil. Financial petroculture's economic cell-form, the derivative gives order, direction, and meaning to energy futures. I am interested in oil's derivation, a market ideology and aesthetic of oil enabled by the infrastructure of financial media. Oil derivatives, otherwise called energy futures, are a critical site for the mediation of crude oil into economic and cultural form. To pursue this line of argument—an infrastructural critique of volatility—we will follow the money from reserve to data centre, from pipeline to pricing formula. Reading this new form of time through visual media, I assess how financial media configures oil's knowability through visual and numeric representation. Thinking with the concept of and market for oil derivatives provides a mediating concept to track oil's translation into finance and culture, and the representations that render it as crude or derived forms.

Chapter five shifts from the visual politics of oil markets to the oil frontier on the permafrost. This chapter is anchored by a close reading of the Larry Fessenden's *The Last Winter* (2006), an ecological horror film situated within a long tradition of frozen and ice-bound horror. This subgenre emerges from an encounter between writers influenced by the polar gothic—Coleridge, Shelley, Poe—and a new geography of geophysical science. Films in this genre are often read as 'revenge-of-nature' narratives and tend to work within a dynamic of surfacing and containment. I will argue that the politics of this subgenre is found in the way that it manages fears of monsters lurking beneath the ice. By contrast, *The Last Winter* refuses the strategies of containment central to this tradition, which I read as a fundamental discontinuity in the meaning of the Alaskan subsurface. Increasingly represented as economic opportunity and national security due to its hydrocarbon reserves, as well as a space particularly sensitive to shifts in global temperature, ice-bound threats become increasingly uncontainable as the permafrost thaws. Reading across ecological and economic registers of the permafrost, my organising claim is that the horror of this film is to be found in delay, and this is registered through spectral hauntings, gory violence, and volatile atmospheres. Delay denotes a desire to remain in one world and shore that world up against the feeling of change. Forming into a set of habits, practices, discourses, affects, and infrastructures, delay is the way a sense of normality adjusts to the geohistorical event of the Anthropocene, registering it as fact but altering the intensity of affective extrapolation. Delay is a historical feeling, and one that should horrify us, but rarely does, as it generates neither dramatic historical scene nor the expectation that change is possible or desirable. In reading for a horror of delay, I aim to apprehend how the contemporary oil economy grounds delay as a social problem, as a fantasy of suspension operative in normal life.

Chapter six aims to read the aesthetic, economic, and political dimensions of solar finance. Solar power often operates as a synecdoche of sustainability. Its exponential growth provides a techno-optimistic, even utopian, economic narrative, in which a market-led revolution in energy generation transforms fossil-fuelled society. Cost of deployment is trending downward, and solar now adds more electricity to grids than any other energy source in the US and Europe. The great success story of green capitalism, the sunlit upland of a solar world promises to leave behind the dirty and exploitative energy forms that have built modernity and plagued its self-image. The first section will turn to photography published by Lightsource bp, a solar energy company and subsidiary of bp (formerly British Petroleum), to analyse the pastoral aesthetic of this novel infrastructure. The second section will show how solar's conceptual abstraction enables narratives of financial accumulation. The third section will look at the discourse deployed by bp when describing their role in the energy transition, and specifically their adoption of a 'Just Transition' framework. I offer a contrasting framework, temporal justice, which aims to supersede the limitations of just transitions as proposed by bp.

Chapter seven concludes the book with a comparative reading of two novels I describe as transitional utopias. If the utopian romances of the nineteenth century turned their presents into the history of a distant future, and the critical utopias of the twentieth projected their alternative systems into contrasting worlds, then the transitional utopias of the twenty-first century narrate the beginnings of a transition towards a different kind of system located in the near future, for which 2050 stands as historical marker. The chapter spends some time discussing forms of transition, a speculative exercise that has a long history in Marxist thought. I argue that the precondition of utopian writing today is, somewhat paradoxically, financial hegemony. Finance represents and is representative of the economy, and as such is understood as a cause of and reflection on historical change. Because of this, its critical negation folds back into the representability of social totality and historical difference. The transitional utopian form is enabled by finance's representational hegemony, which it critically refunctions and negates in the description of transition.

References

Anand, N., Gupta, A., & Appel, H. (Eds.). (2018). *The Promise of Infrastructure*. Duke University Press. https://doi.org/10.1215/9781478002031

Arrighi, G. (2009). *The Long Twentieth Century: Money, Power and the Origins of Our Time: Money*. Verso Books.

Balibar, É. (2007). *The Philosophy of Marx* (C. Turner, Trans.). Verso Books.

Beckert, J. (2020). Anticipating a Future Present. In *Fictions of American Capitalism*. Palgrave Macmillan Ltd.

Carney, M. (2021). *Values: Building a Better World for All*. William Collins.

Coombs, D. S., & Coriale, D. (2016). V21 Forum on Strategic Presentism: Introduction. *Victorian Studies, 59*(1), 87–89. https://doi.org/10.2979/victorianstudies.59.1.04

Crosthwaite, P., Knight, P., & Marsh, N. (2019). The Economic Humanities and the History of Financial Advice. *American Literary History, 31*(4), 661–686. https://doi.org/10.1093/alh/ajz031

Deckard, S., Lawrence, N., Lazarus, N., Macdonald, G., Mukherjee, U. P., Parry, B., & Shapiro, S. (2015). *Combined and Uneven Development: Towards a New Theory of World-Literature (Postcolonialism Across the Disciplines): 17*. Liverpool University Press.

Diamanti, J. (2021). *Climate and Capital in the Age of Petroleum*. Bloomsbury.

Gkanoutas-Leventis, A. (2016). *Spikes and Shocks: The Financialisation of the Oil Market from 1980 to the Present Day:* London. Retrieved from https://www.amazon.co.uk/Spikes-Shocks-Financialisation-Market-Present/dp/1137594608

Harvey, D. (2018). *The Limits to Capital*. Verso Books.

IEA. (n.d.). *Global Energy and Climate Model Documentation 2024*. Retrieved from https://www.iea.org/reports/global-energy-and-climate-model

IEA. (2021). *Net Zero by 2050*. IEA. Retrieved from https://www.iea.org/reports/net-zero-by-2050

IEA. (2023). *World Energy Investment 2023*. IEA.

Imre Szeman, P. D., & Boyer, D. (2017). *Energy Humanities*. Johns Hopkins University Press. https://doi.org/10.56021/9781421421889

Jorgenson, D. W. (1981). Energy Prices and Productivity Growth. *The Scandinavian Journal of Economics, 83*(2), 165. https://doi.org/10.2307/3439894

Konings, M. (2018). *Capital and Time: For a New Critique of Neoliberal Reason (1st edition)*. Stanford University Press.

La Berge, L. C. (2015). *Scandals and Abstraction: Financial Fiction of the Long 1980s (Illustrated edition)*. Academic.

Larkin, B. (2013). The Politics and Poetics of Infrastructure. *Annual Review of Anthropology, 42*(Volume 42, 2013), 327–343. https://doi.org/10.1146/annurev-anthro-092412-155522

Levinson, M. (2016). *An Extraordinary Time: The End of the Postwar Boom and the Return of the Ordinary Economy* (First Edition). Basic Books.

Littlefield. (2013). Security, Independence, and Sustainability: Imprecise Language and the Manipulation of Energy Policy in the United States. *Energy Policy, 52*, 779–788. https://doi.org/10.1016/j.enpol.2012.10.040

Macdonald, G. (2017). Containing Oil: The Pipeline in Petroculture. In S. Wilson, A. Carlson, & I. Szeman (Eds.), *Petrocultures: Oil, Politics, Culture* (pp. 36–76). McGill-Queen's University Press.

Malm, A. (2016). *Fossil Capital: The Rise of Steam Power and the Roots of Global Warming*. Verso Books.

Martin, R. (2002). *Financialization of Daily Life*. Temple University Press.

Marx, K. (1992). *Capital: A Critique of Political Economy, Volume 3*. Penguin Classics.

Mitchell, T. (2020). Infrastructures Work on Time. *E-Flux, New Silk Roads*. Retrieved from https://www.e-flux.com/architecture/new-silk-roads/312596/infrastructures-work-on-time/

Moors, K. (2011). *The Vega Factor: Oil Volatility and the Next Global Crisis (1st edition)*. Wiley.

Nordhaus, W. (1973). The Allocation of Energy Resources. *Brookings Papers on Economic Activity, 4*(3), 529–576.

Pollack, S. (Director). (1975). *Three Days of the Condor* [Video recording]. Paramount Pictures.

Sacco, J. (2020). *Paying the Land* (Illustrated edition). Metropolitan Books.

Solow, R. M. (1974). The Economics of Resources or the Resources of Economics. *The American Economic Review, 64*(2), 1–14.

Spiro, D. E. (1999). *The Hidden Hand of American Hegemony: Petrodollar Recycling and International Markets*. Cornell University Press.

Szeman, I. (2007). System Failure: Oil, Futurity, and the Anticipation of Disaster. *South Atlantic Quarterly, 106*(4), 805–823. https://doi.org/10.1215/00382876-2007-047

Szeman, I. (2018). *On the Politics of Region*. E-Flux. Retrieved from https://www.e-flux.com/architecture/dimensions-of-citizenship/178284/on-the-politics-of-region/

Szeman, I. (2024). *Futures of the Sun: The Struggle over Renewable Life*. Univ Of Minnesota Press.

Szeman, I., & Group, P. R. (2016). *After Oil* (Illustrated edition). West Virginia University Press.

Van Beurden, B. (2021). *Can Shell Transform? Yes. And we will*. Shell.

Watts, M. J. (2012). A Tale of Two Gulfs: Life, Death, and Dispossession along Two Oil Frontiers. *American Quarterly, 64*(3), 437–467.

Wenzel, J. (2014). How to Read for Oil. *Resilience: A Journal of the Environmental Humanities, 1*(3). https://doi.org/10.5250/resilience.1.3.014

Wenzel, J. (2020). *The Disposition of Nature: Environmental Crisis and World Literature*. Fordham University Press.

Wilson, S., Carlson, A., & Szeman, I. (Eds.). (2017). *Petrocultures: Oil, Politics, Culture*. McGill-Queen's University Press.

CHAPTER 2

Plotting Petrodollars: Oil Crisis and the Conspiracy Novel

2.1 Crisis and Credit

The problem of what to do with petrodollars has been an enduring concern since the 1973 oil crisis. At the time, a quadrupled oil price, denominated in dollars, meant a dramatic increase in the currency sent from oil-importing nations to oil-exporting ones. Yet such a surge in capital meant that oil-exporting nations had surpluses well beyond what could be spent nationally, so the petrodollars were 'recycled' through the Atlantic financial system: London's offshore Euromarkets and New York's investment banks. Conventionally understood as a driver of financialisation, this was a period of credit expansion, financial markets, syndicated loans, a debt-led regime, overleveraged investments, and which saw the removal of controls on international financial movement. Flush with petrodollars from oil-exporting states, creditors from the core of the capitalist world-system went off in search of investments in developing countries and the communist bloc (El-Gamal, 2010). Their emergence marks a transition between one era and the beginning of another.

It quickly became clear that creditors found some prospects more pleasing than others. Preferable were relatively stable, low-risk states with industrial development and valuable natural resources. Unsurprisingly, states with proven oil reserves in need of development, such as Mexico, were highly sought after, because they had a future as major oil producers

H. Pitt Scott, *Financial Petroleum Cultures*, Palgrave Studies in Literature, Culture and Economics,
https://doi.org/10.1007/978-3-031-99661-0_2

(Roddick, 1990, p. 28). The oil price was high, and so returns on investment seemed assured. The petrodollar might be thought of as a financial intermediation that separates two moments of extraction: one in the past, and one in a prospective future, represented in the present by financial leverage. A future of (and for) Mexico was imagined, through a financial system that capitalised upon recently discovered oil reserves located offshore. With cheap and abundant capital and a technological revolution in deep-sea drilling, it became possible to imagine and narrate, with a relative degree of certainty and consistency, an offshore revolution and national social transformation.

But whose narrative is this? Moreover, if this imagined future becomes reality, and if finance tries to produce a reality in which its value is realised, to whose benefit is it? This is precisely the sort of inquiry that Mexican novelist Carlos Fuentes brings to bear on the financial narratives created by petrodollarisation in the 1970s in his contemporaneous novel, *The Hydra Head* (1978)—according to the book's dust jacket "probably the first Third World spy thriller". In a scene typical of this thriller about the 1970s Mexican offshore oil boom, two spies, one a Mexican bureaucrat named Felix Maldonado, the other a mysterious British financier, meet in a skyscraper in Houston, Texas, in a clandestine version of what was happening with syndicated loans to developing nations. Gazing out over the skyline, the British spy says to his Mexican counterpart: "look outside, and see the evidence of petrodollars" (Fuentes, 1978, p. 167). I find this invitation to look outwards at a petroleum landscape from within the towering skyscrapers that regularly represent high finance to be an emblematic trope of a financial petroculture and the specific difficulties that petrodollars pose to representation, narrative, and plot. What should be looked at, and which from perspective? How it should it be seen, and what is the evidence of seeing properly? The British spy goes on to foreground the confusion it causes, as "the petrodollars flow in here [Houston] and out there [New York]. Does *anyone* know for whom he's working?" (167).

The representation of finance and the financial representation of the future are, for Fuentes and for us, a narrative problem. The question of what do with petrodollars is an economic concern that becomes a representational one. It becomes a representational concern because petrodollars are a financial instrument, credit that produces narratives.

Crediting this narrative, or not, is an economic—and an aesthetic—evaluation because it increases the likelihood of financial returns. The passage in full reads like this:

> Look outside, and see the evidence of petrodollars. Let's say we play Israel against the Arabs and the Arabs against Israel. Houston is the Arab capital of the United States, and New York the Jewish capital; the petrodollars flow in here and out there. Does *anyone* know for whom he's working? But let's confine ourselves to our game. All scenarios are possible. Even—or especially—one for a new war. Depending on the circumstances, we can close the New York valve and suffocate Israel, or close the Houston valve and freeze Arab funds. Follow the moves in our game, please. Imagine an isolated Israel plunged headlong into a war of desperation. Imagine the Arabs refusing to sell oil in the West. Choose your script, Maldonado... (167).

The act of looking at oil and seeing narrative indexes a financial signifying system. Note the recurrence of narrative forms to describe political possibilities: play, game, scenarios, imagine, script. Note also how the object of concern changes, with no apparent recognition by the speaker: from what is *outside*, the city and its oil infrastructure as the *evidence* of petrodollars, to the various power games possible *inside* the skyscraper, representative of high finance. It is possible to detect, in the shape of the sentence itself, how a financial eye moves, perhaps without recognising it, between infrastructural representation and financial representation. The oil infrastructure is represented and represents value. Financial representation—the scenarios, imaginations, and scripts that represent anticipated value—is enabled by infrastructure, which gives financial anticipation a reality, through the *possibility* of alternative scenarios playing out.

The British spy describes a profitable future and offers up alternative scenarios as threats. It is because such alternative scenarios are imagined that they do not happen and, instead, the anticipated profitable scenario plays out, and this makes them into a sort of currency. They are narratives about value. "All scenarios are possible" (167), Maldonado is told, so he better pay attention.

Such representations are examples of the way finance makes time out of speculative narratives of energy futures. The present is apprehended through financial expectations about how the future will unfold, introducing a specific temporal structure into literature and social life. Financial narratives, inside and outside the text, are not only laid out to make described events happen. Sometimes, as is the case here, narratives circulate as possibilities, to make sure that the described events do not happen. "Conditions resulting from being on the brink of war provide the necessary shock that prolongs an armed peace for fifteen or twenty more years" (167), the British informs the Mexican spy and as a result, the petrodollars keep flowing. Thus, alongside the 'main plot' of a financial form, the financial investment that capitalists hope will pay off, there are any number of 'subplots': scenarios, rumours, speculation, ratings, reputations, created by industry, investors, media, and society. And more distant and abstracted from the particulars of economic development, there are cultural expectations, hopes, and desires summoned and substantiated by financial promises of incoming wealth.

This is the sort of insight that Fuentes's aesthetic mediation of petrodollars generates. It is not because petrodollars are fictitious in the way that a novel is fictitious that is important. What *The Hydra Head* shows is that narratives can be financial forms even if what they narrate never takes place but, through a possible future, anticipation becomes actuality. *The Hydra Head* is a novel about the financial stories about oil, and the reality that such stories make. Narratives *about* oil are (made into) financial forms. The passage cited above weaves together a lot of the strands of this study: financial narrative, architecture, infrastructure, and a feeling of volatility inherent to this newly uncertain world.

Mexico is important to the British spy because, he explains to Maldonado,

> Mexico can't sit forever on the most formidable oil reserves in the hemisphere, a veritable lake of black gold stretching from the Gulf of California to the Caribbean Sea. We simply want to be sure that Mexico profits from it. For the good, preferably. All this can be done without disturbing President Cárdenas's sacred nationalization. Oil can be denationalized, by Jove! without changing appearances (168).

In 1976 Cantarell, an offshore oil field was discovered in the Gulf of Mexico. It was the largest ever discovered at the time, and when it came online in 1981, it was the most expensive. Published in 1978, *The Hydra Head* is forward looking—like the offshore oil industry—and is a narrative about what the extractive future in the Gulf of Mexico will be, to intervene in that prospective future that exists in the present as a financial value. It takes its content and form from its mediation of world-systemic finance. It is a novel about how the present is mediated through an imagined future, in which the petrodollar represents the privatisation of national infrastructure. In 1938 Mexico nationalised oil, and all oil is property of the Mexican state (incidentally Fuentes, son of Mexican diplomats, was in school in Washington when this happened and reportedly became aware of himself as a Mexican in a foreign country for the first time because of how he was treated by American schoolmates (*Carlos Fuentes | Academy of Achievement*, 2021)). Fuentes goes about his mediation of fossil financial forms by asking how international financing and debt-led expansion change national extractive industries, even when it does not change the appearance of infrastructure. Can it really have the same appearance and be denationalised? In which case, his novel is engaged in an aesthetic mediation of financial abstraction and privatisation.

Before proceeding with this question in the form of a close reading of *The Hydra Head*, I want to spend a little time exploring what Fuentes is representing here. What the two men in the skyscraper are discussing is the offshore, and it will help if a little more is said about it. After this digression, we will return to the two spies in Houston with a renewed sense of the mystery the British spy is explaining to the Mexican one.

2.2 Offshore Mysteries

It would be appropriate to begin with a mystery, so let's start with one set in some of the world's largest ports:

> *A ship is mysteriously renamed.* Someone crosschecks cargo manifests, notices a pattern of erratic offshore movement, and begins to construct a story, a suspicious sequence of events, where before there were only lists and voyages, a repetitive and routine industrial series (Sekula, 1996, p. 49).

In Allan Sekula's photowork *Fish Story*, the mystery in the international shipping world is placed alongside photographs taken of workers in shipping ports such as San Diego, Rotterdam, Gdańsk, and Barcelona. The motivation for this is that ports are "a position to see the global patterns of intrigue hidden in the mundane details of commerce". While global commodity circulation is mundane, Sekula's formulation suggests that it nevertheless exerts a palpable fascination, given the way that global commerce and geopolitical intrigue are "pictorially condensed" in settings such as ports, which are the infrastructure of contemporary petrocapitalism (Sekula, 1996, p. 32). The problem that Sekula articulates is one of representation: hidden in repetitive and banal transport are patterns of intrigue, and intriguing patterns, that remain *undetected*. Against the backdrop of the 50,000-strong global merchant fleet, carrying ninety per cent of the world's internationally traded commodities and two-thirds of its oil, it is only through a "pattern in erratic offshore movement", that a plot begins to be constructed. In a different place, he writes that "the oceans remain the crucial space of globalization: nowhere else is the disorientation, violence and alienation of contemporary capitalism more manifest. But this truth is not self-evident and must be approached as a puzzle, or mystery; a problem to be solved" (Sekula & Burch, 2011). Here, Sekula employs a language typical of noir fiction to focus his description of the shipping ports and the events that take place in them; to investigate and detect, as he writes elsewhere, "the world's increasingly grotesque 'connectedness,' the hidden merciless grinding away beneath the slick superficial liquidity of markets" (Sekula, 2002, p. 7). This enables Sekula to connect the very material (yet curiously abstract) world of shipping and the very abstract (but material) world of financial liquidity.

For those working in the Energy Humanities there is perhaps little novelty to this claim, shipping and logistics being of special interest both within the field and in the infrastructural turn more broadly. But scant attention has been paid to the *style* in which Sekula describes his object, which is that of the investigative mystery, because the offshore relies on exclusion, obfuscation, and limited (or ideally no) public oversight. Let's call it the 'offshore mystery', and think of it is a narrative structure capable of representing the networked offshore system and offering a provisional explanation of that system's relative invisibility.

The offshore might provisionally be defined as "a logic through which capitalism carves out and exploits legally distinct and supposedly exceptional spaces" (Potts, 2019, p. 198). The offshore is a logic of extra-territoriality: a juridical-spatial regime that circumvents nation-state regulation through extraterritorial ownership practices, and can include offshore finance, special economic zones, resource extraction, and flagging practices. Flags of convenience, the offshore that Sekula is referring to—and elsewhere described by Sekula as an "ensign of camouflage and confusion" (Sekula, 1996, p. 50), and by historian Rodney Carlisle as "systems of subterfuge" (Carlisle, 1981, p. 179)—effectively conceals ownership of ships, oil-rigs, and other sea-going vessels, through complex systems of incorporation, in order to limit regulation and obfuscate social responsibility (Appel, 2015). While it seems like a topic for dusty textbooks, the offshore has a surprising currency in a subset of noir fiction, set in and around ports, in which 'a pattern in erratic offshore movement' is the key to unravelling a sinister plot.[1]

The offshore can be territorial enclaves such as offshore oil development, or it can have only a virtual existence, such as ship chartering and registering, banking and tax havens. "This strange world of offshore", Palan writes, "is all a fiction. Side by side with the state system, therefore, emerges a virtual world of make-believe, driven by a commodified form of sovereignty" (Palan, 2006, p. 4).

According to Carlisle, flags of convenience were an extension of the American multinational corporate system. The drafting of Liberia's Maritime Code, which would influence the entire legal structure of ship registration including the 1958 Law of the Sea Convention, was checked and approved by the American Overseas Tanker Corporation, Standard Oil and ESSO, who wished to use the Liberia flag to weaken ship workers unions and undermine the European shipping nations (Carlisle, 1981, pp. 110–132). It is a legal structure shaped by fossil capital by creating a juridical realm that circumvents the political and legal risks associated with 'onshore' activity, ensuring that legal titles to valuable oil resources are available to extraterritorial ownership. The offshore reveals that the ocean is not "a formless void *between* societies but rather a unique and specifically constructed space *within* society" (Steinberg, 2001, p. 23); not a *res extensa* but a contested spatial-juridical field used to construct legal distinctions between spaces connected through world-system logistics. 60% of the world oil trade and 25% of the world liquified natural gas trade takes place by sea. Oil is circulated through an environment that is

[1] A small (but by no means exhaustive) sample of these offshore mysteries reveals their broad political geography: Ian Rankin, *Black and Blue* (London: Orion House, 1997), Peter Høeg, *Miss Smilla's Feeling for Snow* (London: Harvill, 1992), Attica Locke, *Black Water Rising* (New York: HarperCollins Publishers, 2009), Kwei Quartey, *Murder at Cape Three Points* (New York: Soho Press, 2014) and Chen Qiufan, *The Waste Tide* (New York: Head of Zeus, 2018); and TV and film such as *The Wire*, dir. David Simon (HBO, 2003), *Syriana*, dir. Stephen Gaghan (Warner Bros, 2005) and *Occupied*, dir. Erik Skjoldbjærg (Zodiak Rights, 2015). This aesthetic extends to non-fiction and muckraking writing too, for which intrigue is of more narrative interest than the quotidian world of oil production. See: Ken Silverstein, *The Secret World of Oil*, (London: Verso, 2014); Christopher Leonard, *Kochland: The Secret Histories of Koch Industries and Corporate Power in America* (New York: Simon & Schuster, 2019).

regulated by the powerful instrument of the offshore. If the ocean is the space upon which fossil capital depends for its realisation, the offshore might be understood as the legal form of fossil capital. In other words, it is a legal framework that expresses the social relations of fossil finance. Legal forms are abstractions from a particular content, the social relations of capital, but objective abstractions, lived concretely.

If what distinguishes offshore is, in one sense, the fact that it is a 'fictional' and 'virtual' realm of tax laws and legal regulations, as Palan suggests, it is no less real because of it. Through these legal representations, the offshore obtains a real existence; it produces space and time, given the preponderance of energy and capital that are circulated through such juridical-spatial regimes. These are the social relationships that Sekula is investigating in *Fish Story*. The 'offshore mystery' is a style employed to provide a situated representation of the world the offshore 'fiction' has built.

The offshore makes obfuscation profitable. It has its own conceptual cartography of "enclaves [that] are increasingly linked up, not in a continuous, territorial national grid, but in transnational networks that link dispersed spaces in a selective, point-to-point fashion" (Ferguson, 2005, p. 380). It insulates interconnected enclaves from democratic oversight, labour rights, taxation, regulation, etc.

At this point it is worth returning to the two spies in Houston. The British spy has invited Maldonado to the office of the company he works for. It is called 'Wonderland Enterprises, Inc.,' an allusion to *Alice in Wonderland,* and it is a shell company. It can disappear and "there will be no trace" (171) it was ever there, Maldonado is told. Shell companies are typical offshore practices, enabling companies to hold assets and investments outside the nation-state in which the main company operates. The spies are in Houston because each is in pursuit of a detailed map of the Mexican oil industry, and "whoever possessed it and deciphered it had all the necessary information for utilizing, interrupting, or—depending on the circumstances—appropriating the function of this machinery" (239). Control of this oil information is the motive of the plot, and pursuit of it leads Maldonado on a journey from Mexico City to Coatzacoalcos, which was at the forefront of offshore development in Mexico. The ring disappears on an oil tanker flying the Panamanian flag. With no way of knowing who owns the tanker or where it is going, Maldonado turns to logbooks, but they provide little information: "It's hard to tell one tanker from another [...] All a tanker has to do is change her name" (147). The tanker is given away by a crime: it changes names and flags to avoid port regulation, concealing its operations from national authorities—the crime, it turns out, is little different from the actual mundane operations of ship registration. Eventually, through a series of literary codes, Felix works out that the tanker has been renamed *Alice,* bound for Galveston and American control. This will lead him down the rabbit hole to Wonderland Enterprises, Inc.

Aside from the fact that this literary geography replicates the transnational offshore network in a way that is, as far as I know, unique in fiction, what is so striking about the 'offshore mystery' in *The Hydra Head* is how it gives form to the differentiation through which the offshore works; and, through that, the problems of how to plot petrodollars. The border between onshore and offshore becomes a moment of narrative tension. Moreover, the novel resituates what critical finance studies understands to be a 'finance fiction', because of how it construes the relationship between representation and finance in fiction.[2] What is financial about the novel form is not, ultimately, the finance in the text, but how it reflects and interrogates financial value representation. This is because the novel's perspective is situated not from Houston, as this scene in the core of the world-system might suggest, but from the semi-peripheral position of a public intellectual and former politician in Mexico, for whom financialisation meant something much different to what it meant in the industrialised core; where finance signals not 'dematerialisation' and 'fragmentation', to note some of the terms critics have used to mediate between the economic and aesthetic of finance, but rather intensified extraction, debt, and dependency on foreign investment.

Back in the Gulf, Felix tracks a spy to the port city of Coatzacoalcos, which he arrives at by plane.

> From the air, [Maldonado] had seen the expanse of the Petróleos Mexicanos refineries in Minatitlán, the stormy Gulf in the background, the industrial capital inland, a modern fortress of towers and tubing and cupolas glinting like tinfoil toys beneath a storm-sated sun, the busy port

[2] If one were to map the geography of texts analysed under the rubric of 'financial fiction', most would be located in the major financial centres of New York and London which, while obviously essential to finance and financial culture, in no sense exhaust its cultural geography or its representation in fiction. Take the focus of three (admittedly excellent) studies of financial fiction, all with a North American focus (La Berge, 2015; McClanahan, 2018; Shonkwiler, 2017).

> with its railroad tracks extending onto the docks, and long, black, sleek-decked tankers [...] Swift glimpses of coconut-palm forests, zebu cattle grazing on brick-colored plains, and the Gulf of Mexico whipping up its early-evening thundershower yielded to a view of a port city with low, ugly buildings, their windows blasted out by hurricanes, and dirty neon signs, unlighted at this hour, a whole consumer society installed in the tropics, supermarkets, television-sale and -repair shops, and in the foreground the everlasting Mexican world of tacos, pigs, flies, and naked children in mute contemplation (121–22).

This aerial perspective captures the vast size of the oil boomtown, the port and the refineries, and its proximity to agricultural and fishing industries. Meanwhile, the offshore rigs, out of sight, are registered under flags of convenience, so exempt from local law and taxation. As with Sekula, who sees in ports the world "pictorially localized" (32), the description tries to capture the entire infrastructural scale of the Gulf. The world of the novel is strange and unfamiliar; in response, the sentences become more certain, abstract, precise. This makes sense, given that our investigator is a bureaucrat, organ of the state apparatus, rationalising space, intervening against the intrusive extraterritorial offshore. Simplistic, bureaucratic, cold: words roll over the landscape, peering into its crevices, describing the banality of pipelines, ports, shipping, decoding the environments they pass through. And this is one of the definitive contradictions that reveal the offshore in the style: the mysterious plot ties together a wide-scale, amorphous and deliberately opaque network of power; and the individual sentence, more localised and small-scale, plods though this epic setting, naming and ordering it, slotting each element into an allotted place, giving meaning to inert, alien infrastructure. This also suggests why noir is particularly useful, because it mediates the scales at which the offshore operates. This is noir's narrative energetics: the incessant plotting of a figure that slowly assembles mysterious pieces together. It expresses how the scalar disorientation created through oil infrastructure precedes and necessitates an entire reorganisation of the perceptual field through which such infrastructure is represented—a gaze that selects what is seen as logistical and restores to it a sense of how to detect the political effects of the offshore.

Maldonado pursues the ring, but it disappears on an oil tanker, bound for Galveston.

> The *cambujo* broke into a run toward the market, swinging the beef carcasses aside, turning over crates, scattering straw in his wake [...] The *cambujo* continued his flight through the market, zigzagging back and forth and sowing obstacles in Felix's path [...] They emerged at the far end of the market onto the railroad tracks, and Felix saw the mestizo bounding along the rails like a rabbit, following the tracks toward the port outlined in the distance by scattered yellow lights [...] The rainstorm had ended with the same abruptness with which it had begun, magnifying to an even greater degree the pungent odors of the tropical port. A moist lacquerlike film shone on the long expanse of dock, the moribund rails, the asphalt, and the distant hulk of oil tankers [...] Felix clasped his machete more tightly in his hand; at any moment the *cambujo* might turn with a pistol in his hand, his pursuer now within sure range. He stopped beside a black rain-washed tanker sweating gray drops of water and oil (136–7).

The port provides narrative excitement. Crashing crates and swinging goods; changes in atmosphere and weather; the sudden inhalation of foreign smells; the threat of violence; and in the distance, ominous oil tankers enclosing the horizon. Unlike the stable panorama from the plane, kinetic energies swirl throughout this scene, from human movement to the olfactory register of climate, commodities, and culture. This is a striking moment: when infrastructure and shipping become a mystery, the offshore system becomes plot.

But why is an oil tanker bound for Galveston in the first place? Because the oil extracted in this region is a heavy, sour oil, called 'Maya crude'. Oil quality and financial evaluation is always given in aesthetic categories: light and heavy, sweet and sour, crude and refined. Heavy, sour crudes are a viscous oil that does not flow well (heavy), and which has high impurity levels (sour). These are more expensive to refine, and are worth less, than sweet, light crudes. For Pemex, this meant reliance on US oil refineries, and so oil flowed from offshore zones into international, then American, spaces. So, oil and logistics is viewed as something both national and international, essential to the nation but part of a wider network of dependency on a more industrially developed neighbour. Resource sovereignty is integral to Mexican nationalism, which makes the offshore a particularly fraught and contested space, given that it undermines a particular understanding of state boundaries, and the relationship between 'national' resources and international industries (Breglia, 2013). Maya crude demonstrates how oil valuation is tied to its material character, the specifics of geography and logistics, which determines its representation in financial markets: a materiality of financial abstraction. This shapes its *literary* and *aesthetic* character as well: the atmosphere of ports, the employment of spaces that represent financial power, and the ever-widening narrative movement, beyond the place of extraction towards distant locations of transport, refining, management, and financing, abstracted from the material flow of oil.

Recall that the British spy has told Maldonado that the Mexican oil "can be denationalized [...] without changing appearances" (168). A sinister *plot* is afoot, to surreptitiously change what is really happening behind the scenes, while keeping appearances the same. The thriller is a genre in which narrative plot is driven by a diegetic plot. Crucially, for both plots to work they must generate excitement for reader and investigator, to drive them towards participation in the narrative, either through reading or uncovering the plot. There must be withheld information or knowledge, which is central to creating motive. One critic argues that is the *potential* for action in thrillers that creates the excitement, the "potentiality [of action] is responsible [for narrative excitement], not its realization" (Palmer, 1979, p. 59). To read a thriller requires speculating on *potential* action; the reader and the spy each speculate on which plots might become real and make judgments about what will help or harm that realisation. Whether or not the story pays off is to do with how well the plot is constructed.

Thrillers are a major genre in financial fiction, because they can enact the "peculiar distortions of space and time, both the secretive post-national space of the offshore and the exuberant futurist time of speculation" (Marsh, 2015, p. 204). Thrillers tend to represent the appearance of normality as a deception, hiding a secretive world that exists beneath the surface or out of sight. This is an effective way of rendering the offshore world in narrative form, even if there is an ambivalence to such writing, given it can mystify in exactly the way that finance might want to be to avoid oversight and transparency.

Maldonado's worry is that debt obligations can lay claim to national resources, providing a financial imagination not of immaterial or deracinated capital flows, but secretive control, paper trails, and covert claims to national resources and land. As Edward LiPuma writes, "nothing defines the field of finance more than the value of knowledge, which correlatively, also imbues deception with value" (LiPuma, 2017, p. 81). Deception is a valuable tool for finance and for literary thrillers because it generates interest and excitement. The worry that Fuentes articulates is that oil narratives are deceptive illusions. This financial mood saturates the novel from its first page, when Maldonado, not yet recruited into espionage, is on his way to work at in the Ministry of Economic Development.

> Felix Maldonado attended a political breakfast every morning. A pretext for exchanging impressions, ordering world affairs, plotting intrigue, conspiring, and organizing cabals. Small early-morning fraternities that serve, above all, as a source of information that would otherwise remain unknown (3).

He meets an old friend, Professor Bernstein, who he will later discover is working to advance American oil interests in Mexico to weaken Saudi influence. For now, Maldonado thinks him only an old friend. They discuss Maldonado's recent transferral from Pemex.

> Ah, the famous Mexican oil reserves! The great mystery. Why did you leave Petróleos Mexicanos?
> "They transferred me," Felix responded. "They have some idea that an official gets stale if he stays in one post too long."
> But you've spent your whole career with Pemex, you're a specialist, what idiocy to waste your experience. You know a lot about the reserves, don't you? (4).

They reflect on politics, financial news, and the nature of information.

> "Just now, as I came in," Felix went on, "I was thinking how you can't understand anything the Mexican press says unless you attend political breakfasts. That's the only way you can understand all the allusions and veiled attacks and unprintable names hinted at in the newspapers."
> Neither do they print important news like the sum total of our oil reserves. It's curious how news about Mexico appears first in foreign newspapers. (5).

This scene is experienced, as it were, twice. On the first read, it appears that the story is focalised through a character who is privy to the sort of information that comes with the privileges of state power, while the national newspapers are, at best, misinformed or, at worst, blind to what is really going on. There is a suspicion that information is being 'leaked' to foreign newspapers whose readership have financial interests in Mexico.

The reader's trust in public information is undermined by the novel, because it suggests that people like Maldonado have it and the reader does not; but the information as it is presented in the novel is confirmed, because we are privy to the privileged conversations of the powerful, through Maldonado. Such a scene is grounded in the imagined community of the nation—the newspaper links these characters to every other Mexican in a morning ritual, conjuring up a national pride and class belonging.

However, when it becomes clear later in the novel that Maldonado has been deceived, he has been transferred out of Pemex to silence him and that Bernstein, his old compatriot, is working against him, this retroactively invalidates the information as it has been presented so far and undermines the solidity of the national community through a global plot. The scene is experienced, firstly, as if it were true, and then secondly, as if our experience of this truth is a necessary fiction that conceals what is really going on. The fiction that Maldonado and the reader gave credit to, turns out to be a fiction that makes a new reality to the extent that it is believed by some but not by others. It is through the fiction that Maldonado has about himself—his confidence in his knowledge and judgement, and his relation to the Mexican oil reserves, of which he is considered a 'specialist'—that conceals from him how oil information is really circulating elsewhere, in foreign newspapers and syndicated loans. Information is to be doubted; but that does not mean that misinformation is without value.

The Hydra Head gives form to an offshore logic because it represents the way political insulation, and a lack of democratic oversight, produces an unevenness of information. Uneven information shapes narrative form and a mode of reading. The way it forces a retroactive rereading of untrustworthy information replicates how the offshore produces disparities from the onshore; any story circulating onshore might be false, or a deception. Maldonado's faith in the national oil narrative is what enables him to be duped by Bernstein. The offshore works because Mexican oil reserves appear to remain the same while being fundamentally reworked through the debt obligations Pemex has to its financial investors, who see it as an investment opportunity. The promise of oil abundance is what grounds national debt as value borrowed from the future.

Moreover, and I think this is crucial, the deception that takes place is not in *contradiction with* the apparent reality and with available information but happens through represented futures of oil abundance, because Pemex really does have unsurpassed oil reserves. The deception is working through the truth, which is that oil is abundant and profitable; it creates value because the represented future of offshore oil development is expected to be realised. But as the fictional becomes reality, this reality retroactively undermined the narrative that a debt-led oil boom would free Mexico from underdevelopment. This turned out be prescient, because in 1982, after the oil price crashed, Mexico defaulted on its debt and this led to structural adjustment programmes, austerity, and to the Mexican state's forced integration with neoliberal policies. I will speak more about 1982 at the end of the chapter. Suffice it to say for now that what the novel's deception shows is how the fiction—the represented future of oil development—worked to produce a future and become reality, but in becoming reality the fictional promises retroactively became untrue; the fiction created the situation in which it became fiction, by becoming real.

2.2.1 International Credit, National Character

The Hydra Head wants the reader to wonder who to trust, which stories to give credit to, and which to see as bankrupt. It also wants us to critically reflect on how potentialities can become effective in the present as valuable information, even when such potentialities remain unrealised. The potential for conflict means narrative mediates financial value precisely because it shapes how oil is valued in the present, and how that present is mediated through volatile futures. Moreover, *The Hydra Head* provides a rejoinder to accounts of finance and postmodernism which, in David Harvey's description, is "dominated by fiction, fantasy, the immaterial (particularly of money), fictitious capital, images, ephemerality, chance" (Harvey, 1991, p. 339). I think this emphasis on the immaterial and ephemeral misses the mark, and cannot account for the relationship between finance, abstraction, and oil. In continuing my close reading of Fuentes, I take up the account of economic and aesthetic form in an era of free-floating currencies, periodising this through the petrodollar revolution. Reflecting on the influential interpretations of Harvey and especially, following him, Fredric Jameson, I suggest that this has produced a structuring blindspot to oil. I am not arguing that oil is invisible *in* or *behind* finance. Rather, 'financial abstraction' constituted as an object of study is structured by this invisibility *to* oil (not *of* oil).

The novel extends a discussion about financial fiction, two instances of which I take as key examples. Ian Baucom's account of the finance, slavery, and historicism in the eighteenth-century world-system shows how bills of payment demanded "a phenomenology of transactions, promises, character, credibility", because such bills relied upon assessing the creditworthiness of the person whose signature guarantees the bill's value. Individuals had to learn to make judgments about whether to trust the bill and the character of its issuer; to accept a bill was to have confidence in one's own ability to "read character" (Baucom, 2005, p. 63). For Baucom, what connects a speculative culture of trust and the insurance contracts of the Atlantic slave trades routes to literary form is the notion of the 'typical' that emerged as a way of seeing financial practices and investments—the typical returns on and risks of cargo, including, centrally for his study, enslaved Africans—and the historicism of the historical and realist novel, which provided characters, as Georg Lukács puts it, as "the embodiment of historical-social types" (Baucom, 2005, p. 40). A related argument appears in Mary Poovey's study of the credit economy in eighteenth and nineteenth century British writing, for whom monetary instruments were value representations that had to be *made* valid by naturalising them as representations, solving the 'problematic of representation'—the gap between sign and referent, between paper money and the value paper money represented. Naturalising value representation was necessary so that individuals would treat these representations as currency, and this meant directing attention away from the medium of money towards how it might be exchanged. As a culture of credit naturalised, and thereby concealed, financial signification, in literary fiction, a "writer might teach a reader to believe once more in possibilities that could not be proved; in so doing, a writer could encourage readers to accept the deferral that was essential to credit, both private and public, without feeling imperiled by risk" (Poovey, 2008, p. 113).

Neither sort of monetary instrument still exists, and the social relationships through which credit is issued in the world-economy are now radically different. However, there is a way that both these accounts help explain what I call 'national character' in twentieth- and twenty-first-century financial forms, and how this economic and aesthetic form became a way for international banks to have the confidence to speculate and engage in issuing credit. What happens to credibility, belief, and character, when the loans are international, and the debtors are states and state companies? What happens when what is loaned are petrodollars and the anticipated future is more oil? To understand this requires knowing how the petrodollar revolution was facilitated by the eurodollar markets, the ending of Bretton Woods, and the dollar denomination of oil revenues, so that we can see how a culture of credit in this period becomes a financial petroculture.

A prelude to the financialisation of the later decades of the twentieth century, the eurodollar markets were an accounting trick—a 'virtual fiction', Palan would say—invented in the City of London in the 1950s that allowed dollars to be held outside the US' regulatory reach. The amount of dollars in circulation around the world was vast, fuelled by the expanding postwar world-economy and the increase in global trade. Because under Bretton Woods all currencies were pegged to the dollar, and the dollar was backed by gold reserves, the boom in the volume of dollars undermined the ability of the US to redeem dollars for gold: there were too many in circulation for the amount of gold held at Fort Knox. In 1971 Richard Nixon ended the Bretton Wood system and "the fiction of the gold-dollar exchange standard" and currencies became 'free-floating', the exchange rate between them settled in financial markets rather than by government decision (Arrighi, 2009, p. 310). The dollar became a fiat currency, whose price might increase or decrease, seemingly without any relation to an objective referent of value, which had been gold. To Joseph Vogl, this "slow but irreversible transition" from commodity-backed money to credit money created a regime of "free-floating signifiers—anchorless and immeasurable [...] a system in which currencies referred only to other currencies" (Vogl, 2014, p. 61). In the conventional narrative told in accounts of postmodernism, severing representation and value meant money dematerialised and became 'more abstract'. As Jameson puts it in his article that practically inaugurated the study of 'Culture and Finance Capital', "free-floating capital [...] will begin to live its life in a new context: no longer in the factories and the spaces of extraction and production, but on the floor of the stock market"; where "nothing is quite so abstract and deterritorialized as the finance capital that underpins and sustains postmodernity as such", a "new ontological and free-floating state" in "a kind of cyberspace in which money-capital has reached its ultimate dematerialization"; ultimately, finance is "a play of monetary entities which needs neither production (as capital does) nor consumption (as money does): which supremely, like cyberspace, can live on its own internal metabolisms and circulate without reference to an older type of content" (Jameson, 1997, pp. 251, 257, 259–260, 260, 265).

But the dollar remained central to the international financial system because oil was sold internationally in dollars and this meant that all oil-importing states maintained a structural need for them, effectively substituting oil for gold as the basis of American monetary power. In 1974 OPEC, led by Saudi Arabia, pegged oil to the dollar, which anchored the dollar as the world's premier currency since (Thompson, 2018, pp. 94–100). The financial system has been structurally integrated with oil since. Finance does appear to be abstract, but this abstraction is a result of oil's voluminous saturation. Capital's 'dematerialisation' occurs, so the argument goes, when value and representation is severed in 1971 at the end of the gold standard. But this 'dematerialisation', which makes finance more abstract because it relates only to itself, is possible only because the dollar was then underpinned by the expansion of very material oil extraction and eurodollar markets. $35 dollars may no longer have been exchangeable with an ounce of gold as they were under Bretton Woods; but dollars were worth what they were worth not because they related only to themselves in a seductive disappearance of the referent, but for the more mundane reason that the world needed to trade them for oil. As Myers Jaffe and El-Gamal note, it was met with some surprise by contemporaries that the world was willing to hold more dollars without backing than dollars backed by gold, and

> in large part, the Dollar's success in expanding its role as global currency was tied to the Kissinger-Simon program for petrodollar recycling, which included investing the proceeds of oil exports in Dollar-denominated assets and pricing oil in Dollars. To some degree, therefore, the term "petrodollar" has also served as a reminder that Dollars were essentially backed by oil, as Saudi Arabia and smaller oil-exporting countries in the GCC have continued to support the Dollar both as a store of value and as a medium of exchange (El-Gamal, 2010, p. 138).

Dollars derive their character from the petroleum's world-economic centrality; because oil is sold in the dominant currency of the world market, oil comes to regulate the money form. Dollars were able to fulfil their function as money because they were an adequate value representation. The 'black gold standard' makes oil into an exceptional economic force because its abstraction into value-form is what grounds world money, making makes oil singularly important to the world-economy's financial architecture. And after 1973 this energised value-form was constituted through the offshore.

Finance became 'more abstract' because it became more extractive, not less. This opens up a different interpretation of financial culture and the historicity of value. Moreover, as I argued above, the fictitiousness of finance becomes most visible when the reality it produces undermines the promises that made that reality desirable; the fiction comes to seem fictional as it becomes real. Because not all imagined scenarios can become true, and most are not meant to, some appear in retrospect only as fictions—but this is how finance makes decisions in an inherently uncertain environment. The question is not *whether* finance is fictitious, but how finance works and so comes to be understood as fictitious. Finance can appear—in reality and in critical finance studies—as fiction, fantasy, or the immaterial *only* because oil backs dollar values, but only *informally*, rather than codified in an institutional arrangement such as the gold-dollar standard. Free-floating finance seems increasingly fictional because Bretton Woods can be distinguished from the petrodollar as a formal, tangible relationship rather than an indeterminate one, thus retroactively making currency in the former gold-dollar regime seem a more real value representation than in the latter. I am not claiming that Jameson's conclusions are wrong, but that his discussion of finance replicates on a cultural level a blindness to the relationship between oil and finance on an economic one. *Seeing* finance as an object in isolation is a resource aesthetic that makes it appear immaterial but which is structurally bound to petroleum.

Nevertheless, as the formally unbacked yet oil-dependent dollar flowed through the offshore network, not only had money changed, but the form in which they were lent changed too. Rather than loans or exchanges made between people who know each other, or even issued by a commercial bank to a private individual, "the 1970s saw groups of lenders banding together to make so-called syndicated loans to Third World governments as sovereign borrowers. The correspondence of the borrower with the state meant that risk adhered to the nation itself as economic actor" (Slobodian, 2021, p. 9). If, as Baucom claims, bills of payment created "a phenomenology of transactions, promises, character, credibility" and, as Poovey argues, "a writer could encourage readers to accept the deferral that was essential to credit", how might an assessment of credit and character take place when what is being assessed is, as Quinn Slobodian puts it, "the nation itself as economic actor" (9)?

I am suggesting we understand the 1970s as a period in which financial signs are dialectically entwined with the specific natural form of oil. If this is the case, then it is perhaps no surprise that petrodollars find a natural home in Petróleos Mexicanos, Mexico's national oil company. Mexico was considered a 'safe' debtor: it had an industrial history and manufacturing base, shared a border with the US and, perhaps most importantly, was a non-OPEC country with huge, recently discovered oil reserves, to which much of the investment flowed (Mahon, 1996, p. 57). Thus the 'problematic of representation', or gap between money and that which guarantees money's value, is solved by the *promise* of future oil revenue because oil is denominated in dollars and dollars are valuable because the demand for oil makes them so. If this sounds suspiciously like tautology, then it is not unsurprising that for a writer like Fuentes it appeared as if petrodollars were little more than an illusion, concocted by capitalists in the core of the world-system who sought to transform Mexican oil into financial returns while underpinning the dollar's value representation. When Maldonado mistakes his specialist expertise for knowledge and so does not realise elements of the Mexican government are conspiring against him to turn financial control of oil over to the Americans, he has fallen for the trick that makes him a good 'national character' for the conspirators: through his belief in the primacy of the state, he has mistaken the world-economic situation, which makes Mexican oil a safe investment.

If Baucom and Poovey describe a culture in which trust and character assessment was to be cultivated between people and perspicacious judgement a quality to be cultivated within the self, then the difference that Fuentes articulates is the alienation of this culture to the interactions between investment banks and the state, in a way that disarticulates what people believe about creditworthiness and what people actually do. What is to be done when you distrust the credit, but the debtor is the state? This is the fiction of credit as it is mediated by the state: the belief is materialised through people acting as if the fiction will become real; but this has the converse effect of making the narrative itself *seem* more fictional, precisely because one is free to not believe it, while this disbelief has no effect on what is happening. This is perhaps a defining element of petroculture's political logic, as financial instruments take on a life of their own. This, I think, is the situation articulated in the novel, through how Maldonado, a 'national character', is treated by representatives of international credit.

Maldonado is initiated into an international conspiracy to publicly assassinate the Mexican president. Upon its completion, he is to be given plastic surgery, a new identity, and documents, and given "a more solid economic and social position" (32) in state employment. The man who promises him this, a mysterious Director General who works in the "deliberately murky penumbra of [a] windowless office" (29) in a Ministry building, assured Maldonado that "we are not interested in you. We are interested only in your name. Your name, not you, will be the criminal" (33). The play of names is part of the enjoyment derived from thrillers, wherein spies and readers enter a game of appearances and attempt to work out the truth behind the mask. Maldonado fails to pull off the assassination, refusing to help those who wish to undermine Mexican state oil control, which thrusts him into an increasingly complicated and opaque world of fake names, doubles, and incomprehensible motives. The British spy he meets in Houston, for example, turns out later on to be an American spy, playing both sides.

Then, in a brilliant twist, it turns out those are both masks for a Mexican petrochemical company owner, who sees business opportunity in the oil boom and its export economy but has to defend this from foreign plots to incorporate him into multinational corporations. "Call me a nationalistic conservative, if you want", he tells Maldonado. "I'd like to conserve *that,* keep the oil ours, and prevent outsiders from playing games with us" (226)—financial games, of course, being all too real. *The Hydra Head*'s character system is structured by the gap between sign and referent that financial value mediation attempts to conceal and naturalise. Moreover, signs and referents are each accorded a different position within the text, as names become 'free-floating' and are detached from the person to whom they refer. After the plastic surgery, Maldonado's name has been criminalised but is told "the man behind the name no longer exists" (69). The question then becomes, for the astute spy and the reader, as to whether the name or the person is creditworthy, and whether belief should be extended to what the name or the person is said to have done.

In addition to the allusions to *Alice in Wonderland,* the novel is replete with references to Shakespeare. The triple spy gives himself the code name 'Timon of Athens', Shakespeare's play about a man financially ruined by giving gifts to his friends. The name that Maldonado is given is Diego Velázquez, after the famous Spanish court painter in the reign of Philip IV (need we mention gold again?), whose masterwork *Las Meninas* (1656) is intended to question perception and representation. Literary jokes have been reduced to clues and codes through which to map the murky world of this mass cultural form, capturing a breakdown between high art and mass culture as high aesthetic status is reduced to a signifier of a world unnerved by this newly volatile political situation. But the literary joke also establishes a distance between this novel and more conventional thrillers (the novels of Ian Fleming, the conspiracy thrillers of the 1970s), because it reflexively identifies its own thematic scaffolding as absurd—discrediting the conspiracy as worldview while maintaining it as narrative form.

Masks, appearances, false doubles, and distorted reflections. To what end? Fuentes's Timon tells Maldonado that "Felix Maldonado is dead and buried. Diego Velázquez is the ideal replacement. No one is looking for him. He has no past. He has no outstanding debts" (241). Because "it's to everyone's best interests that you forget Felix Maldonado and take on a new identity. The perfect spy has no personal life, no wife, no children, no house, no past" (241). The ideal spy is abstraction personified, a total absence of qualities. But Maldonado cannot give up his name and so makes for a poor spy. Maldonado suffers from the difference between his 'real' self and his 'fictional' mask—he is incapable of maintaining his mask, and therefore his place in the symbolic order, inaugurating a gap between symbolic and psychic identities. He cannot reconcile himself with the name and the role he is given. "Who is it who has this power, this power to change lives, twist lives at his whim and make us someone else?" he asks. "I give up" (282).

Maldonado, clinging feebly to his outmoded identity as representative of the Mexican state, cannot see that it is *only* the mask that matters—an appropriate figure for someone unable to discern the fiat dollar's gap between sign and referent, which is guaranteed as value-form and aesthetic logic through the convergence of money and the petroleum economy.

This is how the novel frames petrodollars as an aesthetic problem, to do with trust and credit at the scale of states and financial institutions. Such economic factors are constitutive of the plot as Maldonado mediates between sign and referent. For Maldonado, the lesson is not whether the mask is true or false, but how it works in stabilising the problematic of representation; his character is irrelevant, but it is his structural position as a *national character* that enables him to function as a point of view incapable of seeing the conspiracy and so miss how financial representation is constitutive of oil's social form.

Maldonado, bureaucrat that he really is, is not up to the task of working this out—he is the "James Bond of underdevelopment" (247), according to a rival, "a mediocre economist, a mediocre bureaucrat, a mediocre Don Juan" according to another—hardly spy material. Led on a dizzying chase through the offshore world by Timon, he cannot give up his name, not least because of its association with oil nationalisation. Maldonado "insisted heatedly [...] that he'd been conceived on the eighteenth of March, 1938, the day of nationalization" (218). The triple agent personifies international credit, because in him convergences American oil interests, British financial interests, and Mexican oil export interests. Perhaps it is of little surprise that the national character, Maldonado, unable to separate his name from his person, is duped. But—and this is typical of the thriller genre—it is through being duped that the plot reveals the illusion that structures the social reality. In being deceived by the offshore world and multiplication of masks and social roles, he acts in such a way that he comes to confront the triple agent. The truth is in the deception.

So, what is revealed to our underfunded, under-equipped, and unprepared James Bond? Well, perhaps not that much, but that not much is itself revealing. He has learned that it is oil itself that is the eponymous hydra head. Moreover, the creditworthiness of characters and the scenarios they want to achieve are supported by the promise of oil. But there is another hydra too. The triple agent explains to Maldonado that establishing the relation between sign and referent, or between action and desire, is a fool's game.

> Ah, passion again rears its fearful Hydra head. Cut off one, and a thousand will grow in its place, isn't that right? Call it jealousy, dissatisfaction, envy, scorn, fear, repulsion, vanity, terror; probe into the secret motives of any of who participated in this comedy of errors, Felix, and give to his passion whatever name you will. You will always be wrong, because behind every label there is some unnameable, obscure political or personal reality—makes no difference which—that justly or unjustly—makes no difference which—compels us to disguise as action what is actually passion or hunger or suffering or desire or a love nourished out of hatred or a hatred nourished out of love (244).

The novel is first read as about decoding secret motivations but becomes a message about the loss of knowable motivation as such. It does not matter what characters believe, but how they act as national characters. Indeed, the protagonist's inability to make sense of the conspiracy should be read symptomatically. This is the moment in which the narrative marks a transition, as the capacity to process history—to give aesthetic form to historical time—hits the structural limit of the offshore. The conspiracy narrative is therefore an epistemological solution to an infrastructural problem, and one that captures the historical feeling of financial privatisation, as infrastructures imbued with national symbolism have been transformed into abstract forms that live an invisible life elsewhere.

As the plot unfolds, it becomes clear that it is narrated not by Maldonado, as the reader is led to believe, but by Timon, the agent who it appears, once again, has changed sides. It turns out, he really has been trying to defend national oil resources all along. He "imposed a certain order" on the story—a Freudian secondary revision, the reorganisation of dream-work into a comprehensible narrative, for Maldonado "told his story [to Timon] the way the memory works, in disjointed fragments" (215). The story has been reorganised by the person who the reader is led to think is attempting to deceive them; again, the reader is forced to doubt not only the information that makes up the story but its formal organisation too. Timon's narratorial voice represents and obscures Maldonado's in an act of rewriting that makes us aware of a different version of the story while refusing us access to it. The narrative of the national character has been, from the beginning, organised retroactively and contained within a larger, international fiction. "Which of the two endings would be the real true one", Timon asks himself: "the one I was preparing to invent, or the one [Maldonado] was preparing to live?".

This exemplifies what Franco Moretti describes, in his 'Conjectures on World Literature', as the compromise created by the import of foreign forms to the peripheries of the world-literary system: "foreign *plot*; local *characters*; and then, local *narrative voice*" (Moretti, 2000, p. 65). In my reading, the foreign plot is the thriller and the financial form that make Mexico as a space of international financial investment: petrodollars and plot. The local character is, obviously, Maldonado, the "James Bond of underdevelopment" (247), a character in a foreign form: bureaucrat forced into espionage, a contradiction between state public service and state secret service. He is wholly unsuitable for the job and is allied to a conservative oil nationalist—unlikely spies both. Finally, the local narrative voice is, diegetically, the triple agent, whose compromise is located between his attempt to tell the conventional thriller plot while forcing Maldonado and the reader to constantly, retroactively, reread the significance of events from the perspective not only of the 'national character' but of 'international credit' too, as a game in how to distinguish between them. The narrative voice shifts between petro-nationalist and international investor, which reflects Fuentes' own history as a Mexican diplomat, as a semi-peripheral mediator between core and periphery. He finds in the thriller a form that creates a space of interaction between national characters and international plots, showing how fictional scenarios translate the beliefs of national characters into credible stories for international plots. The social relationships of the petrodollar are not external to the novel, a neutral object of representation, but a problematic internal to its form, that defines its narrative voice and mood, its infrastructural spaces and financial time. The novel shows oil's doubled life in financial representation and infrastructural development, which I have read through the novel's distinction between international credit and national character—and the preponderance of the former over the latter. The novel's ominous threat turned out to be prophetic. Written a few years before the Mexican debt crisis, in which the euphoria of the oil boom would give way a crashing oil price and to state default, austerity, and structural adjustment.

What *The Hydra Head* critiques in content it denies in form. Both detective fiction and thrillers are emplotted through mystery. The detective story uses clues as evidence to reconstruct past events. But the thriller is about stopping something from happening. Its temporal orientation is towards the future, not the past. Debt is a social technology for borrowing from future revenue. But this only holds if that future is expected to come about. *The Hydra Head*'s formal critique is found in the unevenness between the generic expectations of the thriller and the logic of debt-based speculative infrastructures. Maldonado cannot prevent offshore oil development under the control of international credit; foreign form works against local narrative content as he fails to stop the potential becoming real. If the reader is invested in the success of the underdeveloped spy, and therefore the satisfaction produced in the generic structure of the thriller, then this promise has not paid off. In the 1980s, as the oil price crashed and Mexico defaulted on its loans, the financial promises of oil failed to pay off too.

2.2.2 *Conspiracy and Cynicism*

Oil has often been entangled with conspiracy. Consider, for example, the famous cartoon of Rockefeller's Standard Oil, represented as a giant octopus with tentacles wrapped around industry, the U.S. Capitol, a State House, and reaching for the White House. Or think of oilman General Sternwood in Raymond Chandler's *The Big Sleep,* the multinational plot of *Three Days of the Condor,* the accusations of monopolistic conspiracy levelled at OPEC to justify a 'free market' for energy, and anti-war sloganeering in the 2000s that blamed the war in Iraq on an American grab for oil. However, in most of these conspiracies, oil either really means money or power, or it is represented as a sinister agent, in a kind of figurative energy determinism. The narrative function of Maldonado is epistemological: what he 'learns' is that he does not know how to identify petroleum's social form. This is a critical representation of juridical and infrastructural form in a moment of crisis and reconfiguration, attuned to the kinds of narrative that this new infrastructure space enables. Fuentes, in other words, is suspicious—and rightly so—of the narratives of development and wealth that are articulated by a new wave of financialisation and privatisation, two vectors of dispossession that determine the shape of contemporary petroculture (Fig. 2.1).

The Hydra Head is a novel of discontinuities: of national and global; past and future. It is concerned with the new trajectories and temporalities implicit in the prospective endeavour of offshore oil development as this extractive space is animated by the promises and profits of financial capital. Mexican offshore oil development retained its projected value as long as the path from the present to the future was understood to be stable. When the oil market price crash of 1981 meant that future was no longer credible, the temporal form that structured the relation between present representation and the future dissolved—to be retroactively understood as a fiction.

The petrodollar introduced new temporal forms to petroculture, as market abstractions and media speculations began to write energy futures in the language of spot and future price, risk, volatility, and interest rates. The conspiracy narrative I have been reading provides a cognitive map of this moment of discontinuity, because its narrative structure marks out the financial speculations that flow around offshore infrastructures and the juridical blockages that produce its relative hiddenness. It plots a multi-scalar convergence of finance, infrastructure, markets, and media,

Fig. 2.1 Keppler, Udo's political cartoon of Standard Oil (1904). *Source* Wikimedia Commons

and a narrative impasse central to the social and political production of petroleum's market future. Oil is a financial form not only because its pricing in dollars maintains the value of the period's premier currency and universal equivalent, and therefore all kinds of other financial activity, but also because extraction is a prospective endeavour, oriented towards achieving profit and therefore return on investment. As a genre capable of making plot out of financial speculation, *The Hydra Head* is suspicious of how information in market media might have begun to reorganise oil into information (or misinformation), making narratives valuable in a new way. It therefore articulates a narrative logic that corresponds to the macroeconomics of oil as it becomes the basis of the value-form, as its market abstractions become a hegemonic object and condition of representation (Diamanti, 2021).

I have been arguing that Fuentes is trying to represent his own historical present, and that he makes use of suspicion and conspiracy as a strategic mode, a form that enables a hard-nosed, critical and even cynical disposition to petroleum. This is the case in at least two senses. Maldonado is a cynic: he disdains the disguise he is supposed to wear, horrified and outraged by the attempt to transform national symbol into international resource. But the novel is structurally cynical, in a way that makes it critical of the typical form of closure of the thriller: the resolution of the threat. This symbolic resolution was unavailable to Fuentes as a satisfactory resolution to the plot, which pushes the novel into a political cynicism indistinguishable from fate and predestination. The novel concludes with the following lines:

> But beneath the land of the Malinche lies riches greater than all of Moctezuma's gold. Sealed in geological pits more ancient than the most ancient empires, the treasure of Chiapas, Veracruz, and Tabasco is a promise in a sealed bottle: to seek it is to pursue an invisible cat through subterranean labyrinths. The patient drillers penetrate two, three, four thousand meters deep into the sea, into the jungles, into the sierra. The discover of one fertile well compensates for the failure of a thousand sterile ones.
>
> Like the Hydra, the oil is reborn, multiplied, from a single severed head. Dark semen in a land of hopes and betrayals, oil fecundates the realms of the Malinche beneath the mute voices of the stars and their nocturnal portents (292).

On the one hand, this is the trap of genre: either the spy does or doesn't stop the threat. Here, that failure is cast in world-historical terms, as colonial extraction (Malinche, Moctezuma) is repeated in a new form of financial plunder, or accumulation by dispossession. But on the other hand, it suggests how easily political cynicism falls into a kind of energy determinism, as all historical content is displaced through the nigh-on mythic figuration of invisible cats, subterranean labyrinths, and hydras. This shift in tone, from the cynical voice of the triple agent to the distant, mythical, and abstract, are not so much a stylistic contradiction as a logical consequence; different registers through which to express a world-weary disposition towards petroleum as fate. It is cynical, too, in its failure to resolve the plot, as it becomes clear that the national bureaucrat, and by extension the state, are ultimately subordinated to international interests.

Yet, for all that, the novel remains committed to making knowable the problem that financialised petroleum poses to national development. For this alone, it remains of a hopeful disposition. After all, why make something legible if you don't think that doing so will effect a change? Despite the emotional tenor, then, the desire to intervene remains central to this historical sensibility when it comes to petroleum's new inflection and directionality as financial form. Caught between mystery, conspiracy, and cynicism, Fuentes named, in its emergence, the crisis that continues to unfold as the form and content of our historical present.

References

Appel, H. (2015). *Offshore Work: Infrastructure and Hydrocarbon Capitalism in Equatorial Guinea*. Life Worlds of Oil and Gas. Cornell University Press.

Arrighi, G. (2009). *The Long Twentieth Century: Money, Power and the Origins of Our Time: Money*. Verso Books.

Baucom, I. (2005). *Specters of the Atlantic: Finance Capital, Slavery, and the Philosophy of History* (Illustrated edition). Duke University Press.

Breglia, L. C. (2013). *Living with Oil: Promises, Peaks, and Declines on Mexico's Gulf Coast (Reprint edition)*. University of Texas Press.

Carlisle, R. P. (1981). Sovereignty for Sale: The Origins and Evolution of the Panamanian and Liberian Flags of Convenience. FisicalBook.

Carlos Fuentes | Academy of Achievement. (2021). https://achievement.org/achiever/carlos-fuentes/

Diamanti, J. (2021). *Climate and Capital in the Age of Petroleum*. Bloomsbury.

El-Gamal, M. A. (2010). *Oil, Dollars, Debt, and Crises: The Global Curse of Black Gold*. Cambridge University Press.

Ferguson, J. (2005). Seeing Like an Oil Company: Space, Security, and Global Capital in Neoliberal Africa. *American Anthropologist, 107*(3), 377–382.

Fuentes, C. (1978). *The Hydra Head*. Redburn Wood Limited.

Harvey, D. (1991). *The Condition of Postmodernity: An Enquiry into the Origins of Cultural Change* (1st edition). Wiley-Blackwell.

Jameson, F. (1997). Culture and Finance Capital. *Critical Inquiry, 24*(1), 246–265. https://doi.org/10.1086/448873

La Berge, L. C. (2015). *Scandals and Abstraction: Financial Fiction of the Long 1980s (Illustrated edition)*. Academic.

LiPuma, E. (2017). *The Social Life of Financial Derivatives: Markets, Risk, and Time*. Duke University Press Books.

Mahon, J. E. (1996). *Mobile Capital and Latin American Development*. Pennsylvania State University Press.

Marsh, N. (2015). Finance, Fiction, and the Genre of a World Economy. In *The Cambridge Companion to British Fiction since 1945*. Cambridge University Press.

McClanahan, A. (2018). *Dead Pledges: Debt, Crisis, and Twenty-First-Century Culture*. Stanford University Press.

Moretti, F. (2000). Conjectures on World Literature. *New Left Review, 1*, 54–68.

Palan, R. (2006). *The Offshore World: Sovereign Markets, Virtual Places, and Nomad Millionaires (Annotated edition)*. Cornell University Press.

Palmer, J. (1979). *Thrillers: Genesis and Structure of a Popular Genre*.

Poovey, M. (2008). *Genres of the Credit Economy: Mediating Value in Eighteenth- and Nineteenth-Century Britain* (Illustrated edition). University of Chicago Press.

Potts, S. (2019). Offshore. In *Keywords in Radical Geography: Antipode at 50*. Wiley Blackwell.

Roddick, J. (1990). *The Dance of the Millions: Latin America and the Debt Crisis* (P. O'Brien & J. Painter, Eds.). Latin America Bureau.

Sekula, A. (1996). *Fish Story*. Distributed Art Pub Inc.

Sekula, A. (2002, October). Between the Net and the Deep Blue Sea (Rethinking the Traffic in Photographs), *102*, 3–34.

Sekula, Allan and Noël Burch (2011). 'The Forgotten Space', *New Left Review* 69.

Shonkwiler, Alison (2017). *The Financial Imaginary: Economic Mystification and the Limits of Realist Fiction*. University Of Minnesota Press.

Slobodian, Quinn (2021). 'World Maps for the Debt Paradigm: Risk Ranking the Poorer Nations in the 1970s', *Critical Historical Studies*, 8, 1.

Steinberg, Philip E. (2001). *The Social Construction of the Ocean*. Cambridge University Press.

Thompson, Helen (2018). *Oil and the Western Economic crisis*. Palgrave MacMillan.

Vogl, Joseph (2014). *The Specter of Capital*. Stanford University Press.

CHAPTER 3

Architecture of the Offshore: Lloyd's in Transition

3.1 Architectural Atmospheres

Early in the morning of 18th October 2023, protestors made their way to the centre of London to disrupt the funding of fossil-fuel infrastructure. Mobilising members from activist groups Extinction Rebellion and Fossil Free London, this coordinated action had begun the previous day by disrupting the 'Energy Intelligence Forum' (recently rebranded from the much more accurate 'Oil and Money Conference') at the InterContinental London Park Lane Hotel, where oil executives, CEOs, state representatives, and investment banks had planned to meet. This action succeeded in shutting down the conference, with important guest speakers electing to pull out or appear online instead. On the 18th, however, the targets were different. While the Metropolitan Police headed off to secure the conference, most protestors were heading to a different destination: the City of London, the financial centre of the city and the heart of the fossil financial system.

The objective was to occupy the offices of ten major insurers of fossil fuels, located in the esteemed Lloyd's of London. Blockading the entrance and occupying the halls, the protestors had two demands. Stop underwriting the West Cumbria Coal Mine, the first coal mine to be approved for development in the United Kingdom for thirty years, and the East African Crude Oil Pipeline (EACOP), a 900-mile heated pipeline

H. Pitt Scott, *Financial Petroleum Cultures*, Palgrave Studies in Literature, Culture and Economics,
https://doi.org/10.1007/978-3-031-99661-0_3

(the longest in the world) originating in Uganda's Lake Albert oilfields, traversing around Lake Victoria and through Tanzania to the port of Tanga, where the petroleum will be sold on world markets. While it seems like the West Cumbria Coal Mine will not go ahead, EACOP, controversially, is still in development. The proposed construction runs through ecosystems central to the livelihoods of millions. The risk of spills and ecological destruction threatens the human rights of communities along the logistical corridor through land acquisition and right of way, and a long list of endangered animals in protected and key biodiversity areas. Protestors in Uganda and Tanzania have faced violence, arrest, and threats of criminal charges. While the development of new fossil infrastructure threatens the increasingly unachievable goal of keeping the planet to under two degrees of warming.

What XR and Fossil Free London have identified is a crucial financial dimension to fossil capital. An army of actuaries, surveyors, analysts, accountants, lawyers, bankers, and assessment bodies are required to lay out the legal and financial terms that shape the petroleum infrastructures that connect extraction zones to ports and financial centres. Thus, as members of socialist organisation rs21 noted when reflecting on this action, "by targeting these spaces [the City of London], not only might we disrupt the flows of oily money but we also expose them to the light of day" (rs21, 2023). This militant practical theorisation in situ offers an incisive appraisal of the political economy that links Lake Victoria's socio-ecological vulnerability to London's financial accumulation. Its dual purpose of disruption and visibility articulates an infrastructural environmentalism whose causality runs from insurance policy and pipeline to climate crisis; that sees financial infrastructure as enabling the physical dimension of the energy system. Oil's material flow is only one site open to sabotage, blockage, and disruption, as the exposure of finance located many thousands of miles from extraction sites pulls into visibility. For the protestors, the prospect of a volatile future is the basis for a new and global form of solidarity, where finance opens a new terrain of political struggle over the coming energy future.

Lloyd's of London is the focus of this chapter. I have chosen Lloyd's not just because of its historical importance, but due to the fact that architecture has a privileged relation to financial petroculture: a social practice concerned with producing cultural and economic settings that enable financial accumulation. Architecture is designed, planned, and invested with temporality: to enable Lloyd's to "play to the full its international role in the 21st Century" (Powell, 1994, p. 1). It is also an environment that facilitates financial time into socio-spatial experience, as subjects learn certain habits, expectations, and values. Architecture design is also a practical way of thinking energetically: "architecture can be understood as a *material* organization that regulates and brings to order to *energy* flows; and, simultaneously and inseparably, as an *energetic* organization that stabilizes and maintains *material* forms" (Fernández–galia, 2001, p. 5). The junction of architectural, energy, and financial time provides a way of seeing a kind of juridical spatiality immanent to petroculture that is designed to be difficult to think about at all.

For most of its history, the Lloyd's of London building has not been representative of fossil finance. Instead, it has been a signature example of the 'International Style', sometimes known as 'High-Tech', an architectural style that came to define the corporate architecture of the 1980s. A fictionalised version of Lloyd's, renamed Kesselers, is described very differently in Alan Hollinghurst's *The Line of Beauty* (2004), a historical novel of the Thatcher years:

> When the day came Nick turned up early at the bank and waited under a palm tree in the atrium. People hurried in, nodding to the commissionaire, who still wore a tailcoat and a top hat. On the exposed escalators the employees were carried up and down, looking both slavish and intensely important. Nick watched the motorbike messengers in their sweaty waterproofs and leathers, and heavy boots. He felt abashed and agitated by closeness to so many people at work, in costume, in character, in the know. The building itself had the glitter of confidence, and made and retained an unending and authentic noise out of air vents, the hubbub of voices and the impersonal trundling of the escalators. Nick craned upwards for a glimpse of the regions where Lord Kessler himself might be conducting business, at that level surely a matter of mere blinks and ironies, a matter of telepathy. He knew that the old panelled boardroom had been retained, and that Lionel had hung some remarkable pictures there [...]
> It was nearly all men in the restaurant. Nick was glad he'd worn his best suit and almost wished he'd worn a tie. There were sharp-eyed older men, looking faintly harassed by the speed and noise, their dignity threatened by the ferocious youngsters who already had their hands on a new kind of success. Some of the young men were beautiful and exciting; a sort of ruthless sex-drive was the way Nick imagined their sense of their own power. Others were the uglies and misfits from the school playground who'd made money their best friend (Hollinghurst, 2005, pp. 203–204).

Lloyd's, in this retrospective telling of the cultural and economic shift into neoliberalism from the perspective of a young, gay man on the peripheries of Thatcherism and the financial boom, expresses the spirit of that transitional decade, as the gentlemanly City of the postwar years is slowly transformed by a competitive, ruthless, and individualistic financial culture. It is as if the building's confident indifference to its occupants has imprinted on the financiers and insurers who pass through its doors every day; its rupture with the older architectural style of the City—a curiously modernist gesture, as we will come to see—emblematic of a new kind of man (and they are mostly men, in this period); where a kind of self-importance, in the preservation of the old boardroom, coheres into an insular atmosphere.

But it is now necessary to describe the building, designed by Richard Rogers and opened in 1986. Lloyd's was considered a pioneer of the High-Tech style, a type of design that separates 'served' and 'servant' spaces (an influence of modernist Louis Kahn) (Fig. 3.1). The piping, heating, elevators, and service sectors are all placed on the outside of the building, rather than in the internal structure. This bold, dynamic façade has a dramatic effect on the inside, by creating a large, adaptable, and flexible space, capable of change and unconstrained by infrastructure. This central space is called the 'Underwriting Room' and is overlooked by a series of galleries that are given light by the barrel-vaulted glass roof (Fig. 3.2). In the uninhibited interior, which contains only eight concrete pillars and a central clock, insurance stalls and intersecting elevators sit in a light and open marketplace. The light and unimpeded interior emphasise smoothness, mobility, and dynamism. The exterior is a striking combination of steel and glass, as the functional infrastructure, such as elevators and pipes, disrupt its smoothness with turret-like shafts. According to Kenneth Powell, it is a symbol of the City of London, because "its flexibility, environmentalism and responsiveness to the changing shape of services, electronic and non-electronic", provided an influential architectural model (Powell, 1994, p. 45).

While relatively rare in the 1980s, the stylish large-office buildings pioneered by Rogers dominated London's financially driven boom years of the 1990s and 2000s, of which 88 Wood Street (1993–99) and the Lloyd's Register Building (1993–2000) are examples. It remains a popular style, with the Leadenhall Building (2010–14), another Rogers design, now standing opposite the Lloyd's Building and dwarfing it in

Fig. 3.1 The Lloyd's Building. 'High-Tech' is known for its 'inside-out' style, the servant spaces visible on the façade. *Source* Lloyd's Website

size. The other most famous example of High-Tech is Norman Foster's HSBC Main Building in Hong Kong (1978–85).

Lloyd's took on its globally significant role in financial petroculture because of a convergence of economic, political, infrastructural and architectural shifts. In this chapter, I want to trace that conjuncture as a prehistory of our volatile present, before finance gets resignified as a driver of climate catastrophe. I am interested in this formation and eventual discontinuity because the story of Lloyd's is of the rise of the offshore to a place of central importance to financial petroculture.

3.2 High-Tech Dreams

I began my account of financial petrocultures in the Gulf of Mexico, which I read as a site in which petrodollarisation became legible as a new kind of financial, legal, and infrastructural form. Across the Atlantic, the United Kingdom was undergoing its own offshore revolution. In the 1950s, while Bretton Woods was still in effect, bankers in the City of

Fig. 3.2 The Atrium. The 60m high Atrium is the central to the building, providing both light and a complex air-conditioning and heat system through air circulation

London discovered a loophole that allowed them to hold dollars that were not regulated by the Bank of England or the US. Called the 'Eurodollar' market, it was home to stateless money that existed on the sidelines of nation-states and slowly undermined the Bretton Woods gold-dollar standard. By 1971 there were so many Eurodollars in petroleum markets that the US could no longer redeem international dollars with gold. Much of the oil rents accrued in economies unable to invest the vast sums in production, a tendency that greatly accelerated after the 1973 oil shock. Eurodollar markets operated as a channel through which to circulate petrodollars and by the 1970s, the volume of monetary transactions through this financial offshore network exceeded the value of world trade (Arrighi, 2009, p. 308). Britain became central to the creation of opaque networks of insulated legal and financial jurisdictions. Meanwhile, offshore oil and gas discoveries in the North Sea were parcelled up, sold, and development began, an industry that had, and maintains, deep political and financial ties to the City of London (Cumbers, 2012).

Lloyd's had specialised in marine insurance since the seventeenth century, and until as recently as 2018, when it was subject to huge losses as a result of natural disasters, it was the largest insurance market in the world. An important player in the insurance markets of shipping, it has had a hand in almost every economy of the British Empire, including the slave trade. Since the mid-twentieth century, marine insurance has also included offshore oil exploration and production, while it now has significant amounts of contracts in shipping, aviation, energy and motor insurance, and a very large reinsurance market. With Lloyd's at the forefront, the shipping insurance market boomed in the 1970s as it underwrote the logistical revolution and the oil tanker boom. The offshore expansion was driven by the need for new prospects amid the 1970s price boom, and the vast sums of money required to fund tough offshore extraction meant that Lloyd's became deeply entangled with this oil boom. Construction on the new building began in 1978 and opened in 1986, a month after the London Stock Market deregulation known as the 'Big Bang'. This decision by Thatcher's government to deregulate financial markets transformed the City of London into a global financial services centre and a hub of global petroculture.

Lloyd's does more than insure oil extraction. Its Joint War Committee (JWC) is one of the key arbiters in deciding the risk associated with different shipping routes, gateways, and corridors. The JWC, connected to military security in NATO, make threats to maritime trade—piracy, labour disputes, environmental catastrophe, terrorist attacks—an object of financial governance. Lloyd's and NATO turn this incalculability into a logic of 'risk-embracing', leading them to "shape a security apparatus to enable the profitable operation of their insurance venture", actively contributing to the marine environments in which risks to oil capital are managed (Lobo-Guerrero, 2012, p. 74). Oil flows securely through militarised ocean routes because of insurance markets in the City of London.

Lloyd's rise coincided with the relative decline of the British industrial economy on the world stage. Since the 1986 opening, three broad economic trends have shaped the United Kingdom. Manufacturing nearly halved and labour productivity (economic output per unit of labour time), once the highest in Europe, did not keep pace with other industrial economies (and has been almost stagnant since 2008) (Department for Business Innovation and Skills, 2011). Since 2008, it has had negative average productivity growth. Between 1986 and 2008, financial services as a percentage of total UK exports rose from under 10% to 29%, with a growth rate far outstripping manufacturing growth, driven primarily by overseas demand. The United Kingdom became a 'service economy', with services accounting for two-thirds of the economy in 1986, and four-fifths in 2011. Meanwhile, North Sea oil and Gulf petrodollars propped up sterling value as the UK's manufacturing export sector weakened, effectively offsetting the balance of payments deficit that threatened to undermine the economic power of the UK (Wearing, 2018, p. 1).

Lloyd's explicitly positioned themselves as historic pioneers of this process. In a special report published in 1986 to advertise their new building, Peter Miller, then chairman of Lloyd's, wrote that

> Lloyd's has always led the way in innovation. When sail gave way to steam, Lloyd's was there to underwrite the newcomer. When the horse and carriage was replaced by the motor, Lloyd's undertook the insurance. Today the trend continues, with offshore drilling rigs and satellites in space figuring prominently in Lloyd's business (Lloyd's (Firm), 1986, p. 1).

Lloyd's represents its history as a key player in the transition from wind to coal, coal to oil, and oil to offshore oil. They commissioned a new building, in part, because of this last shift: they had outgrown the previous, which was not large enough to house the booming insurance market.

The commission was first advertised in 1978, and Richard Rogers and Renzo Piano had completed the Centre Pompidou in Paris just the year before. A public library, museum, and centre for the arts, this building pioneered a futuristic and utopian style that positioned architecture at the forefront of a democratic culture. Playful and entertaining, this building was a rich engagement with a number of modernist styles such as Futurism and Archigram. It was to be accessed by the public and so represented and facilitated a civic identity, while its internal spaces were flexible and could change according to public need. At the end of the Centre Pompidou project and at the tail end of the UK's 1970s recession, with less work available for architects, the then Richard Rogers Partnership (now Roger Stirk Harbour + Partners) applied to design the new Lloyd's Building. Representative of mass culture, the Centre Pompidou was to Rogers's disadvantage in this respect, because Lloyd's wanted a design more in keeping with the austere nature of its role as insurer. At the same time, Lloyd's wanted an impressive and innovative visual monument, with the future building positioning the institution at the cutting-edge of architectural development (Powell, 1994, p. 25). When Rogers won the contract, he found himself in a contradictory position: at the forefront of a so-called radical architectural movement, High-Tech, with a background interest in structural simplicity and energy efficiency, but commissioned to design buildings for not only *for* a financial institution, but to employ the architectonic innovations in service to the forms of financial work that Lloyd's demanded.

he 1970s was a strange architectural climate for an architect like Rogers, who wanted to maintain the social and cultural importance of the modern movement even as it went into terminal crisis in Britain. The economic crisis, triggered by oil crisis, had effectively ended the modern movement that defined the UK's postwar architecture scene, which had been dominated by the welfare state's planned economy (Kaminer, 2011, p. 4). For David Harvey, this meant "a break with the idea that planning and development should focus on large-scale, technologically rational, austere and functionally efficient 'international style'" to seek "some kind of accommodation with the more flexible regime of accumulation that has emerged since 1973" (Harvey, 1990, p. 253). Modernist projects—the notorious concrete high-rises—were no longer seen as an architectural solution in the wake of the crisis, stagflation, and economic downturn. Critiques of modernist urban planning and architecture were formulated in both economic and aesthetic terms. 'Non-Plan: An Experiment in Freedom' (1969), exemplified this critique because of its attack on the UK's postwar development which it saw as the destruction of local particularity, democratic participation, and popular sensibility. The influential article, is taglined "Why not have the courage, where practical, to let people shape their own environment?" By "find[ing] out what people would want [...] one might discover the hidden style of mid-twentieth century Britain" (Sadler, 1999).

The authors quote Frank Lloyd Wright approvingly, who said that "the gasoline service station may be seen the beginning of an important advance agent of decentralisation", a nod to the effects of automobility on the geographical dispensing and distribution of forms of social life that were once centrally bound to American city centres (Sadler, 1999). The contrast, for the Non-Plan authors, between East and West Midlands industrialisation—between Birmingham's industrial concentration and a regional industrial decentralisation—is that the former deepens the town-country divide while the latter accommodates the difference through automobility. They take inspiration from American petrocultural suburban sprawl and adapt this to a British context; an uneven and combined petroculture for an English countryside, encompassing suggestions from Vegas-style strips around airports to a cybernetic revolution in planning and even, bizarrely, thermal-controlled domed nudist beaches. Petroculture changes architecture not only because of the modes of planning petroleum's capacities make available, but because architectural space and experience can be imagined differently through automobility. Decentralisation mediates the economic and aesthetic needs of a motorising British society and culminates (in England) in specialist automobile manufacturing of Jaguar-Land Rover, which hardly resembles the Ford River Rouge Plant so exemplary of centralised Fordism. Decentralisation becomes an imaginary resolution to a localist environmentalism that sees modernist planning as a destructive and anti-democratic extension of industrialisation, resolving the divide between country and city at a regional level, while generalising it at a global one.

Enabled by the new decentralised geographies of petroculture, 'Non-Plan' crystallised in architectural critique an economic and aesthetic anti-statism that could be valenced into a pro-market position, populism, pop culture and advertisements, or an English environmentalism of country preserved against industrialisation. It is a perspective that accounts for oil as the fuel of what would later get called postmodernism, first in architecture and then, later, late-capitalist culture as a whole. It captures the exciting influence of American petroculture—still an import at the time—while articulating the limits of the nation-state as a framework from which to make sense of the changes ushered in by oil. Whatever came after architectural modernism, so the argument went, would have to be suited to a different society than that centred on the nation-state.

This culminated in the Thatcherite revolution, the transition of Britain to a petroculture, and the return of British finance to world-systemic importance. After 1973, the national economy no longer provided a coherent object of governance as it gradually reintegrated with the world-economy, and London became a major financial centre (Edgerton, 2018, pp. 295–297). When oil came online in 1975, oil revenues supported sterling value and made Britain into a major energy producer again, in the North Sea rather than its coalfields, restoring Britain's place as a net-energy exporter for the first time since the end of empire. But as is regularly noted in historical scholarship, oil did not enter into British national image and identity. Expertise and infrastructure for offshore development were imported from abroad, the industry workforce remained small and fairly non-unionised, and so did not cohere into a culture like those who worked in coal capitalist industries did (Harvie, 1995). The offshore enables a transition between a national and an international orientation because it represents some activities as external to the nation-state. The offshore shows that the *social* character of the state is distinct from its *spatial* character, as its juridical domain does not correspond with its territorial one. This means that oil is better grasped in British petroculture not as a symbol or through its direct representation but as a cultural logic modulated by Britain's offshoring economy, and that architecture and architectural critique is uniquely sensitive to this.

It was against an architectural sea change that Lloyd's new building was conceived. At the time High-Tech was an innovative and distinctive vision. The style, which combined industrial functionality and flexible adaptation, captured the transition the UK was experiencing. What is conspicuous about this building for the argument I am pursuing is that Rogers's design combines distinctive, at times oppositional, styles. Postmodern architecture, which came into fashion in the 1970s, emphasised context and historicism, so that buildings 'fit in' with their immediate environment (generally conceived as a reaction to modernism's desire to make the new). To an extent Rogers employed this through the fidelity with which the building is aligned and ordered with the curvature of the historic mediaeval Leadenhall Street and Market. But he combined this with an anti-historicist style that does not reference its immediate environment. It clearly does fit within an alternative, modernist tradition—and so draws on the energetic materialism implicit in the building's modernist predecessors. It is also an environmentally conscious building, responsive to problems of energy exchange (such as heat loss and lighting) between internal and external environments, especially as these relate to power usage and air conditioning, which were newly relevant as computers became increasingly common. Within the building's enclosed space is a secure environment shaped by techno-environmental adaptation and invention, where light and heat are rationally and seamlessly integrated into, but differentiated from, the external environment—a means of managing exposure to the outer elements. There is a nascent environmentalism here, even if it is contained within a larger system of environmental destruction. Moreover, Rogers had to contend with the naturally conservative clients at Lloyd's, many of whom were uncomfortable with modernist architecture. But economic necessity drove the compromise, because in the 1970s Lloyd's needed both a much larger space and to remain within the City, where most of its business clients were located.

At first glance what is most striking about the Lloyd's Building is the steel exterior. External infrastructure appears to ground the vault atrium, as if, without it, the entire building itself would float off. This is a modernist impulse, expressed in the anti-historicist symbolism of steel. Stainless steel, unlike concrete, does not bear the mark of time through discolouration, as if the material itself is both inside and outside of historical change. Along with its externalised infrastructure, which gives Lloyd's its definitive outline, the steel skin conveys a tensile energy, of weighty permanence with a sense of motion—especially as one moves around it, the outside rippling as the silhouette shifts the visible material. The infrastructure—elevator shafts, pipes, service towers and cranes—are connected by concrete joints, which gives the building a high degree of articulation and a distinctive geometrical precision. But it is not symmetrical, given its fit into the curved mediaeval street and uneven tower height, and this asymmetry makes it visibly unique. This distinguishes it from the postwar high-rise (especially those influenced by the International Style, but also the Brutalism prevalent in British cities) whose architectural language is monolithic, uniform, and abstract. Lloyd's is distinguished from its environment not through abstraction but through particularity. Lloyd's iconic power as a symbol of the City and its architectural innovation as energy efficient and environmentally consciousness gives it the curious status of unique and ecological yet modernist and anti-historicist.

Rogers would later recount the purpose of the inside-outside design and the large open space inside: "[We] kept the floors clear because Lloyd's said they wanted two things [...] They wanted a building that would last into the next century—we met that one—and they wanted a building that could meet their changing needs". Building the services and infrastructure on the outside "create[d] uninterrupted spaces inside. This is similar to the Centre Pompidou, and has equally uncluttered and highly flexible internal spaces" (Crook, 2019). Uninterrupted, uncluttered, highly flexible, adaptable, but contained within a structure of relative permanence and spatial order: the internal space is non-programmatic and open to transformation. It can expand or contract, if necessary, by developing or retreating from different floors. The purpose of this flexible design was to make Lloyd's future-proof, able to accommodate the ongoing boom in financial services well into the twenty-first century.

Resolving incongruities of environment and social function might describe Rogers's architecture in general, which has always developed under contradictory impulses. In a speech in 1988, Rogers says that the work of his firm is

> a continuation of the Modern Movement, trying to expand its approach to meet constantly changing needs. We are searching for a more open and dynamic yet harmonious order which offers the user freedom from the constraints of finite form: a geometry which may be modified by new experiences allowing for planned and unplanned evolution but in which the totality has complete integrity at any one time (Rogers, 1988, p. 873).

Most clear in the building's ordered arrangement of service sectors, made from pre-assembled 'kit-of-parts', this modernist dynamism negotiates newness and change through a historicity of obsolescence. This became essential once the City moved from the call-and-response paper-based financial trading to digital trading, as the kit-of-parts infrastructure easily allowed for the installation of digital technology infrastructure such as power and wiring. This is precisely the 'freedom from the constraints of finite form' Rogers describes, and which must also be read as an insight into the nature of architectural value to finance, because mitigating obsolescence is a speculative practice that offers a vision of what the economic future was thought to look like in the 1970s. Meanwhile the usage of innovative technology to invite light into the building and an advanced, energy-efficient heat-control system creates an adaptable and flexible Underwriting Room capable of supporting the work of six-thousand people (which expanded to over five times that number by the mid-1980s). Rogers finds a geometrical order for the "programmatic indeterminacy" of financial space: the unity of "planned and unplanned evolution" is a striking anticipation of the future world of finance (Rogers, 1988, p. 876). In recognising that the need for power might dramatically expand through digital electrical financial infrastructure, the design theorised the new energetic and material forms necessary to infrastructure the coming electrified finance economy.

That this infrastructure promised the future is a result of the strong Futurist influence on the design of the façade. Rogers was an admirer of the work of Antonio Sant'Elia, who wrote the 'Manifesto of Futurist Architecture' and whose *Città Nuova* (1914) has a recognisable influence on the Lloyd's Building (Fig. 3.3) . While Sant'Elia envisaged his design at city scale, the description he offers has startling similarities with Lloyd's:

> We must invent and reconstruct the futurist city on the model of an immense, bustling shipyard, every part agile, mobile and dynamic; the futurist house must become a kind of gigantic machine. Lifts mustn't be hidden away like solitary worms in stairwells, stairs—now obsolete—should be abolished, and lifts should wriggle up façades like steel-and glass snakes. The concrete, steel and glass building, bare of painting and sculpture, enriched only by the inherent beauty of its lines and modelling, will be extraordinarily brutal, ugly in its mechanical simplicity and as tall and large as necessary, unlimited by municipal building restrictions (Sant'Elia, 1914).

Sant'Elia's Futurist architecture captures the speed, scale, and dynamism afforded by electricity and fossil fuel; a radical break with the non-modern city, expressed by the smooth surfaces, volumetric form and stark silhouette of the drawn building, which dwarfs the circulation of pedestrians, trams and automobiles in scale. Rogers adapts the expressive Futurist energies, including the external shafts—Sant'Elia's steel-and-glass snakes—their visible mechanics a celebration of automated movement, but totally repurposed. For Sant'Elia this was an embodiment of industrial

Fig. 3.3 Città Nuova. In 1914 Antonio Sant'Elia, Futurist architect, lived in modernising Milan undergoing its own version of the Plan, the 'Beruto Plan', loosely based on Haussmann's work in Paris. He designed a building with external elevators shafts as part of his Città Nuova (1914). Most of the drawings are of power plants. While it was never built, the similarities with the Lloyd's Building are striking. *Source* Wikimedia Commons

progress, the city resembling a factory, its inhabitants trained for modernity through the rational integration of the entire city environment. But in Lloyd's the façade differentiates *between* the city and the internal financial space, suggestive of an infrastructural insulation of a post-imperial resurgent financial sector from the surrounding urban environment. This design is not some great social utopian vision in the style of Sant'Elia or Le Corbusier, of a city remade and life reinvented. It is precisely the discontinuity with such a vision that must be emphasised.

Indeed, Rogers's modernist design was resisted by Lloyd's on several occasions. Amazingly, at the centre of this Futurist-inspired building, lies the Committee Room, an eighteenth-century banquet hall disassembled, transported to the eleventh floor and reassembled, to satisfy the conservative Lloyd's membership. This unevenness was created by the conflict between modernist architect and conservative client, times out of joint but connected by the Futurist steel-and-glass snake elevators, as automation intersects, literally, with the structured hierarchical space. What is fascinating about this conflict is that it reveals how necessary the modern design was for it to be accepted and yet so strongly resisted. It had to be accepted, because the flexible space afforded by High-Tech could not be compromised if Lloyd's was to retain its (literal) place as lead insurer in the City (Fig. 3.4).

While the façade and internal space suggest transparency and openness, in a way that is opposite to offshore secrecy, the private nature of finance contained inside makes this transparency into a spectacle, a site of visual attraction, rather than having any democratising effect on the form of work it contains. This contradiction surfaces and indeed becomes part of the visible surface of the building in the elevator design. Up to the fourth floor is a semi-public space. The fifth and upward, although encased in glass, are private. They are accessible via the external glass elevator, and thus they are visible from outside the building, as its users move upward into a private sphere. The new elevator technology enables a design that allows the private and the visible to briefly meet. This architectural language of surface and transparency coexists with the Futurist spectacle of innovative technology on the outside. As one leans back and watches individuals flicker in and out of visibility as they disappear into private space, transparency dissipates into technological marvel (Fig. 3.5).

If the great circular service towers draw the eye upward in one moment, they are drawn downward to a subterranean space in another. One need only view the building lit at night in cool blue and green hues, its exterior shafts appearing like drills thrust into the earth, to get a sense of the building as an industrial spectacle. High-Tech expresses a futuristic industrial mood. At night, the pipes and lighting create an effect evocative of a spaceship landing from a distant, chromatic future. It combines

Fig. 3.4 The external elevators. *Source* Lloyd's of London website

Fig. 3.5 The Underwriting Room. With the building's infrastructure on the outside, this open, uninterrupted space can expand or contract, flexibly accommodating to the needs of the insurance market. *Source* Lloyd's Website

material experimentation and formal coherence: echoes of modern utopianism reinterpreted as a flexible but harmonious order between the planned and unplanned, the public and the private. It is perfectly adaptable to financial infrastructure, facilitating financial exchange in an internal competitive market. It is adaptable to an uncertain future yet able to weather economic risk.

If difference was the watchword of modernism, then for High-Tech it might be dynamism. It is here that Rogers's influence by the 1960s Archigram movement is most clearly discernible. Archigram was a modernist style updated for the technological moment of the 1960s. The movement wanted a dynamic, technologically advanced, and modular architecture, inspired by the new commodities created by postwar chemicals, electronics, and aeronautical industries. Against the social fixity embodied by the image of concrete high-rises, and what it perceived to be the excessive arrogance of the top-down plan, Archigram saw the future of architecture in mass-produced, malleable pre-cast building materials that could be widely, cheaply and democratically distributed—suitable to the changing needs of a consumer society (these appear in Lloyd's concrete kit-of-parts columns). As was written in the *Archigram* Magazine in 1963, "Through every level of society and with every level of commodity, the unchanging scene is being replaced by the increase in change of our user-habits—and thereby, eventually, our user-habitats [...] We must recognise this as a healthy and altogether positive sign. It is the product of a sophisticated consumer society" (Sadler, 2005, p. 95). Archigram's speculative energies ran on petroculture's abundance and plasticity, as well as economic worries about obsolescence, the drag of fixed capital, and built environments unsuitable to support the society of the future. The focus on automation, movement, interchangeability, plasticity, and fluidity speculated on future spatial form and cultural practice. Meanwhile, the connection between colloquial habits and habitats in Archigram is suitably elastic to encompass notions of both a culture of mass democracy and of mass consumerism.

Archigram positioned itself as an avant-garde *against* the British architectural establishment, preserving the futurity of modernist architecture in an era in which modernists had become dominant. In his book-length study of Archigram, Simon Sadler writes that the movement "contended that architecture should not create fixed volumes of space to be mutely inhabited, less still shaped masses of masonry, but must provide the equipment for 'living', for 'being'" (Sadler, 2005, p. 5). For Archigram, living was equated with the plasticity of life, work, and space, reconfigured by new postwar petroleum technology. The movement expressed a structure of feeling expressed through a non-linguistic form of spatial imagination (the kit-of-parts, malleable space, endless variation), connecting the consumer society and mass democracy to the capacity for oil's derivative forms to give material shape to daily life.

Archigram had its heyday in the 1960s. But as 1970s stagflation put paid to its social visions, the prospect of endless expansiveness and total urban reorganisation through modular component parts turned out to be architectural science fiction. But it had a lasting impact on High-Tech. One of Rogers's earlier designs was a prefabricated house with an interior space capable of reorganisation according to the needs of the inhabitants. It was mass-produced but non-standardised and assembled from energy-efficient resources. Rogers found inspiration in Archigram but moderated it with an economy of material for the energy-anxious culture of the 1970s. Such design was unburdened from social history and top-down planning, with little concrete in sight; and, in a great irony, Lloyd's remains to this day an energy-efficient building. While the infinite expansion of malleable material was never realised, the interior spatial flexibility that Archigram desired became essential to Rogers's project, equally useful in the democratic Pompidou Centre as the electricity-intensive Lloyd's Building.

Archigram functioned as 'vanishing mediator', criticising an outmoded architectural modernism and providing the formal innovation for new spatial organisations of work, after which it dissipated and disappeared into architectural history. While the Archigram movement maintained a Utopian impulse in envisioning non-alienated environments for life adapted to the changing needs of a new consumer society, in effect they provided Rogers with the inspiration for creating spaces suitably elastic for financial petroculture. This no doubt is the reason why High-Tech has become a global icon of corporate architecture. Archigram, tempered into High-Tech through the energy crisis decade and an austere financial culture, provided a transitional form between democratic and financial space. Echoes of bricolage, present in Centre Pompidou, are shorn of playfulness by an austere formalism of contrasting material, between steel and glass, weight and light. This combined multiple styles: the industrial energy of Futurism, the consumerist plasticity of Archigram, and the modernist weightiness of towers of concrete and steel.

To really see the building, you have to move around it. The entrance is relatively concealed, and inaccessible to the public. The admirable physical features, spatial order, and innovative flexibility offer aesthetic enjoyment but also a sense of powerful, permanent concealment. The façade turns function into an assertion of self-reliance, the detachment of the Lloyd's Building from its immediate setting. The outside is modernist monumentality, communicating certainty and power, yet the internal space celebrates cultural flexibility and technological revolution, suggestive of the dialectic of permanence and change Rogers identifies as the heart of his architectural vision. The building actualises a flexible space enclosed and differentiated from the rest of the world; an offshore enclave materialised in the heart of the London.

3.3 Grand Visions

The Lloyd's Building provides a way of discerning how the offshore is formative of financial petroculture. Lloyd's has played a historic role in fossil capital's expansion in the era of 'tough' oil, offshore manufacturing, and global connectivity. Given the exorbitant cost of tough oil extraction, underwriting is the precondition for financial investment in oil extraction. It gives shape to the typical and expected. Ian Baucom writes that "Insurance's condition of possibility is a way of seeing within the particularities of any given contemporary life, commodity, or venture it is called on to underwrite, the typical structures of mortality, exchange, or history that circumscribe these things and operate as their historically peculiar circumstances" (Baucom, 2005, p. 40). Tough oil means huge quantities of capital must be invested in oil extraction, and insurance determines the risk of such activity. A financial representation of space is necessary to transform energy into economic form. Insurance is an economic and narrative form about how that future is expected to happen. The offshore is a space available for resource extraction through underwriting: the description, measurement, approval, and signing of typical risks—a kind of financial infrastructure for investment, a genre helping to produce the world it describes.

It is for this reason that Lloyd's was an essential player in the formation of an offshore world. Oil was crucial to the British transition into neoliberalism, offering an alternative energy form to coal, which was the basis of working-class union militancy, and a new front for privatisation. The North Sea development was driven by a short-termist perspective which, supported by Margaret Thatcher's government, encouraged rapid exploitation. High oil prices after the 1979 Iranian revolution, and constant anxieties about supply disruptions from the Middle East meant that oil from the United Kingdom was expected to be safe and profitable, which incentivised getting it out of the sea as quickly as possible. This required a dependency on overseas American expertise (Brotherstone, 2012, pp. 77–78). In Britain in the 1980s, undergoing a revolution in the role and function of the state, "the post-war model had been turned on its head. In place of nationalisation and statutory monopoly, privatization and competition became the driving forces of energy policy. Security of supply would no longer be driven by government, but instead would be the outcome of market forces" (Helm, 2003, p. 2). The transformation of the offshore into an infrastructure for typical investment (in economic rather than cultural perception) made for conditions that described speed as something that made capital safe. Viewed through the frame of a volatile high oil price, the North Sea was seen through the short-term need to extract as much value as possible; and insurers, desperate to invest capital in a burgeoning reinsurance market—in which A reinsured B who reinsured C who reinsured A—which actively shaped the offshore into a market setting, described and therein produced this new norm.

Yet if the political-economic logic of offshoring intends to separate, enclose, and spread risk, the volatility of petroleum often spills out of containment. It was against this background that the worst disaster in the history of oil industry took place, the Piper Alpha disaster in 1988. What made Piper Alpha exceptional was the temporality of insurance, which made the offshore typical. Insurers at Lloyd's decided to underwrite Piper Alpha, which opened it to investment and development, while American oil companies, with an anti-trade-union culture, side-lined union ability to set health-and-safety policy. Oil production started in 1976. In 1988, the platform set on fire, with one hundred and sixty-seven deaths and sixty-five injuries. The disaster led to a reformation of offshore manufacturing and what Lloyd's calls "exposure management", how risk is measured in offshore energy industries. This was the largest insured man-made catastrophe to date, estimated at $1.4 billion—due to a huge quantity of cheap insurance contracts related to Piper Alpha, primarily because underwriters were desperate for profit and "saturated with exposure" to the oil market (Hales, 1995, p. 258). Just two years later, the *Exxon Valdez,* also insured at the prestigious market, struck a reef off the coast of Alaska, causing the largest oil spill to date and splashing the environmental consequences of petroleum across the front pages of the world's media.

The connection between Lloyd's, Piper Alpha, and the *Exxon Valdez* disaster shows how important insurance markets are to determining the relative visibility of offshore spaces. These disasters spilled into wider cultural visibility and, due to oil's parallel existence as financial form, led to financial crisis, as lack of regulation and large investment in reinsurance led to significant exposure to oil disasters. This relay between infrastructure crisis and financial form illuminates the newly volatile landscape of financial petroculture. Price signals, market forces, and the political need to develop alternative energy forms to those associated with working-class power (the 'enemy within', in Thatcherite Britain) generated the offshore as a political and financial solution to national political and economic crisis.

If the new economy of oil enabled by soaring oil prices had fuelled Lloyd's' boom, it nearly spelled its end, as few syndicates had the requisite reserves to meet these liabilities (alongside others such as hurricanes, asbestos claims, and the gulf war) and the market seemed on the point of collapse. It weathered the financial storm through litigation settlement, market reform, and the introduction of corporate investors. The New Labour government subjected it to independent regulation by the Financial Services Authority in 1998. But for twenty years, Lloyd's embodied the spirit of unregulated financial accumulation, trusting its syndicates to self-regulate because of their individual expertise, long-standing position, and deep knowledge of the market. As market experts, they were presumed to know the risks.

The idea that financial experts were best left to themselves, and that the market would best regulate them, was certainly in the air in the Thatcher years. A heady mixture of neoliberal ideas was being unleashed on British society, leading to privatisation of state companies (such as BP between 1979 and 1987), and the deregulation of London Stock Exchange in 1986, enabling the shift from open outcry to electronic trading. The neoliberals intended to encase markets against the threat of democracy; the function of the state was conceived as securing the role of markets in governing the allocation of resources (Slobodian, 2018). This was a vision of political order that challenged the prevailing wisdom of state planning. One of the political movement's most prominent thinkers, Friedrich Hayek, argued that the problem with planning was that it was always consciously directed by an individual with incomplete knowledge, while a complete knowledge of the totality of economic relations was impossible. All plans were destined to distort the more efficient mechanism of the market order, which utilised the aggregate knowledge "dispersed among uncounted persons" and regulated by price mechanisms (F. Hayek, 1974). Instead of a planned economy, what was required was an economic order insulated from state planners intending to interfere with the operations of the world market. This "communication systems we call the market, he argued, "turns out to be a more efficient mechanism for digesting dispersed information than any that man has deliberately designed" (F. Hayek, 1974). Thus the market provided a grand economic vision in which modelling, description, and price signals are sufficient for rational economic activity.

If this kind of thinking would dominate the 1980s, it was prevalent in Lloyd's for at least a decade prior, due to its unique market structure.

Because of the introduction of very high investment income tax in the UK (98%), there was a strong incentive for joining Lloyd's, because syndicates could make use of insurance contracts to, in effect, convert investment income to capital gains, which was taxed at a much lower rate (40%). Other financial techniques such as rollovers, where insurance premiums were rolled over across often fraudulent contracts to avoid tax entirely, contributed to turning Lloyd's into a tax haven (Duguid, 2014, p. 27). These loopholes channelled money into vast dark pools of capital adrift in the unregulated offshore, on the edges of the system of interventionist nation-states central to the postwar system. Thus, neoliberalism arrived early in places like Lloyd's, whose market structure had found a way of encasing money from state politics.

I am interested in the architectural form of this financial imaginary. Our understanding of architectural space is enhanced if we understand the kind of imaginary it anchors, both materially and discursively. Lloyd's was architecturally suited to this new neoliberal world; indeed, it arrived there first, via the offshore, as the volume of monetary transactions necessitated a transformation in architectural space to make room for their exchange. I have sought to show how the conjuncture of an offshore oil boom, financial tax havens, neoliberal deregulation of finance, and a crisis in architecture produced this world-historic space for financial petroculture's anchoring of pipelines to price mechanisms—a design that Rogers articulated ideals of flexible adaptation to a booming financial future and a practical vision of the electrical infrastructure to enable it. It is a conjuncture that makes legible the mutual determination of architecture form and financial ideology.

This economic configuration can be felt in the role that Lloyd's has assumed in the climate crisis, as a key arbiter in the management of climate risks. The Task Force on Climate-related Financial Disclosures (TCFD) was established in 2015 by The Financial Stability Board (FSB), an international organisation composed of the G20 central banks and the European Commission to address the challenges of the 2008 financial crisis. The TCFD produced a report that synthesised an investigation into the needs of major financial actors in a transition, which it used to provide shared strategies for central banks, major investment banks, and asset managers. Their remit was to "enable stakeholders to understand better the concentrations of carbon-related assets in the financial sector and the financial system's exposures to climate-related risks" (Task Force on Climate-Related Disclosures, 2017, p. 2). Risk is the economic category that sustains the imagined possibility of growth in a world after oil, a financial abstraction evidenced in bank statements, press releases, political institutions, and events such as COP26.

To do this, TCFD developed a risk typology. It is widely adopted in the literature and the financial industry. They distinguish between 'transition risks' and 'physical risks'.

> Transition Risks. Transitioning to a lower-carbon economy may entail extensive policy, legal, technology, and market changes to address mitigation and adaptation requirements related to climate change. Depending on the nature, speed, and focus of these changes, transition risks may pose varying levels of financial and reputational risk to organizations.
> Physical Risks. Physical risks resulting from climate change can be event driven (acute) or longer-term shifts (chronic) in climate patterns. Physical risks may have financial implications for organizations, such as direct damage to assets and indirect impacts from supply chain disruption. Organizations' financial performance may also be affected by changes in water availability, sourcing, and quality; food security; and extreme temperature changes affecting organizations' premises, operations, supply chain, transport needs, and employee safety (Task Force on Climate-Related Disclosures, 2017, p. 5).

The terms 'transition risk' and 'physical risk' aim to expand the conceptual field through which social and ecological events are brought within financial temporality. If companies are inadequately preparing for the energy transition, so the argument goes, it is because they have not yet developed the tools to make climate visible. As BlackRock (who, incidentally, now advise the EU on climate strategy) notes, "This causes investors to discount pressing climate-related risks already lurking in portfolios" (Blackrock Investment Institute, 2019, p. 2). The risks exist as social and biophysical things, but not (yet) *to,* and therefore *as,* capital—that is, not yet incorporated within financial value signification. That the anticipated future lurks *within* portfolios suggests that what is being registered here is a growing awareness of a structuring blind spot to hydrocarbons in a financial vision. Motivating financial institutions to reorganise the biospheric and social dimensions of energy into a typology of risks. This is not just a question of description. It is a form of descriptive organisation, backed by banks, corporations, and states.

This is finance reflecting upon its own ground, upon the process that renders the world in capital's image, in a moment when a geological epochal shift represents the difficulty of positioning value's climate future. What gets rendered in this genre of financial writing is the generic: risk works to the extent that a representational system can generalise a means of tracking the constitutive grounding force of fossil energy in the financial economy. And this is a process that gives physical and transitions risk a general equivalence and substitutability: reducing physical risks, the economic effects of climate change, increases transition risks, the economic effects of transition, and vice versa. This formal equivalence is the precondition of financial imagined transitions, which balance the ecological and economic from the perspective of value. This means that it is possible to weigh up the costs to capital posed by different kinds of investment risks and decide climate catastrophe is a better bet—after all, atmospheric instability offer a dynamic practically the opposite of capital's need for regulated material abstractions.

Take Lloyd's of London's 2017 risk report on *Stranded Assets: The Transition to a Low Carbon Economy*. While not exactly a gripping read, what is fascinating about this report is how the catalogue of potential stranded assets relevant to Lloyd's insurance ventures (energy, property, and shipping), and the scenarios used to narrativise potential values, enable the representational reduction—the real abstraction—of climate to risk.

> Risks: Government regulations. Effect: Climate change. Response: limit increase in global average temperatures to 2°C. Result: Reduction of global emissions, fossil fuel reserves could remain unburned.
> Risks: Societal norms change. Effect: Climate change. Responses: Divestment from fossil fuels. Result: Reduction of investment in the fossil fuel industry (Caldecott et al., 2017, p. 4).

This representation, sparse as it may be, marks a transformation in thinking that indexes the historicity of modes of interpreting climate. This is a description of value: fossil fuel reserves, the market value of fossil-fuel companies, leveraged in the present through stock markets. Subsequent revaluations of what is insurable and credible are therefore confirmations of the imagined effects of climate change on an economic horizon. Transition becomes internal to the real abstraction of value through risks that can be moved from columns labelled 'assets' or 'liabilities', marking an emergent situation in which transition has shifted to a calculative and imaginative practice internal to financial knowledge. It matters that this genre of financial writing is a crucial part of a financial media culture that has been regulated by, and productive of, petroculture since the middle of the twentieth century. Energy, and now climate, regulate financial representation, in a mode that becomes effective through leveraging a relationship between an uncertain present and uncertain future. Risk becomes the basic economic and cultural dimension of representations that support and structure a financial reality, building its very sense of transition. Financial risk and its value-forms are abstractions that constitute the objects represented as risks. In shaping spaces for representing transition, a financial media culture produces the scene and temporality in which climate is signified as a financial object.

In a famous address at Lloyd's of London on the topic of climate finance adaptation, Mark Carney, governor of the Bank of England (BoE) between 2013 and 2020, warns his audience of insurers that "while the sector is well-placed to respond in the near-term you should not assume your ability to manage risks today means the future is secure". However, insurers are "amongst those with the greatest incentives to understand and tackle climate change in the short term". His solution is a predictable one: "With better information as a foundation, we can build a virtuous circle of better understanding of tomorrow's risks, better pricing for investors, better decisions by policymakers, and a smoother transition to a lower-carbon economy. By managing what gets measured, we can break the Tragedy of the Horizon" (Carney, 2015).

Under Carney's stewardship, this has become an important concern at the BoE, and one of the problems identified in *The Future of Finance* is the failure to "take account of longer-horizon forward-looking information such as climate change" (van Steenis, 2019, pp. 85–86). Sustainable growth requires the representation of climate and carbon in information that can be used to govern investment. According to this report, one of the primary reasons that climate change has not been factored into long-term investment strategies is information shortage. It is because the future does not look enough like the past—the problem of representation at the heart of this book—that a Hayekian logic of information gets imagined as a solution. If the risks of the lower-carbon economy are the content of financial transition representations, then information is its form, how it is mediated through financial environments. From the same report:

> the Bank must take steps to ensure systemic risks from climate change are addressed and the safety and soundness of regulated financial institutions upheld. This means making sure risks are properly managed. It requires a strategic approach to account for the distinctive features of climate risks. These features arise from the breadth of industries and geographies, the magnitude of the impact climate-related events can have on the economy and their foreseeable nature. Most importantly, short-term actions today are determining the size of future impacts. So the uncertain time horizon of climate risks needs to be brought into traditional business planning cycles (Carney, 2015).

This imagined transition runs from ensuring the safety of financial institutions to the management of risk, necessitating a new strategic approach that registers impacts on 'the economy' and the foreseeable nature of such risks. There is an implied ratio between present action and future impact, and the coordination of financial and climate time horizons. Information becomes the key leverage point between present action and future impact, a framing suggests that climate information, if disseminated across the sector, will generate the effect of climate change in the economy now, leading to a smooth and rational transition from a high- to a lower-carbon economy that avoids the shocks of stranded assets and the devaluation of carbon-intensive infrastructures. Risk is both a thing to be measured but also a representation that makes the future intelligible to financial governance, while enclosing and protecting infrastructure from external shocks posed by governments, workers, or activists—securing finance against disruption.

According to the BoE the responsibility for investing in the future "falls to the financial sector: to banks, and to investors in companies' equity and debt. The scale of that task would be challenging even if the path to net zero were certain. But it is not—so investors must also manage the potential for significant losses on their assets, as and when more aggressive policies to reduce emissions come on stream, or physical climate events grow in intensity" (Hauser, 2021). For Carney this means creating an investment climate to make "sustainable investment commercially viable" (Carney, 2021, p. 362) through private–public partnerships and changes to market structure, sustainable revenue capture and growth. Daniela Gabor claims that the state is thereby envisioned as 'derisking' the world for transition: using public finance to make up shortfalls to expected commercial rates of return (Gabor, 2023). This is a descriptive account of the decline in economic growth in a world after oil, integrating the state into sustaining the monetary environment through offsetting the risks of a low growth economy. The threat is that finance will withdraw slowly and inefficiently, interrupting financial flows towards transition infrastructure. The measurement of risk is of central importance to financial sabotage. By refusing to invest unless infrastructures are arranged to serve the needs of finance's value-forms, capital's abstractions, written in future perfect tense, determine the form of transition in its planning and financing stage, before it takes material shape.

Energy futures interface with information processing through climate modelling, the basis of the IPCC (Intergovernmental Panel on Climate Change) and IEA reports that fundamentally influence this archive of financial writing about climate, and through the attempt to render climate visible to finance and therefore accountable: to reflect climate in prices. This is an attempt to construct a monetary environment that will become self-regulating through the dispersal of knowledge through the price system. Making transition fit a market price system demonstrates how financial models do not just model the world but produce techniques of governance that create effects in, and constitute, the reality they model. My conceptual touchstone for understanding how this financial writing produces a temporality of governable risks has been the philosopher of the price system, Hayek, for whom

> The process of adaptation operates, as do the adjustments of any self-organizing system, by what cybernetics has taught us to call negative feedback: responses to the differences between the expected and the actual results of actions so that these differences will be reduced. This will produce an increased correspondence of expectations of the different persons so long as current prices provide some indications of what future prices will be, that is, so long as, in a fairly constant framework of known facts, always only a few of them change; and so long as the price mechanism operates as a medium of communicating knowledge which brings it about that the facts which become known to some, through the effects of their actions on prices, are made to influence the decision of others (Hayek, 2012, pp. 283–284).

Attaining certainty over the future requires, paradoxically, that the negative feedback of disappointed expectations gets communicated through prices to all participants. In this cybernetic logic, general knowledge of climate change has no effective advantage over a knowledge concentrated in a class of technical and financial specialists, because it is the investors who will adapt to the risks and opportunities of energy transition, as measuring the risks to carbon-intensive assets will force them to. Even they need not know how the price of forms of capital reflects a new climate reality or understand conscious direction or design. This addresses epistemological and political questions, of how to make the climate communicable through markets, and how to establish this as the basis for a mode of financial domination.

3.4 The Outsider's View

I want now to return to the character of Nick, the focal character from whose perspective we see Lloyd's in *The Line of Beauty*. Nick is a gay man from a middle-class background who learns to rub shoulders with the British elite at Oxford, which leads him to reside in the home of a Tory MP, father of an undergraduate friend. He half-befriends a number of young men who go on to the kinds of people who stride confidently into Lloyd's; new men of the Thatcher decade, whose access to wealth necessitates the appearance of sophistication even as, in the novel's diagnosis, this is a sort of veneer over much uglier qualities of avarice and arrogance. By contrast, Nick, an aesthete from a small business-owner background (Thatcher's people, in other words), is invited in as a guest, a small investor, and escorted round, but never asked to stay. His sums, a gift from a secret, wealthy lover, are too small, and his presence accepted only as a sort of favour from a friend of his undergraduate days. Nick's life is speculative and at risk—it is not, in other words, underwritten by the kinds of financial reserves available to his peers (Alderson, 2017, p. 137).

While the novel does not dwell over the building in the way that I have in this chapter, it captures that strange mixture of the new and the old: "When the day came Nick turned up early at the bank and waited under a palm tree in the atrium. People hurried in, nodded to the commissionaire, who still wore a tailcoat and a top hat [...] There were sharp-eyed older men, looking faintly harassed by the speed and noise, their dignity threatened by the ferocious youngsters who already had their hands on a new kind of success" (Hollinghurst, 2005, p. 203). This architectural chronotope captures the right-wing movement diagnosed by Stuart Hall as a combination of "organic Toryism—nation, family, duty, authority, standards, traditionalism—with the aggressive themes of a revived neoliberalism—self-interest, competitive individualism, anti-statism" (Hall, 2021, p. 48). The novel's historical atmosphere—that Hall named 'authoritarian populism', and we might now call neoliberalism—is nevertheless encountered from the perspective of an outsider. He feels it as a kind of exclusivity that seems to produce a distancing effect, as if the everyday reality of financial petroculture is filtered through a pre-existing detachment, to be only observed. Of course, to be habituated to this separation is to, in effect, have grown accustomed to the frictions of an offshore world, to no longer register it as significant. Nick, who bristles at his exclusion, has his entire experience coloured by this barely perceptible differentiation between himself and those at home in this space. His feelings, which are hardly political in an obvious sense, nevertheless capture something of the way that the offshore attempts to escape and elude representation; how it enables zones insulated from the national political territories in which they are otherwise embedded. This is what is registered by Nick's unease at his outsider status.

As the offshore is more of a logic than a nominal space, fiction is often best poised to concretise the kinds of abstraction—financial and spatial—that reconfigure this social dimension. This reconfiguration gives social reality a particular dynamic across disparate practices, organisations, and conventions. This can be seen in differentiation of space, which architecture gives us a particularly privileged way of thinking. A social act of categorisation before it is a spatial phenomenon, this social form is structured by an internal dislocation, a distinction between inside and outside. My point is that the offshore alerts us to a fundamental antagonism in the age of financial petroculture, between those who govern the flow of capital into our imagined futures and those who suffer structural consequences. While it may be imagined as an external space, offshore is really a logic in which exclusivity, secrecy, and flexibility become profitable; where financial representation enables the real abstraction of value; and where energy is mediated into cultural form.

In the Lloyd's Building, architectural form seems to diffract the heaviness of fossil infrastructure and the electric lightness of a newly wired world. The question this poses, then, is what kind of society is ratified when architecture and architects ask us to equate freedom with flexibility; when observers are asked not to think about the differentiation that structures the social? What underwrites such a view of the social? Lloyd's is an architecture of transition: a promise about how to get from a present crisis to a financial energy future. Its energy future moves laterally, as it were, through the offshore, in which it sheds the social promise of modernism and emerges instead as a financial promise; rather than a utopian space made universal, it offers an exceptional space made typical. And what is typical can be accommodated and tolerated—if not completely ignored—as it is woven into the fabric of a whole way of life.

To return, then, to the protestors that opened this chapter: in storming the entrance of this exclusive space, they have identified the centrality of financial mediation to the volatile future of energy. They offer a practical theory of financial time, through demands not for the closure of existing but the cancelling of future infrastructures that exist only as plans, designs, and contracts. The wager of such blockading is that these spaces represent nodes of critical vulnerability that might be leveraged into political demands over the future of energy. They threaten with reputational rather than logistical risks, but this follows logically from a terrain of struggle inclusive of past, present, and future carbon-emitting infrastructures. This disruption makes visible the logic of financial time and a form of solidarity that might challenge it. I have aimed to provide a genealogy of this conflict over the infrastructures of the coming decades, through a conjunctural analysis of political economy and architectural form as these converge in Lloyd's of London in the era that followed the oil crisis.

References

Alderson, D. (2017). Attachment and Possession: The Romance of Family, Politics and Things in The Line of Beauty. In *Sex and Sensibility in the Novels of Alan Hollinghurst* (pp. 129–149). Palgrave Macmillan Ltd. Retrieved from https://research.manchester.ac.uk/en/publications/attachment-and-possession-the-romance-of-family-politics-and-thin

Arrighi, G. (2009). *The Long Twentieth Century: Money, Power and the Origins of Our Time: Money*. Verso Books.

Baucom, I. (2005). *Specters of the Atlantic: Finance Capital, Slavery, and the Philosophy of History* (Illustrated edition). Duke University Press.

Blackrock Investment Instititute. (2019). *Getting Physical: Scenario Analysis for assessing climate-related risks*. Global Insights. Retrieved from www.blackrock.com/us/individual/literature/whitepaper/bii-physical-climate-risks-april-2019.pdf

Brotherstone, T. (2012). *A Contribution to the Critique of Post-Imperial British History: North Sea Oil, Scottish Nationalism and Thatcherite Neoliberalism*. Studies on the Socio-Economics of Oil and Gas. Pluto Press.

Caldecott, B., Dericks, G., Pfeiffer, A., & Astudillo, P. (2017). *Stranded Assets: The Transition to a Low Carbon Economy*. Lloyd's of London.

Retrieved from https://assets.lloyds.com/assets/pdf-stranded-assets/1/pdf_stranded-assets.pdf

Carney, M. (2015). *Breaking the Tragedy of the Horizon—Climate Change and Financial Stability—Speech by Mark Carney*. Retrieved from https://www.bankofengland.co.uk/speech/2015/breaking-the-tragedy-of-the-horizon-climate-change-and-financial-stability

Carney, M. (2021). *Values: Building a Better World for All*. William Collins.

Crook, l. (2019, November 19). *Lloyd's Building is Richard Rogers' First High-Tech Office Block*. Dezeen. Retrieved from https://www.dezeen.com/2019/11/19/lloyds-building-richard-rogers-high-tech-london/

Cumbers, A. (2012). *North Sea Oil, the State and Divergent Development in the United Kingdom and Norway*. Studies on the Socio-Economics of Oil and Gas. Pluto Press.

Department for Business Innovation and Skills. (2011). *UK TRADE PERFORMANCE OVER THE PAST YEARS* (No. BIS/11/720). Department for International Development.

Duguid, A. (2014). *On the Brink: How a Crisis Transformed Lloyd's of London (2014th edition)*. Palgrave Macmillan.

Edgerton, D. (2018). *The Rise and Fall of the British Nation: A Twentieth-Century History* (1st edition). Allen Lane.

Fernández–galia, L. (2001). *Fire & Memory—On Architecture & Energy: On Architecture and Energy*. MIT Press.

Gabor, D. (2023). The (European) Derisking State. *SocArXiv*, Article hpbj2. Retrieved from https://ideas.repec.org//p/osf/socarx/hpbj2.html

Hales, K. (1995). Insurance—Piper Alpha "et al." *Energy Exploration & Exploitation, 13*(2–3), 253–260. https://doi.org/10.1177/0144598795013002-314

Hall, S. (2021). *The Hard Road to Renewal*. Verso. Retrieved from https://www.versobooks.com/en-gb/products/1252-the-hard-road-to-renewal

Harvey, D. (1990). Flexible Accumulation through Urbanization Reflections on 'Post-Modernism' in the American City. *Perspecta, 26*, 251. https://doi.org/10.2307/1567167

Harvie, C. (1995). *Fool's Gold: The Story of North Sea Oil* (New edition). Penguin.

Hauser, A. (2021). *It's Not Easy Being Green—But That Shouldn't Stop Us: How Central Banks Can Use Their Monetary Policy Portfolio to Support Orderly Transition to Net Zero*. Bank of England. Retrieved from https://www.bankofengland.co.uk/-/media/boe/files/speech/2021/may/its-not-easy-being-green-but-that-shouldnt-stop-us-speech-by-andrew-hauser.pdf?la=en&hash=6859472C053CB4130189220C3141648C0AADF5C2

Hayek, F. (1974). *The Sveriges Riksbank Prize in Economic Sciences in Memory of Alfred Nobel 1974: The Pretence of Knowledge*. NobelPrize.Org. Retrieved from https://www.nobelprize.org/prizes/economic-sciences/1974/hayek/lecture/

Hayek, F. A. (2012). *Law, Legislation and Liberty: A New Statement of the Liberal Principles of Justice and Political Economy (1st edition)*. Routledge.

Helm, D. (2003). *Energy, the State, and the Market: British Energy Policy Since 1979* (Revised ed. edition). OUP Oxford.

Hollinghurst, A. (2005). *The Line of Beauty* (Reprints edition). Picador.

Kaminer, T. (2011). *Architecture, Crisis and Resuscitation: The Reproduction of Post-Fordism in Late-Twentieth-Century Architecture (1st edition)*. Routledge.

Lloyd's (Firm). (1986). *Serving the World: The New Lloyd's Building*. Lloyd's of London Press.

Lobo-Guerrero, L. (2012). LLOYD'S and the Moral Economy of Insuring Against Piracy. *Journal of Cultural Economy*. Retrieved from https://www.tandfonline.com/doi/abs/https://doi.org/10.1080/17530350.2012.640555

Powell, K. (1994). *Lloyd's Building: Richard Rogers Partnership*. Phaidon.

Rogers, R. (1988). *2. Belief in the Future is Rooted in the Memory of the Past on JSTOR*. Retrieved from https://www.jstor.org/stable/41374749

rs21. (2023, November 5). Oily Money Out—A leap forward for British environmentalism. *Rs21*. Retrieved from https://www.rs21.org.uk/2023/11/05/oily-money-out-a-leap-forward-for-british-environmentalism/

Sadler, S. (1999). *Non-Plan: Essays on Freedom, Participation and Change in Modern Architecture and Urbanism* (J. Hughes, Ed.; 1st edition). Routledge.

Sadler, S. (2005). *Archigram: Architecture without Architecture*. MIT Press.

Sant'Elia, A. (1914). *Manifesto of Futurist Architecture*. R / D. Retrieved from https://www.readingdesign.org/manifesto-futurist

Slobodian, Q. (2018). *Globalists: The End of Empire and the Birth of Neoliberalism*. Harvard University Press.

Task Force on Climate-Related Disclosures. (2017). *Recommendations of the Task Force on Climate-related Financial Disclosures*. TCFD. Retrieved from https://assets.bbhub.io/company/sites/60/2020/10/FINAL-2017-TCFD-Report-11052018.pdf

van Steenis, H. (2019). *Future of Finance Review on the Outlook for the UK Financial System: What it Means for the Bank of England*. Bank of England. Retrieved from https://www.bankofengland.co.uk/-/media/boe/files/report/2019/future-of-finance-report.pdf?la=en&hash=59CEFAEF01C71AA551E7182262E933A699E952FC

Wearing, D. (2018). *AngloArabia: Why Gulf Wealth Matters to Britain* (1st edition). Polity.

CHAPTER 4

Derivative Aesthetics: Representing Volatility

4.1 Market Mediations

On 13th June 2019, the US Military released footage of an attack on an oil tanker they claim was sabotaged by Iranian special forces in the Gulf of Oman. The grainy, black-and-white footage appears to be taken from a surveillance plane, and so it is a representation of events from a military logistical perspective. 30% of ocean trade is oil, and 60% of oil is traded by the sea. Securing oil flow is key to American naval policy, and historically the Gulf has been critical to world energy supply, as much of the world's oil and liquefied natural gas passes through it. When the video circulated through global media outlets, the price of oil shot upwards. What it represents opens up the potential for intensified Iranian-US conflict, the possibility of embargos, and oil trade disruption (Guardian, 2019).

Despite the threat, no conflict took place. But to the futures markets, the *possibility* is what counts. The video indexes an act that can be, and therefore is, interpreted as the potential for war. It does not even need to be convincing. Energy traders only need to anticipate what the average trader is anticipating, or what the average trader expects the average trader to anticipate.

For the attacker, despite the fact that the *Kokuka Courageous* is not American—it is Japanese-owned and flies under the Panamanian flag of convenience—it is in an American-secured energy corridor, and so within

H. Pitt Scott, *Financial Petroleum Cultures*, Palgrave Studies in Literature, Culture and Economics,
https://doi.org/10.1007/978-3-031-99661-0_4

the logic of energy territoriality it is quasi-American. It is not the oil per se, but the potential for political and financial contagion that makes such ships into strategic targets. There is a curious abstraction at work here, from what the video is *of*, to what it represents *for* the financial markets. The attack, reported and circulated in global media outlets, becomes a quasi-financial thing, an event unfolding through market mediations. The video offers an example of how financial markets value information about oil, even if those circulating it are not involved in financial markets at all. All images and narratives of financial assets have the potential to affect their valuation (La Berge, 2015, p. 119).

This chapter is about what volatility does to time as capital is recomposed in form, setting, and representation by the globalisation and financialisation of oil. It focuses on the derivative, a financial contract used to trade expectations about the future price of oil. Financial petroculture's economic cell-form, the derivative gives order, direction, and meaning to energy futures. I am interested in the practice, logic, and forms of oil's derivation, as a market ideology and aesthetic of oil enabled by the infrastructure of financial media. Oil derivatives, otherwise called energy futures, are a critical site for the mediation of crude oil into economic and cultural form. To pursue this line of argument—an infrastructural critique of volatility—we will follow the money from reserve to data centre, from pipeline to pricing formula. The market volatilizes the material—the commodity, the oil barrel—dispersing into a medium of economic activity.

Petroculture is a world derived from oil: "oil-derived lubricants are indispensable for countless industrial tasks, modern transportation infrastructures are unthinkable without oil-derived paving materials, and syntheses of scores of plastics begin with oil-derived feedstocks. All these benefits derive from resource extraction not renewable on a civilizational timescale" (Smil, 2008, pp. 163–164). But it is through the financial derivative that oil markets become a cultural-economic dominant, a leading representation or synecdoche of the petroleum system. Just as oil infrastructure is deliberately designed to keep crude oil out of sight, so financial media configures oil's knowability through visual and numeric representation. Thinking with the concept of and market for oil derivatives provides a mediating concept to track oil's translation into finance and culture, through the representations that render it as crude or derived forms.

To start, take Ursula Biemann's remarkable two-channel video installation documentary *Black Sea Files* (2006), which provides a visual exploration of the messy human geographies linked by the development of the Baku–Tbilisi–Ceyhan (BTC) pipeline. The social and political dimensions of petroleum infrastructure come into focus through the frictions generated by construction, and encompasses a cast of migrants, fishermen, oil workers, and sex workers; figures that fade to the background in global media stories of progress and development, if they appear at all. In a scene focused on an oil terminal, Biemann's voiceover informs us that "there is a growing tension between the messy resource fringe in remote places and the clean world of digital users", and that the secretive offshore terminal is a major node in connecting these two sites. Visualising what Jeff Diamanti has called a 'terminal landscape'—infrastructural sites that process crude materiality into market form—*Black Sea Files* provides lingering shots of tankers, on which is superimposed a scrolling ticker tape (Diamanti, 2021). Capturing the chronotopes of oil's material and financial circulation in image form as they converge at the terminal, the film relates an often-invisible infrastructure to the visual and financial media that organises our perception of petroleum.

What is interesting about this gesture to the spectral abstraction of the stock market at sites of concrete materiality is how it uses the ticker tape and the electronic display board as signifier. The electronic display board is a financial technology of representation that numerically depicts and shapes the market. It also signifies the market in cultural representations of finance. Sometimes it is as object of narrative interest, something the characters care about, defining them as a particular kind of person. At others, it is part of a setting, used to generate historical atmosphere. Just as often it is a narrative device for cutting time into discontinuous unities, as event sequences are syncopated to price movements. Sometimes it is all three (see *Wall Street* (dir. Stone, 1987)). As object, setting, or actant, the electronic display board functions as a metonym of the market. Even media critical of this dislocation of financial wealth and peripheral exploitation like *Black Sea Files* makes use of this metonym. The humble computer terminal is therefore central to the rise of the ticker tape as a representational dominant; a technology of representation actively shaping the market abstractions of petroculture and entailing a whole new communication infrastructure of its own. Oil's coordination by the financial sector might be understood as the migration of financial promises into a temporality of future expenditure. This is a story of formulas, algorithms, and terminals as much as it is of pipelines and ports, as these emerge out of the intersecting crises of energy, capital, and finance in the 1970s.

In the late 1970s, the US was at an energy crossroads. The unwinding of the OPEC system, and the entailing economic crisis, had forced energy to the centre of political debate. In 1979, Jimmy Carter gave his famous 'Malaise speech', in which he lamented, among other things, a loss of faith in an energy future: "We believed that our Nation's resources were limitless until 1973, when we had to face a growing dependence on foreign oil". Looking forward, Carter saw rapidly shrinking resources and constraints on the American way of life, as national resources dwindled and dependency on oil imports increased. Casting the oil crisis in the gravest terms, he saw this as a symptom of a deeper problem, a moral and spiritual crisis for which the evidence was profligate energy consumption far above the resources available to the nation. Economic crisis, joblessness, environmental destruction, and international conflict would all follow. Most importantly, it was a crisis of confidence in the American future: "Confidence has defined our course and has served as a link between generations. We've always believed in something called progress". As faith in the future weakens, so Carter asserted that the values of hard work, family, community, and God were being replaced by consumerism. Cast in the gravest terms, Carter saw a moral duty in the shift to solar and coal, as the fact of future depletion—or peak oil—and the "excessive dependence on OPEC" became the guiding narrative of America's decline. He exhorted the American people to conserve and reduce their energy use; to transition away from depletable, artificially cheap, and unsustainable forms of energy. The future of the US was at stake, and for Carter this would necessarily be a future after oil (Carter, 1979).

In contrast, in a famous lecture given in 1978 in San Francisco, famed advocate of the free market and figurehead of the Chicago school of economics Milton Friedman, drew quite different conclusions from the ongoing crisis of confidence in America's energy future. His central claim was that it was impossible to predict the future of recoverable reserves. Making reference to William Stanley Jevons, who in *The Coal Question* famously lamented the depletion of coal in Britain as an immediate horizon of political and economic decline, Friedman argued that calculated figures of known reserves were entirely unreliable. Noting that reserve quantities are better thought of as iterative and recursive predictions relative to new technological and infrastructural developments, he said that, instead of relying on the gloomy guesswork of engineers and geologists, who were constantly revising expectations because of new discoveries, a far better mechanism for regulating the future of energy already existed,

> namely the price mechanism, which successfully steered us over several centuries from wood to coal to whale oil to petroleum to natural gas. That is a mechanism in which it is in the self-interest of hundreds and thousands and millions of people to make their best guesses about the future, in which it's unnecessary to have a single blueprint, in which you have an automatic adjustable mechanism as things develop. If we have a problem today in the energy area, as we do, it is solely in my opinion because that system has not been allowed to work (Friedman, 2013).

This built on a decade-long push to introduce futures markets to currencies (which kicked off in 1972 after the end of Bretton Woods). In Friedman's account, the proper way to mediate value was in the privatisation and deregulation of financial instruments known as derivatives. Mediation of value would be assured through rational self-interest, ***and*** it would ensure that the US financial sector maintained its important in governing flows of trade across the financial world-economy. A stable price, settled through the exchange of currency futures, would ameliorate the anxieties caused by the uncertainty of currency fluctuations. Speculation was, therefore, a social good, and a stabilising influence, in the context of deepening international trade. Moreover, this was a *nationalist* claim: against the threat to the US dollar posed by the Eurodollar markets and the anti-colonial OPEC nations. American finance would play this mediating role. Friedman was making a political claim cloaked in an economic one: currency markets were the only source of price stability, and therefore only American finance was up to the task. This would ensure that the dollar remained the dominant currency, even after the end of Bretton Woods, because oil would be priced in dollars and oil-importing nations would therefore require dollars. Because currencies needed to be fixed against each other, at least temporarily, for the purposes of trade, derivatives would mediate between the floats and the dollar (Friedman, 1971).

Likewise, Friedman supported the introduction of energy futures markets, which were argued for in moral as well as economic terms. Against the solemn predictions of exhaustion and decline, the market stood as an emblem of progress and growth; against the chaos and volatility of short-sighted bureaucrats stood the efficient mechanism of the market and its avatar, the well-meaning speculator, who would introduce the future into the present in a rational, profitable, and frictionless way precisely because of his self-interest. By locating a path through the crisis, the market was imbued with optimism and hope. Friedman suggested that little had to change in the use of energy, as the major shift would come through distribution and ownership. This would protect the consumer from the unpredictable, secretive cabal of foreign oil producers, whose price-setting power distorted underlying true values of resources. This understanding of the energy crisis as a financial crisis with financial solutions became the dominant discursive framing, not Carter's (Wellum, 2020, p. 23).

But it is the infrastructure of this discursive rupture that interests me, because that is how market temporality begins to shape aesthetic form. Breaking from the producer-controlling pricing system of the previous fifty years, the 1970s saw the beginning of the spot market in crude oil. Oil futures were first traded on NYMEX, unsuccessfully, in 1974. The market did not have enough volatility—price fluctuations to incentivise speculators—or liquidity—enough speculators and market-makers—to effectively represent oil's price. It wasn't until 1981–3 that the volume of transactions became sufficient for a free-market pricing system to take over the governance of oil's future. This occurred through the establishment of a new benchmark financial contract and a new delivery point for this contract: the West Texas Intermediate (WTI) and the storage hub at Cushing, Oklahoma, now known as the pipeline crossroads of the world. At the nexus of thirty pipelines and sixteen storage terminals, this hub of the global oil market enabled the real abstraction of crude into an exchange contract of nominal thousands of barrels, to be settled at a future date. In 1988, Brent Crude (from the North Sea) would begin to be traded on the London International Petroleum Exchange (now the electronic Intercontinental Exchange), eventually established as a global benchmark. Roughly eighty per cent of all types of crude are pegged to Brent. If I wished to trade Mexican Maya, Angolan Nemba, Russian Siberian Light, or Indonesian Minas, I would reference Brent, which trades in US dollars. Oil markets have a global and extranational geography, but finance makes these hydrocarbon spaces distant and proximate. The market proved so successful that by 1988, OPEC, which had attempted to assert resource sovereignty through oil as a strategy for decolonisation, had fixed the price of their crude to Brent. This genre of financial contract began to write its future in the language of oil, continually engaged in the description, representation, and evaluation of the global energy landscape, to translate into price.

After 1971, the ability to pump out oil without a fall in prices depended on the ability to pump out dollars, as unbacked credit money, without a fall in their value. The dollar's new status as world money and universal value-form was secured in a flood of oil onto world markets. But the oil price shock posed a real inflationary threat, threatening to weaken dollar values. Something was required that could hedge rising oil prices without lowering dollar values and therefore the value of the dollar-denominated financial assets of such importance to the accelerating financial accumulation. The new financial mechanisms to represent the bankable value of dollar-denominated oil assets were derivatives. In effect, derivatives stabilised oil production, financial accumulation, and the value-form, because it enabled financial instruments, and therefore oil assets, to become representations of the swelling value of oil without requiring actual dollars (although they remained priced in them). Financial liquidity enabled oil to keep flowing *and* dollars to function as a value-form without suffering inflationary devaluation. Derivatives provided stores of value that did not need to be held in cash, while enabling financialised markets to extract value from the ongoing volatility and spread of oil prices. Oil's mediation of the value-form opens up a global space for market volatility to become a cultural logic.

According to its proponents, WTI enabled the price signal to scale use according to supply and demand, incentivising the discovery of new reserves, and balancing the market during normal and volatile times. Even as financial contracts were reorganising the spatio-temporal coordinates of oil capital, the introduction of a price-finding mechanism to a substance central to social reproduction increasingly integrated the market into the concerns of daily life. As longtime WTI trader Thomas McMahon notes,

> Because the downstream relationship—the power, energy, and transportation—is in everybody's lives whether you're a small business operator or you've got to drive your kids to school every morning. The cost of energy became embedded in our lives. WTI represents that. It is price discovery and it became ingrained in our lives (McMahon, 2023).

This was conceived as a democratising process. Anyone could participate in the trades facilitated by the clearing house through electronic screens, viewing the fluctuation of oil prices in real-time. In the words of one trader, the new contract "allowed the grocer or the barber (as one used to say) to get involved in the dynamics of the oil market, to have an opinion about OPEC and to feel him or herself adequately informed after reading the news" (Carollo, 2011, p. 100).

But if oil markets made oil newly visible in financial form, the mechanisms that generated this representational ubiquity have remained relatively opaque. Anyone with an internet connection or access to a news channel can view oil prices. Even as markets impose a temporal logic on the social life of oil, it is not possible to see the institutions, the traders, the engineers, software developers, the anonymous and impersonal computer systems, data servers, undersea cables, transmission towers, terminals, software programs, algorithms, and HFT firms in the screens that constitute financial media today. It is to the shaping of this socio-technical system that we now turn.

Traders in futures markets profit from volatility in a process called *arbitrage*, making money from minor differences in 'future' and 'spot' price: the predicted price represented by the derivative and the actual price at the end of the derivative contract. To encourage participants who wish to hedge against risk and speculators who wish to profit from it, oil's smooth circulation requires price movement, or volatility. This results from the distinction between the actual volatility of a financial instrument, a measure of its past prices, and implied volatility, a measure of expected future variation. Implied volatility is modelled through the Black–Scholes-Merton (BSM) derivatives model, to create predictions of future prices. For example, political disturbances in the Straits of Hormuz, a particularly cold winter driving up demand for gas heating, unpredictable weather in the North Sea, and a boom in Chinese demand for engine oil are each comparable because all are concrete risks to potential value, priced and exchanged in futures markets.

Donald MacKenzie has provided a persuasive account of how derivative models actively shape the reality they purport to describe, because they govern how actors interact with the market. Implied volatility is a theoretical notion that cannot be calculated without a model, and this modelling recursively shaped energy futures because the model became embedded in how market participants see and interact with the market. Models are representative abstractions; theoretical representations that bring about and impose an empirical state they were meant to describe (Mackenzie, 2006). What I am calling oil's derivative aesthetic is characterised by this abstraction as a dominant form *in*, not *from* a social reality flooded with energy derivatives. Derivatives are present representations of future value that recursively shapes model and market.

As trader Elie Ayache puts it, "Derivatives prices (or, generally, prices) are the forward-looking narrative [that] literally help us infer the future" (Ayache, 2010, p. 21). Volatility structures oil's economic representation, inaugurating a temporal logic in which the present is mediated by narratable futures. Again, according to MacKenzie, the historical importance of volatility is due to its 'cognitive *simplicity*': "The underlying mathematics might be complicated, but the [BSM] model could be talked about and thought about relatively straightforwardly; its one free parameter—volatility—was easily grasped, discussed, and reasoned about" (Mackenzie, 2006). By abstracting oil to price, volatility becomes a way of knowing a world saturated by petroleum, bridging the gap between abstract model and vernacular description.

The calculative models used to produce financial time relied on advances in financial software. The BSM formula created a perfectly hedged portfolio that would earn a riskless rate of interest. It took advances in computer modelling to provide the technological capacity to produce large amounts of options prices so a trader can create a 'spread'—holding different positions on the same underlier with different prices and expirations as a hedging strategy.

By the 1980s, advances in computer technology and changing market regulations meant computational finance was no longer just needed for churning out options prices, because trading itself went digital. Pits and trading floors were slowly replaced by trading desks, computers, and offices. As dynamic, flexible spaces were required, architecture adapted to computational requirements. High-frequency trading (HFT) began, although with trade times of milliseconds, not nanoseconds, as it is today. The humble computer terminal became a world-making technology, articulating the abstraction of oil into commodity-form to the predictive logic of volatile markets.

CME Group, owner of NYMEX and the world's largest operator of futures exchanges, operates two data centres in the US, one in Aurora, Illinois, a back-up centre in Manhattan, New York, and another in Britain, in Slough, a large town west of London. Hosted by Equinix, a data centre provider, this market infrastructure enables ultra-low latency electronic exchanges, to allow for algorithmic high-frequency trading. In contrast to stock exchange and investment bank buildings in New York and the City of London, these nondescript warehouses are located on the peripheries of major financial cities, postindustrial zones that provide infrastructural services to the new economy. While not exactly secret—CyrusOne London I, as the one in Slough is called, can be found on Google Maps—they do not draw attention: no climate protestors have yet assembled outside its gates. Its architectural form refuses the sort of criticism that major financial architecture in the City invites. More interesting is how it is advertised to potential users and how its internal space was digitally mediated.[1] The site contains its own electrical substation and generators. This is to power the computer room air conditioning (CRAC). High density data storage requires energy, emitting heat, and so dedicated heat extraction is required to monitor and maintain temperature. Requiring little staff except for maintenance and security, the major running costs of data centres are their electrical bills, making cheap power a requirement. Alongside the fact that such buildings do not advertise their contents to the public, critical as they are to the financial economy, the warehouse architecture is shaped to minimise heating and therefore cost. Cooling plants enclose each data hall, which are independently regulated, with heat vented through the roof. They are individually linked to battery management systems to prevent cascading failure and power surges, with an autonomous back-up system and fire suppression. Security, automation, and energy efficiency is the name of the game. The economic logic of financial data centres turns on its relation to electricity, while its media logic shapes financial media and modelling. Whereas the latter is where the drama of the stock market is represented, the former is where it is sited.

The foreign exchanges hosted in Aurora and Slough are as much part of the petroleum world as oil terminals located in the Caspian Sea, because each mediate oil into its value-forms. To say that financial markets *rely* on digital servers and computational power is a mistake. Trading takes place in data centres like the one owned by CME Group. Financial digital media is the interface of its technical operation, a mode of networked social connectivity that organises market perceptibility. From

[1] A virtual tour of CyrusOne London II can be found on YouTube. < www.youtube.com/watch?v=-RZQaApgb7k > .

the models to the optic cables, ocean cables, satellites, microwave transmissions, server warehouses, to the code, information, signals, relays, and the digital market itself and those who work within it, the coders, traders, quants, server providers and maintenance, the computational infrastructure of finance *is* the market. Oil is mediated by media, which establish representations inseparable from the materiality of circuits, hardware, silicon, copper, plastic, and electricity.

Developed initially so that those involved in the physical production of oil could reduce exposure to market volatility, oil derivatives opened the market to financial speculators who had no interest in taking physical oil deliveries. Instead, they saw commodity indexes as an investment, taking speculative positions on market volatility. In fact, 99% of exchanges on NYMEX are settled through what is called 'offsetting', having buys and sales on the same day so that no physical settlement takes place, effectively turning short contracts into long-term investments. This means that market participants who have no interest in settling contracts through physical delivery can nevertheless exchange 'paper barrels'. These might be speculators such as hedge funds, or more traditional institutional investors such as pension funds who see commodity futures as safe assets in a portfolio (this was the case from roughly 2000–2007). Because contracts can be purchased and sold continuously, traders are encouraged to constantly recalibrate the contracts they hold in accordance with market movement. Financial institutions have reshaped the fundamental structure of commodity markets, introducing a speculative dynamic, more concerned with the financial performance of the market than the commodities being traded. The interest shifts to market performance as a mediator of value, to the models and narratives that make up how market performance is communicated and understood.

Derivatives remake the world through the 'blending' different units of capital into a single measure, making an economic equivalence between the natural distinctiveness of things: "They make it possible to convert things as economically nebulous as ideas and perceptions, weather and war into commodities that can be priced relative to each other and traded for profits" (Bryan & Rafferty, 2005, p. 12). This real abstraction provides a concrete "'essence'—a sort of DNA of capital—that all particular capitals share in common" (Bryan & Rafferty, 2007, p. 142). They dissemble and unbundle capital into smaller, tradeable elements, without trading the underlying asset itself, fixing in financial instruments what had hitherto only been present in capital in the abstract; not an abstraction from an underlying reality but value's real abstraction. This matters to oil because, within the signification of financial markets, it is abstracted from its social particularity.

Derivatives are useful channels of financial accumulation because what is traded is not the underlier, but a contract derived from it, and so it is possible to take out as many contracts as there are market participants willing to purchase them, leading to derivatives markets having a notional value many times greater than the values of the underliers to which they refer. As the oil price reached its highest recorded amount in 2008, each barrel of oil in physical circulation was being sold on average ten times per day in the exchanges. Contracts can be sold many times over without the physical commodity changing hands. Yet if the term, derivation, points towards origins, the abstraction into nominal barrels makes it impossible to know the source and location of the represented crude; a conceptual, infrastructural, and aesthetic separation begins between sites of physical and financial flow.

I have been describing something of a double abstraction: of the market from trading pit to electronic medium; and of petroleum into units of exchange on an open market, such that it is impossible to know the origins of the traded commodity. There is a methodological difference, however, La Berge claims, between finance being abstract and finance representing an abstraction (La Berge, 2019, p. 58). In this understanding, derivatives are a mode of representing and materialising abstractions in market forms. Derivatives do not abstract a newly immaterial finance from the material world, so much as reorganise the spatio-temporal form of petroleum's interrelated circuits of accumulation; a new medium in which crude materiality gets modulated into petroculture. Financial abstractions (yield, interest, risk, volatility, etc.) are not the same sort of thing as aesthetic abstraction in the conventional sense. I have tried to think abstraction conjuncturally, identifying the situations and sites that generate its modalities. Abstraction must be *modally specified,* otherwise one risks making an abstraction of abstraction and dubious claims about correspondences between its modes. The volatility abstraction drives representation towards mathematical accuracy and scientific realism, not figuration, expressionism, and the departure from realistic representation, as might be expected if one thought that financial abstraction was homologous with aesthetic abstraction. The point, then, is not to get 'behind' the derivative aesthetic to see 'oil itself' in unmediated form but rather to show that this resource aesthetic is at work in the world.

As Jameson argues, "We can think abstractly about the world only to the degree to which the world itself has already become abstract" (Jameson, 2002, p. 58).

The cultural work of the oil market was to stabilise the meaning of oil in a period of its economic resurgence after a decade of crisis. If it worked, petroleum could recede to the background, a distant concern that remained so as long the price at the pump or in the pension fund stayed stable. Oil became both intimate and distant; a matter of concern filtered through the particular lens of price, through which it took on social meaning, as gas, electricity, or inflation. From this derivative aesthetic—this way of rendering and knowing oil—denotes a politics and infrastructure of habituated separation. I now aim to track this aesthetic across two distinct time signatures, volatility and convolution, to map the landscape of financial petroculture.

4.2 Volatility and Crisis

Take the narrative volatility of some scenes from Stephen Gaghan's geopolitical thriller *Syriana* (2005). The film opens with lingering shots of a desert somewhere in the Gulf, evoking a speculative gaze on what the landscape contains, on its surface and under the ground. This dissolves into a long shot of South Asian migrant workers, nameless and unidentifiable, competing to get onto a bus to work at a new oil development. Into this volatile world, a CIA operative and an energy analyst each pursue different, but related, plots: illegal weapons trading and the financial backing of oil development. The film's setting is a fog of uncertainty—the intrigue of oil companies, petrostates, and a terrorist network connecting exploitative Saudis and disaffected workers—requiring specialist expertise to uncover.

Terrorist threats and nationalist projects contribute to the disorder of things, and one way the film imagines the re-establishment of political stability is through a drone strike, which eliminates an Arab political opponent threatening to nationalise oil and disrupt pipeline construction to Europe. The form of this bloody *denouement*—but, importantly, bloodless through satellite image sightlines, which promises violence in which there *will not* be blood—perceives the energy world from above, even if it is morally inflected with an anti-imperialist message. The target for assassination is an emir who wishes to modernise his unnamed Persian Gulf state, articulating a belated nationalism similar to that which motivated

Fig. 4.1 Syriana's drone strike, a familiar visual motif of late twentieth-century warfare

OPEC in the 1960s. Some forty years later, and in the wake of the Gulf War and Iraq War, such nationalist messages meet the advanced American war machine (Fig. 4.1).

Of interest here is the visual form through which such discordant encounters are ordered, and certain forms of visual and informational abstraction. For Sekula, the aerial wars of the late twentieth century were 'wars without bodies', where "bodies [are] redefined as mere matter in space, mere *occupied volume*". Environments are viewed through the energetic abstraction of sightlines. Militants are represented "by the quality of being 'soft' rather than 'hard,' and thus vulnerable to different intensities and distributions of destructive force" (Sekula, 1991). Space and time are viewed through devices that represent strategic environments through heat, light, vibration, and sound. Such warfare has its origins in the Gulf War, in which combat was envisioned through the principle of overwhelming force to minimise risk of casualties—limiting exposure to volatile political extremes. Begun in 1991, Operation Desert Storm was, from the perspective of the USA, primarily an aerial war.

In *Syriana*, the satellite shots are mimetic of aerial warfare's visual abstraction. This is a gaze that is mediated by technology and the image; environments are fields of perception, surveyed by representational technologies such as cameras, satellites, gunsights, sensors, thermographic, and light-sensitive images. It is a crenellated visual field established through limited information. The narrative logic is that of uncertainty, possibility, and risk. The assassination of a political opponent condenses, in *Syriana's* final, uncomfortable moments, the temporal logic of the pre-emptive strike. It anticipates an imagined future, summoning the spectre of a return to the nationalist volatility of the 1970s, then forecloses this future by isolating and eliminating an extreme risk whose volatility might disturb the balance of power in the Middle East. It is perhaps unsurprising, then, that the final shot concludes with an American energy analyst returning to the comforting embrace of his family: suburban middle-class America, safe from systematic volatility.

The figure of the energy analyst is important, too, in Joseph O'Neill's *Netherland* (2009), a realist novel about a Dutch man living in New York after 9/11 who, split between the pressures of his career and his family, finds an outlet in the underdeveloped New York cricket scene. This analyst, mulling on the geopolitics of the post-9/11 world-system, thinks:

> I could take a guess at the oil production capacity of an American-occupied Iraq and in fact was pressed at work about this issue daily, and stupidly. ('What are you saying, two and a half million barrels or three million? Which one is it?') But I found myself unable to contribute to conversations about the value of international law or the feasibility of producing a dirty bomb or the constitutional rights of imprisoned enemies or the efficacy of duct tape as a window sealant or the merits of vaccinating the American masses against smallpox or the complexity of weaponising deadly bacteria or the menace of the neoconservative cabal in the Bush administration, [...] In this ever-shifting, all-enveloping discussion, my orientation was poor. I could not tell where I stood. If pressed to state my position, I would confess the truth: that I had not succeeded in arriving at a position. I lacked necessary powers of perception and certainty and, above all, foresight. The future retained the impenetrable character I had always attributed to it. Would American security be improved or worsened by taking over Iraq? I did not know, because I had no information about the future purposes and capacities of terrorists or, for that matter, American administrators; and even if I were to have such information, I could still not hope to know how things would turn out. Did I know if the death and pain caused by a war in Iraq would or would not exceed the miseries that might likely flow from leaving Saddam Hussein in power? No. Could I say whether the right to autonomy of the Iraqi people—a problematic national entity, by all accounts—would be enhanced or diminished by an American regime change? I could not. Did Iraq have weapons of mass destruction that posed a real threat? I had no idea; and to be truthful, and to touch on

my real difficulty, I had little interest. I didn't really care (O'Neill, 2009, pp. 96–97).

Because the analyst encounters only derived forms, he has to make no decision about the events, only about whether the events will affect his firm's financial investments. Concerned only with data useful to his work, which shapes decisions made by his investment firm, "powers of perception and certainty and, above all, foresight", are surrendered. Later, he describes himself as "an analyst—a bystander" (O'Neill, 2009, p. 99). Perception does not yield insight but information. The description *Netherland* offers suggests how financial mediation inculcates not the absence of knowledge but an indifference to it: a by-stander, unable to step into the flow of the market for fear of being swept away. Put differently, it alerts us to the division of labour of writing energy fiction and energy financial contracts, which is the precondition for a novel in which a character's distance from the derivative contract's underlier—the political economy of oil production—becomes a source of personal crisis. *Netherland* shrinks from financial drama, watching the market at work but maintaining a distance from it. Unlike financial thrillers, which operate through excitement and crisis, this novel better captures the way that markets exist as a kind of background setting that resist imaginative and symbolic engagement. Oil is not repressed or invisible—after all, he is an expert. Rather, the novel captures something an aesthetic in which oil appears distant and of little concern. This feeling of distance from, and the meaning of, oil to everyday life is a mode of experience in which oil only ever appears in derived forms.

It is against this background of dull, quotidian reproduction of oil markets in formulas, automated exchanges, and price spreads that the narrative of crisis becomes a temptation. *Big Men* (Dir. Rachel Boynton, 2013), a documentary about an American oil exploration company called Kosmos Energy (incorporated in an offshore financial centre, Bermuda) as it begins offshore oil development in Ghana, shows what this narrative form looks like, as it narrates the shock and excitement of oil price volatility. It opens, in 2007, with uncertainty over whether oil will be struck. Oil is found and development begins. Narrative tension is generated through negotiations between the founders James Musselman and Brian Maxted, representatives of the Ghanaian government, and the company's New York investors. The company received favourable business terms, justified, according to Musselman, who is interviewed throughout the documentary, by the extraordinary risk they took in exploration. However, an upcoming election threatens to overturn this deal, and the loss in potential profits affects the company's valuation, upsetting the financial backers. There are corruption rumours, and Musselman is forced to step down from his role as company figurehead.

Two other plots are entwined with this one. Firstly, there are scenes shot in the Niger Delta, where corruption, sabotage, and violence are represented as a conflict over the region's oil profits. This functions as a cautionary tale in the documentary, the spectre of a resource curse which provides a warning about what the future of oil in Ghana might be like, if managed poorly. The other one is the 2008 financial crisis because, in the backdrop of Ghanaian oil development is an oil price drop that dramatically decreases potential oil profits and threatens to bring the development to a halt. Because of long-term downward pressure on financial assets in the twenty-first century associated with declining profits, the migration of finance into oil, which remained highly valuable, added to the price shock that contributed to the 2007–8 financial crisis (Gkanoutas-Leventis & Nesvetailova, 2015).

Big Men is not only a narrative in which financial valuation threatens to destabilise oil extraction, but, because it was filmed between 2007 and 2011, when oil fell from \$147 to ~ \$30, it is a narrative in which financial volatility displaces drilling as the central loci of plot. Contrasting shots juxtapose mask-wearing militias in the Niger Delta and people syphoning highly flammable condensate from pipelines with shots of skyscrapers, ticker tapes awash in red, stunned traders and news clips about the scale of the financial crash. The oil price crash superimposes the volatile disunity of abstract and physical oil onto the same narrative frame.

As oil prices impact projected profits, the global energy landscape and its market becomes the backdrop against which the action is interpreted. The narrative is structured through financial volatility and nationalist politics, distinct events comparable in effect. Firstly, the risk posed to international business by potentially destabilising claims to national resource sovereignty, as the incoming President, John Atta Mills, threatens to renege on the earlier financial arrangement between Ghana and Kosmos Energy. There is social unrest and potential future threat of sabotage and militant violence represented by Nigeria. Finally, there is financial volatility in the oil markets. The way this undermines the company's projected future is what gives the narrative its conflict, tension, and resolution. As the oil price drops, so does the financial value of Kosmos Energy on the stock market; with the risk too high, they try to sell to ExxonMobil, who eventually drop out due to geopolitical conflict in Ghana. The film concludes with Kosmos Energy listed on the New York Stock Exchange: financial success, despite the crisis.

Following this plot requires following the oil market, which means recognising volatility as a narrative about the future. It is impossible to look at an oil barrel and see how much value it contains. The oil market does not exist in the oil itself: it is a social not a natural form. Neither it is possible to see oil infrastructures in financial signifiers, nor a crashing oil price makes no physical change to an oil barrel. It remains what it is, crude in a metal drum. Following the oil market entails observing financial markets and seeing them as a document of a reality that cannot be captured by the direct representation of oil extraction, pipelines, or offshore development. This crisis in the representation of oil's value becomes, for the documentary, a way of figuring financial petroculture as a whole, with moral and political consequences. As a lesson in whether to trust the financial representation of oil, *Big Men* wants the viewer to think about whether the market is adequately representing oil value. This is to the documentary's strength, but it takes place entirely within the representational logic of the market itself. The adept market reader sees through the temporary misrepresentations of financial volatility documented in the film to the 'real' value that finance is meant to, but failing to, represent.

The film opens with a quote from Milton Friedman that reads "Tell me, is there some society that you know that doesn't run on greed?" According to the film's cultural logic, greed and speculation are the cause of resource misfortune and the disparity between price and value. This is as true in Nigeria, where corrupt elites syphon oil profits for personal gain, as it is on Wall Street, where the celebratory ending of men dressed in suits sits uncomfortably alongside the reality of poverty, crime, and underdevelopment in Nigeria and Ghana. This causal claim is wrong, of course, but it provides the narrative with shape and message. Moralising finance during moments of crisis provides a way of simplifying political economy to plot. If all societies run on greed, then the specificity of an oil society is subsumed by an ideological critique that is diffused by its lack of historicity. As the backdrop of the petroleum industry is brought into the foreground at a critical moment, oil itself is relegated to a secondary role, a figure for the greediness that all societies run on. Here, a critical representation of oil at a moment of crisis symptomatically confirms rather than confronts the political dimension of oil markets. Critiquing oil *through* the market via a too-quick identification of greedy speculators confirms the framework of the market as the ultimate index of oil's reality.

If, in *Big Men*, physical and financial form are brought into representational focus through a crisis in financial signification, I have been asking a more expansive question about the social forms and representational logics of financial petroculture. I have named this a derivative aesthetic, the politics of which is capable of managing critical breakdowns as well as quotidian financial accumulation. Because if energy futures link disparate spaces, they also produce a real separation between physical and futures markets, each of which possess their own spatio-temporality. Mazen Labban writes that

> introducing financial logic to the study of oil engenders a space-time parallax between oil's representation as a physical commodity circulating in physical (and financial) markets and its representation as a financial asset circulating in financial (and physical) markets. This is not a dualism between a 'real' space-time of material circulation and a 'fictitious' space-time of financial representations. Both are real enough and have their own materiality, but each alone is an abstraction incapable of standing in for the oil market, whose objectivity is produced from the incessant displacement between two space-times of circulation (Labban, 2010, p. 541).

The oil market attains social objectivity through these two interrelated circuits of accumulation. Energy futures are not an abstracted or distorted representation of a 'real' physical market, but rather a real space–time of financial circulation essential to the objectivity of the physical and financial oil market. Volatility is the concept, form, and vernacular of a financial culture invested in keeping physical and paper barrels flowing.

Whether it be plot, object of interest, or atmosphere, volatility is a temporality immanent to a derived world. The concept and form of derivation lets us cognitively map financial petroculture without relying on moments of critical breakdown as a dramatic revealing of uncovered mystery—even if we understand such narrative logics as symptomatic of the difficulty in situating oil in modernity. No moment of criticality will disclose the shape of the future because crisis is the volatile logic of energy futures, its mode of financial reasoning.

4.3 Convoluted Time

If, as neoclassical economists tell us, dramatic oil price increases become the mechanism by which demand for energy is curtailed, and there is not the capacity to replace it with other energy or political structures to ensure just distribution, then it is likely to produce significant political backlash from those for whom energy price increases mean increases in living costs, economic hardship, and falling living standards. While the management of volatility might be profitable for financialised oil markets, the failure to manage it is hardly good for environmentalist politics, because surging prices get mediated into everyday life, which offer obvious solutions: increase oil production. Energy transition is shaped by the way that financial markets engineer the visibility of oil and mediate between producers and consumers. This means oil markets have become their own justification: in a volatile world, cause and effect blur into a structuring blockage that is sustained by a volatile futurity. We might, then, think the present as a derivative of the 1970s, a kind of repetition that sustains itself through the logic of volatility as it structures energy crises so that the only way out is to restore the conditions that create the crisis. If this makes a smooth transition out of oil unlikely, it demonstrates that a political culture unequipped to deal with volatility reproduces the economic and aesthetic force of oil in moments that otherwise appear to threaten it. Crisis and conflict justify energy futures and creates political backlash against curtailing oil demand. The effect of energy crises in oil markets exerts a conservative force over energy futures because it links depletion to loss of prosperity, while offering no channels of recourse or alternative modes of life.

Why is oil uniquely vulnerable to these derivative disasters? The material ecology of petroleum is sustained so effectively through financial assets due to oil's 'stock' quality: it can be left untapped or stored, while its flow can be easily directed, modified, controlled, and sabotaged. While hydroelectric dams, watermills, wind farms, solar panels, and land itself can circulate as legal title, fictitious commodity, and rent, the flow of energy, unless stored or used, is lost. Stock energy, on the other hand, is a resource that must be extracted through enormous quantities of fixed capital and human labour and subjected to heat and refinement to become useful. For Malm, fossil energy's "most concrete quality was abstractness, permitting it to circulate through nature rather than around predetermined places in the landscape" (Malm, 2016, p. 302). This material abstractness is what makes fossil energy so effective as the energetic substrate of capital. Because fossil energy is mobile, divisible, and latent, it can be stored, moved, and burned in places distant from its extraction. It has a spatio-temporal profile unlike that of energy flows, which is rooted in particular energy landscapes. This material abstraction creates specific political-economic relations between capital and labour.

Because stocks are predictable, abstract sources of *potential* energy, they can be used at a future date according to economic need. Energy contracts can circulate in the present because of the predictable energy expenditure, known in advance by proven reserves. Reserves are stores of value in their own right, because their material abstraction lends them to financial abstraction as known future value. Like derivative options to purchase a given stock, share, or commodity at a future date, oil stocks are stores of energy that can be transformed into work when needed (unlike energy flows which flow regardless of capture or not). Proven reserves can be sold and traded without their extraction or used as collateral for loans. The equivalent kilojoules of energy flow cannot. Financialised oil blurs the distinction between extracted and yet-to-be extracted energy. As long as there is a promise of future extraction, oil futures can circulate on international stock exchanges while the physical oil it represents is still in the ground. Thus, for example, pension funds began to invest in energy futures markets in the early 2000s because unextracted oil abstracted into financial form represented a safe investment (O'Sullivan, 2014, p. 107). Fossil finance is dependent upon fossil energy's spatio-temporal characteristics. The stock market swells with fires of the future.

But unlike coal, which is a static stock, oil's materiality means its moves under its geological pressures: it rises to the surface, seeps through the ground, and flows through pipelines and into tankers. What makes it useful as a fuel also makes it dangerous to store. Petroleum flows easily and is safest on the move. This movement also makes it safer from disruption, as workers or protestors have a harder time disrupting the flow to make political demands—shaping a resource aesthetic in which, for many, crude is only experienced as the price of Brent or WTI. But what I want to emphasise here is how this materiality of oil means geological and economic knowledge has a latent imprecision—or 'convolution'—that is repeatedly transformed into macroeconomic and political effects.

Oil reserves are not fixed, definitive amounts of crude. They cannot be measured directly and so are inherently uncertain. Companies use reflection seismology to get an estimation of oil reserves. Sound waves are generated at the surface from different positions and sound receivers record the seismic reflections returned from rock formations, which generates a 3D image of subsurface deposits. This generates a series of different representations of the same subsurface space. Because these sound-waves each produce a distinctive space, a 'convoluted' image is built, a technical term that expresses how each seismic image trace is distorted by overlapping representations of the same seismic space. This superimposes different representations in the same location that both generates the reality of a represented space and confuses it. Computational power is required to 'deconvolute' these representations, removing the distortions which both obscure the space and constitute the raw data out of which seismic maps are created. A stable, if inherently imprecise, 3D representation emerges from a saturating process that mediates constitutive distortions into the imaginary appearance of a singular geological shape. This 3D visualisation is supplemented with 4D surveying, which tracks changing heat, pressure, and movement, enabling geologists to anticipate reservoir flows (Smil, 2008, pp. 84–87). An image series is taken across a period of time to visualise oil's flow. No one sees proven reserves—they are convoluted representations. This digital revolution in seismic mapping, developed in the 1960s, predominantly offshore in the Gulf of Mexico, was an early form of digitalisation, and advances in computing power gave a more refined interpretation of the subsurface (Priest, 2021, p. 180). This reduced the financial risk of wildcatting, especially in expensive offshore extraction. In reducing costs of project financing, advances in seismic mapping made returns on oil investments more certain, in an industry in which smaller businesses were likely to be bankrupted by too many dry holes.

The convolution of petroleum stock and flow is more than a problem of geophysical representation, but something like the central problem of an oil market in which each energy future generates a shape that is both focalised and distorted by the presence of other futures. Energy futures are always functionally modified by other futures, and these internal modifications cannot be removed because without them each representation would insufficiently render the future and be useless as a critical and cognitive map. Which means that oil's convolutions—in the seismic sense, but also in the sense of a knotted complexity that is difficult to follow—is a distortion that is constitutive of our energy futurity, because of the objectivity of petroleum's market mediations. Convolution names the fact that petroleum always slips away from thought, exceeds its grasp; it is a seismic subsurface whose echoes we can measure and assemble into derivatives, but never be immediate to, immersed in. Financial markets translate this constitutive gap between objectivity and representation into implied volatility. Seismic and financial representations of oil are not modally distinct: geological and financial spaces are socio-technically constituted and related to one another. This is exactly what Friedman meant when he said that "The calculated figures on reserves I have no confidence in; they have been revised over and over again, and who knows where they will be the next time they are revised?" (Friedman, 2013). They are a cascade of internally related representations of a substance that is impossible to deconvolute absolutely. Our futures are written in a language that reverberates with seismic echoes: reserve estimates, flow rates, seismograms, price spreads, and volatilities.

While the technical capacity to render subsurfaces dramatically improved through advances in microprocessor technology, it could not eliminate the risks of drilling or provide a totally deconvoluted geological map. Which means that estimates given by state companies and publicly traded oil companies can never be fully deconvoluted: they are open to obfuscation, either through overestimating reserves in order to push up stock market valuation or shrinking it to reduce taxes. Much of it is sealed in confidentiality agreements. It is not just scientific uncertainties, and the amount of proven or unproven estimates of a given oil field, but technological capability, extraction costs, taxation, environmental impacts, and investor confidence. A document on petroleum reserves states that a "key problem in structuring information about reserves is that relatively objective estimates of reservoir characteristics must be combined with subjective forecasts of project feasibility and commerciality" (Mitchell, 2004).

Proven reserves are revised in the wake of macroeconomic shifts, which contributes to changing expectations about future prices, creating volatility—the justification for futures markets and arbitrage. Higher prices bring more expensive wells online. Expectations of future production are the basis of oil company stock market valuations, so the interface between society and geological strata operates through a logic that synchronises with financial uncertainty. The socio-natural properties that make oil into a speculative resource make abstract volatility an inevitable feature of an oil market. All the ideological precepts of financialisation are embedded features of the oil industry: high-risk plays, uncertain futures, volatile markets, technological mediation, and technocratic expertise. As it drifts offshore and gets caught up in the digital revolution, this financial logic justifies the private world of fossil finance at an ideological level, while its convolution is the means of its control at a strategic level. Oil is an inherently forward-looking business, not only due to the fact that extractive industries require new sites as old ones run dry, but because proven reserves are a key resource for subjective forecasts of an oil company's ability to generate future profits, which are essential to reward shareholders and maintain share price. This is true in reverse of course, and exactly the crisis that Kosmos Energy faced in 2007, as the oil price dropped and the prospective value of their find declined. Seismic mapping can produce a convoluted zone whose imprecision and volatility sustain financial accumulation across stock and futures markets precisely because there is a financial certainty maintained in geological imprecision. If the present is too volatile for a stable future, then, contradictorily, instability is the mode of its reproduction.

Portfolio managers such as BlackRock are particularly interested (and invested) in algo-driven climate finance: an index fund that selectively moves investments across assets in accordance with algo-modelled climate scenarios is optimised to profit from shifting investment climates. Here is Rhodium Group's description of its computational rendering of the future: "To create probabilistic, asset-level risk information across all of these impact categories, Rhodium Group uses a distributed cloud computing environment. Our results represent the synthesis of millions of individual simulations covering many sources of uncertainty. These include the degree of temperature change, variability in local weather, changes in hurricane activity, variability in hurricane genesis and behaviour, and uncertainty in the impact of extreme weather events" (Rhodium Group, 2019, p. 8). It renders a convoluted future in which information-saturated and algorithmically organised price signals have internalised capital's climate externalities by tracing the unfolding molar and molecular structures of climate adaptation. They measure capitalist time from high-frequency trading to the long-term costs of energy transition, effecting changes in configurations that are beyond common capacity to conceptualise but nevertheless modulate social allocation of capital and resources. The beauty of it, for the investor worried about climate change, is that even under conditions of declining profitability—almost guaranteed as energy expenditure declines—capital can continue to exist, automatically metastasizing across networks of data, alighting on islands of profitable assets before drifting onward in the pull of computational reasoning.

Cybernetics becomes a site of connection between an economy wired for growth and a global ecology measured for homeostasis through a shared logic of feedback loops. The recursion of the feedback loop becomes a figurable form of the relation between society and climate. BlackRock's cybernetic logic of market abstraction is a new interface of algorithmic mediation, a relation to nature that posits it as financial information to be represented, linking atmospheric feedback loops to data centres and algorithms of financial accumulation. The cybernetic points to an assemblage in which energy/information flows become syncopated to an ecology animated by the geological force of capital. Retrofitting Hayek for the Anthropocene can be seen as an epistemological and political outcome of the market internalisation of climate temporalities.

In the IPCC AR 6 report, the temporal form of the climate is figured through intensity and frequency: "With every additional increment of global warming, changes in extremes continue to become larger. For example, every additional 0.5 °C of global warming causes clearly discernible increases in the *intensity and frequency* [emphasis mine] of hot extremes, including heatwaves (*very likely*), and heavy precipitation (*high confidence*), as well as agricultural and ecological droughts in some regions (*high confidence*)" (IPCC Working Group, 2021). The IPCC AR 6 scenario narrates what would have to happen to keep planetary warming within 2 °C and concludes that it is technically possible—if CCUS comes online at industrial scale by 2030 and countries cut deep into their carbon output—but politically very unlikely: 3–4 °C is a better bet. The IPCC AR 6 is probably our best ideology critique yet, the success of which only alerts us to the fact that the reproduction of fossil capital does not happen at the level of ideology at all. Moreover, it means that 2 °C financial scenarios are energy futures already receding into our past, as the carbon budget of ~ 1100 Gt CO_2 (including 220 Gt carbon capture) will likely be surpassed by mid-century, and the temperature threshold not far behind. Neither the threshold nor its effects are stable temporal forms, and IPCC narrating the limits of narrative becomes the raw material for financial speculation about how to frame uncertainty when a convoluting future does not cohere through the political economy of fossil fuels.

For BlackRock, this is a problem inasmuch as the ecological rhythms of a warming world are not yet economic ones: "Extreme weather risks already threaten utility stocks—and are set to *rise in frequency and intensity over time* [emphasis mine]—but are not fully priced in" (Blackrock Investment Instititute, 2019, p. 16). BlackRock use the example of 'storm shocks' as epicentres from which imagined weather extremes can be seen to flow through infrastructure in its physical and financial form. If a hurricane makes landfall and halts power plant operations for a measurable duration, then the value lost can be approximated. The less predictable, more frequent, and more intense such landfalls become, the harder it is to measure financial impact. More climate data must be internalised in stock prices to offset the financial volatility they cause. At stake in the transitions emplotted through tipping points and sudden devaluations is a literal *peripeteia*, a reversal of fortune, as the ecological ground of value overwhelms the numerical figures that represent it. We have, then, a financial imaginary in which the response to this can only be imagined as the extension of information into the atmosphere. Thus, BlackRock posits its own feedback loop as the justification of its role in transition, as each incremental change necessitates more and more data filtered into market forms. Emissions are cumulative even if the effects on the atmosphere are nonlinear, and risk becomes the fundament of economic reason for knowing this moving background. BlackRock's market abstractions enframe a climate at risk of exceeding the forms of financial thought that have governed the relation between energy and economy since the 1970s.

In this chapter, I have used volatility to map the landscape of financial petroculture, which I have theorised through a derivative aesthetic. Szeman argues that one of the central structuring beliefs of petroculture is that there will always be enough energy, but that energy plays only a minor role in the drama of human history (Szeman, 2011, p. 324). I have attempted to show that financial environments are necessary for petroleum to appear only as a background condition of modernity, structured economically and aesthetically through derivatives as part of the financial landscape. This happens best when oil circulates smoothly in stock exchanges and oil tankers, portfolios and pipelines. Much of what makes fossil fuel valuable is that is not represented, but remain enclosed in tankers, storage facilities, and registered offshore. This absence of oil's crude form exists in distinct contrast to the representational dominance of derivatives: prices, stocks, and shares; gasolines, fertilisers, plastics; the media, materiality, and economy of petroculture.

Oil is a unique material. Its material character means that it, like finance, can be both stock and flow: it can be treated as an asset and unit of exchange across a global economy that has burned more carbon since the beginning of energy futures trading than in the entirety of human history prior. But the propensity of this liquid to flow in and out of subterranean estates means that movement is generative of our problems of knowing oil and its future. Attempts to gain clarity on that future means recognising the fact that it is already saturated by financial writing that determine how investors allocate capital and value financial assets in relation to energy. Think of millions of traded futures contracts, oil reserve predictions, scenarios, company outlooks, climate modelling, speculative fiction and non-fiction, and so on: the density of that represented space we call the future cannot be deconvoluted without dissolving into anaemic abstractions; any single future is only a function of the distortion that the series of futures must necessarily be in order to attain sufficient representational saturation to shape our relation to it. While it might be literally true that proven reserves are finite, the measure of finitude is insufficient to prevent extraction at quantities that amount to climate catastrophe. The addition of more reserves and advances in extraction technology has meant there is about two-and-a-half times more proven oil than there was in 1980—in other words, Friedman was right—which means that hope an *external* limit will bring an end to oil extraction is desperate political fantasy (the same is true of coal) (Dale, 2015, pp. 3–8). Neither will Nature itself march onto the stage of history as its new subject and bring about the oil's end. Between the apocalypses of limits and limitlessness is a future of *too much*, a volatile excess much harder to narrativise. Petroleum surges through the financial system whether it has been burned or not, inflating the share values of oil companies through the promise of future combustion. Reckoning with oil's convoluted ontologies means thinking about how oil gives narrative structure to energy futures that make oil visible, but visible in a way that makes it harder to imagine a future beyond the volatile abstractions we continue to live as our ongoing warming present.

The future of energy seeps into the present, through project financing and markets as much as through the cumulative emissions that trap heat in the atmosphere. The materiality of oil writes our present into the future and our future into the present as much as financial contracts, in the signs we learn to read of a warming world: uncanny weather, wildfires, floods, and droughts. Every trajectory plotted out of petroculture runs into financial or atmospheric volatility. The problem is how to thread a path between crises that entrench fossil fuel usage further or the political fantasies of an orderly transition that does not move fast enough. The purpose of this chapter has been to show that these are not representational distortions of our future that can be scrubbed out as we proceed from ideological ignorance to knowledge of our oil ontology. They are constitutive of a convoluted reality that we must critically register if we are to build a world after one derived from oil.

References

Ayache, E. (2010). *The Blank Swan: The End of Probability (1st edition).* Wiley.

Blackrock Investment Instititute. (2019). *Getting Physical: Scenario Analysis for Assessing Climate-Related Risks.* Global Insights. Retrieved from www.blackrock.com/us/individual/literature/whitepaper/bii-physical-climate-risks-april-2019.pdf

Bryan, D., & Rafferty, M. (2005). *Capitalism With Derivatives: A Political Economy of Financial Derivatives, Capital and Class (2006th edition).* Palgrave Macmillan.

Bryan, D., & Rafferty, M. (2007). Financial Derivatives and the Theory of Money. *Economy and Society, 36*(1), 134–158. https://doi.org/10.1080/03085140601089861

Carollo, S. (2011). *Understanding Oil Prices: A Guide to What Drives the Price of Oil in Today's Markets (1st edition).* Wiley.

Carter, J. (1979). *Crisis of Confidence | American Experience | PBS.* Retrieved from https://www.pbs.org/wgbh/americanexperience/features/carter-crisis/

Dale, S. (2015). *New Economics of Oil.* Society of Business Economists Annual Conference, London. Retrieved from https://www.bp.com/content/dam/bp/business-sites/en/global/corporate/pdfs/news-and-insights/speeches/new-economics-of-oil-spencer-dale.pdf

Diamanti, J. (2021). *Climate and Capital in the Age of Petroleum.* Bloomsbury.

Friedman, M. (1971). *The Need for Futures Markets in Currencies.* Retrieved from https://papers.ssrn.com/abstract=2251345

Friedman, M. (2013, February 27). Classic 1978 Milton Friedman Lecture on the Future of Energy. *American Enterprise Institute—AEI.* Retrieved from https://www.aei.org/carpe-diem/classic-1978-milton-friedman-lecture-on-the-future-of-energy/

Gkanoutas-Leventis, A., & Nesvetailova, A. (2015). Financialisation, Oil and the Great Recession. *Energy Policy, 86*, 891–902. https://doi.org/10.1016/j.enpol.2015.05.006

Guardian. (2019, June 14). *Footage US Military Claims Shows Iranian Patrol Boat Removing Limpet Mine from Tanker—Video*. The Guardian. Retrieved from http://www.theguardian.com/global/video/2019/jun/14/footage-us-military-claims-shows-iranian-patrol-boat-removing-limpet-mine-from-tanker-video

IPCC Working Group. (2021). *IPCC AR6 Working Group 1: Summary for Policymakers*. Retrieved from https://www.ipcc.ch/report/ar6/wg1/chapter/summary-for-policymakers/

Jameson, F. (2002). *The Political Unconscious (2nd edition)*. Routledge.

La Berge, L. C. (2015). *Scandals and Abstraction: Financial Fiction of the Long 1980s (Illustrated edition)*. Academic.

La Berge, L. C. (2019). The Rules of Abstraction: Methods and Discourses of Finance. In *In the Mind but Not from There: Real Abstraction and Contemporary Art*. Verso.

Labban, M. (2010). Oil in Parallax: Scarcity, Markets, and the Financialization of Accumulation. *Geoforum, 4*(41), 541–552. https://doi.org/10.1016/j.geoforum.2009.12.002

Mackenzie, D. (2006). Is Economics Performative? Option Theory and the Construction of Derivatives Markets. *Journal of the History of Economic Thought, 28*(1), 29–55. https://doi.org/10.1080/10427710500509722

Malm, A. (2016). *Fossil Capital: The Rise of Steam Power and the Roots of Global Warming*. Verso Books.

McMahon, T. (2023). *Q&A with Pioneering Oil Trader Thomas McMahon—OpenMarkets*. Retrieved from https://www.cmegroup.com/openmarkets/energy/2023/qa-with-pioneering-oil-trader-thomas-mcmahon.html

Mitchell, J. (2004). *Petroleum Reserves in Question*. Oxford Institute for Energy Studies. Retrieved from https://www.oxfordenergy.org/publications/petroleum-reserves-in-question/

O'Neill, J. (2009). *Netherland* (1st edition). Harper.

O'Sullivan, D. (2014). *Petromania: Black Gold, Paper Barrels and Oil Price Bubbles* (Illustrated edition). Harriman House.

Priest, T. (2021). Seismic Innovations: The Digital Revolution in the Search for Oil and Gas. In *Energy in the Americas*. Calgary University Press.

Rhodium Group. (2019, April 3). *Clear, Present and Underpriced: The Physical Risks of Climate Change—Rhodium Group*. Retrieved from https://rhg.com/research/physical-risks-climate-blackrock/

Sekula, A. (1991, November 8). War Without Bodies. *Artforum*. Retrieved from https://www.artforum.com/features/war-without-bodies-203869/

Smil, V. (2008). *Oil: A Beginner's Guide*. Oneworld Publications.

Szeman, I. (2011). Literature and Energy Futures. *PMLA*, *126*(2). https://www.jstor.org/stable/41414106

Wellum, C. (2020). Energizing Finance: The Energy Crisis, Oil Futures, and Neoliberal Narratives. *Enterprise & Society*, *21*(1), 2–37. https://doi.org/10.1017/eso.2019.26

CHAPTER 5

Delay: Horrors on the Permafrost

5.1 Permafrost Time

In March 2023, President Biden approved a controversial oil prospect on Alaska's North Slope. Situated in the National Petroleum Reserve, the largest tract of public land in the US, the ConocoPhillips Willow Project is expected to produce an estimated 576 m barrels of oil over the next thirty years. Despite objections from climate activists and local campaigners, who say that it threatens climate goals and the local landscape, it has been justified through a conventional rhetoric of energy security and independence, and the promise of economic development for the local area.

Like most of Alaska, this is an area where rising temperatures have led to permafrost thaw. While this is recognised as a key tipping point in climate change science, it creates a more local problem for ConocoPhillips. The previously solid ground is becoming too unstable to support the gravel roads to extraction sites, and too soft to embed the well casings that hold oil wells in place. ConocoPhillips' solution is to instal giant passive thermosyphons that circulate heat out of the ground and into the air. The purpose of these so-called 'chillers' is to refreeze the permafrost in areas adjacent to infrastructure, delaying the thaw. Unsurprisingly, this has caused some uproar, as the company freezes the permafrost while extracting the stuff that causes its melting. By the time

H. Pitt Scott, *Financial Petroleum Cultures*, Palgrave Studies in Literature, Culture and Economics,
https://doi.org/10.1007/978-3-031-99661-0_5

ConocoPhillips has drained the last drop of oil from the Willow Project around 2050, as much as 50% of Alaskan infrastructure may be damaged or inoperable because of thaw; the coast will be vulnerable to storms; and traditional food systems will be under threat or destroyed. The arctic is heating faster than anywhere else on earth, with an average temperature rise of three degrees in the last sixty years.

Defined as any type of ground, from soil to rock, that is continuously frozen for over two years, permafrost is significant to the climate because it operates as a carbon trap. When plants and animals die and are decomposed by microbes, they release carbon dioxide and methane. In arctic climates, a deep freeze arrests this process of decomposition, locking these greenhouse gases into the ice. Permafrost is packed with millennia of life, making it a planetary morgue estimated to hold as much as twice the amount of carbon in the atmosphere. At current thawing rates, some 92bn tonnes of CO_2 is expected to be released by 2100, twenty per cent of the amount released by human activity since the start of the Industrial Revolution. Carbon emissions are no longer solely a human affair.

Permafrost is a climate barometer, a setting in which the history of fossil fuels weighs heavily, and a site for speculation about economic resources. Because the primary driver and consequence of thaw is global temperature rise, we are all in relation to permafrost. But permafrost tends to pass beneath cultural or critical notice. As Charlotte Wrigley writes, it is "dull and marshy. It is largely hidden under snow for much of the year, emerging in the brief summer months infested with mosquitoes, fetid and humped" (Wrigley, 2023, p. 2). Underground, out of sight, and far away, it is invisible to the naked eye, contained below layers of active soil, and its effects are measured through ground shifts or things long dead rising to the surface. The slow transition from ice to water, and the steady release of invisible gases, is hard to dramatise. By contrast, collapsing icebergs, used to figure the changing climate for decades, generate a sublime awe. The language of horror has often been deployed in the imagination of ice-bound regions. For example, Coleridge's icebergs are figured as monstrous.

> The ice was here, the ice was there,
> The ice was all around:
> It cracked and growled, and roared and howled,
> Like noises in a swound!

Like recent concerns over 'zombie viruses' frozen in ice, threatening to unleash new pandemics, there is no shortage of terror to be found (Mckie, 2024). While the gothic has often been associated with ice-bound regions, its focus has been drawn to the sublime majesty of the iceberg and the icesheet, where the endless expanse of ice surpasses imagination. We'll let Caspar David Friedrich's *The Sea of Ice,* which covers my copy of *Frankenstein,* stand in for this tradition, which includes Shelley, Coleridge, and Poe (Shelley, 2012).

Permafrost, by contrast, tends to invite reflections on time. If Thomas Pynchon writes in *Bleeding Edge,* "the future is out there on the permafrost" (Pynchon, 2013), it is also a space that, in the words of Kathleen Jamie, "the past can spill out of the earth, become the present" (Jamie, 2019). Time expands and contracts: the past surfaces; the future arrives too early. It requires diachronic and dialectical thinking, imagining relations across time and space, and through elements, infrastructures, and financial abstractions.

This chapter will be anchored by a close reading of the Larry Fessenden's *The Last Winter* (2006), an ecological horror film situated within a long tradition of frozen and ice-bound horror. This subgenre emerges from an encounter between writers influenced by the polar gothic—Coleridge, Shelley, Poe—and a new geography of geophysical science. Films in this genre—and I'll discuss some of them shortly—are often read as 'revenge-of-nature' narratives and tend to work within a dynamic of surfacing and containment. I will argue that the politics of this subgenre is found in the way that it manages fears of monsters lurking beneath the ice.

By contrast, *The Last Winter* refuses the strategies of containment central to this tradition, which I read as a fundamental discontinuity in the meaning of the Alaskan subsurface. Increasingly represented as economic opportunity and national security due to its hydrocarbon reserves, as well as a space particularly sensitive to shifts in global temperature, ice-bound threats become increasingly uncontainable as the permafrost thaws. The film exhibits a contradiction between ecological attention and financial representation that gets rendered aesthetically as volatility. I will argue that volatility is a problem for narrative form that gets resolved in horror through setting, atmosphere, and the dynamics of narrative endings. Reading across ecological and economic registers of permafrost time, my organising claim is that the horror of this film is to be found in delay, and this is registered through spectral hauntings, gory violence, and volatile atmospheres. By paying attention to the dialectic of delay and volatility, we notice how they combine into narratives and affects that sustain commitments to financial petroculture *despite* its horrifying violence; managing horror, in other words, is of utmost importance to its persistence and reproduction. Interpreting *The Last Winter* as a film of financial petroculture makes available a critique of the material, abstract, and narrative function of volatility.

As we shift into an era in which climate change is becoming an ecological and political reality, the major obstacle to addressing it is not climate denial but climate delay (Lamb et al., 2020). Delay denotes a desire to remain in one world and shore that world up against the feeling of change. Forming into a set of habits, practices, discourses, affects, and infrastructures, delay is the way a sense of normality adjusts to the geohistorical event of the Anthropocene, registering it as fact but altering the intensity of affective extrapolation. But if delay is about extending the now into and against an uncertain future, the now is exactly what is called into question by the cumulative emissions of centuries of fires: "We can never be in the heat of the moment", writes Andreas Malm, "only in the heat of this ongoing past" (Malm, 2017, p. 5). Delay is a historical feeling, and one that should horrify us, but rarely does, as it generates neither dramatic historical scene nor the expectation that change is possible or desirable. In reading for a horror of delay, I aim to apprehend how the contemporary oil economy grounds delay as a social problem, as a fantasy of suspension operative in normal life.

Even when we do see oil, we tend to focus on what Frederick Buell calls exuberant or catastrophic moments, missing the forms of energy that give shape and character to contemporary life (Buell, 2012). Automobility, plastics, economic growth, national security, and the recurrent fear of exhaustion and depletion, oil enables the times and spaces of modernity in ways that we are only beginning to reckon with. Over all this hovers the spectre of a volatile future, which reconfigures the prehistoric and historic past, the globalised present, and the ecology of the distant future. My methodological claim here is that horror is a genre finely tuned to infrastructure failure, which appear as rifts in social time and habitus as the ambient environment of daily life breaks apart. Horror twists infrastructural environments into spaces of terror, locating a nightmarish quality inherent to technological systems, the "embedded strangeness" of the built environment that is "invisible, part of the background for other kinds of work"(STAR, 1999, p. 380).

The wager of this chapter is that horror's infrastructuralism can track the passage of volatility into daily life, because it is able to dramatise the feeling of unease central to maintaining the fictions of energy futurity that continue to dominate our social horizon. Our energy culture is premised on preserving a tolerable level of volatility, contained and managed by financial markets, which are meant to regulate present to future. That it might be unable to do so at the permafrost: this is the critical mediation captured by the genre best able to conjoin negative emotions to the infrastructures that write our climate future in the language of flood, melt, thaw, and drought.

5.2 Infrastructural Horrors

The Last Winter takes place at a prospective oil frontier. In the film, an oil company has just received a licence to begin drilling in the Arctic National Wildlife Refuge. Setting up a research station not far from the original test well, a group comprised of oil workers and scientists monitor the local area. Ed Pollack, the oil company representative, is pushing to expand necessary infrastructure for drilling, such as ice roads. The scientists are hired by the oil company to write an environmental report to show that the impacts of extraction will be minimal. James Hoffman, the head of the scientific team, concerned about the effect that a warming climate is having on the Arctic ecosystem, worries that the heavy vehicles required to transport drilling equipment will further accelerate the thaw. Much narrative energy is invested in subsurface speculation, a space once described by Pablo Neruda as a "world of sinister depth" (Neruda, 2000, p. 176). It is a space where the promise of infrastructure and the threat of climate change are immiscible.

A young member of the oil company team, Maxwell, begins to see things around the test well. He insists everyone leave, which the hard-headed Pollack refuses to do. Visiting a site where he is collecting permafrost temperature data, we observe Hoffman make records in a journal in which he notes that subsurface temperatures are rising, and that "*some thing* is being unleashed from the permafrost". Shortly after, Maxwell sees something emerge out of the ice at the test well. Using a crane shot, the camera adopts the perspective of the thing, which remains out of view. The camera moves upward from the well, towards the young worker, and then quickly away into the white snow and towards Hoffman in the data collection site. He too begins to see things.

It is some time before this monster appears to others in the group, and this gives the characters time to reflect on what they have seen. Maxwell, the first to be exposed to the curse, becomes increasingly convinced the well is haunted, while Pollack does his best to contain the contagious fear. Others suspect that methane leaking out of the thawing ground is leading to hallucinations. Maxwell tolls Hoffman: "It's coming out of the ground. Ghosts. I mean, what is oil anyway, but fossils, plants and animals from whatever millions of years ago?" Here, the film establishes a gothic ecology of oil curses, as extractive infrastructures intermingle with deep pasts and deep futures.

In a later scene, another scientist visits Hoffman's data collection outpost and reads his diary. The film cuts rapidly between geological maps and frantic scribblings. Hoffman's voice informs us that something is off: in the numbers—the temperature of the permafrost—but also in feeling, mood and atmosphere. Sensing this disturbance like a background hum, he asserts that there is 'no way home': the permafrost has become uncanny, out of joint. Laid over shots of crude oil bubbling out of the ground, the voiceover asks: what would it look like if oil came out of the ground willingly to confront humanity?

The Last Winter finds a novel kind of historical feeling on the permafrost, as oil's invisibility is registered in the spectral and fantastic. Temperature data has not yet become narrative, but it has unsettled the ordinary enough to encourage speculation. Lauren Berlant calls this a crisis within ordinariness: a historical present is felt when an event directs us towards sensing an emerging historical environment atmospherically (Berlant, 2008, p. 5). As is to expected in a horror film, this takes on form through monstrous figures. The monster comes from up the drill shaft. Maxwell, convinced that he can see a ghostly presence, walks onto the ice naked, in his final moments capturing a spectre on camera. Of course, the remaining crew fail to heed this warning, and as the conventions of the genre dictate, this condemns them to death.

In his influential account of American horror, Robin Wood argues that the basic formula of the horror film is that "normality is threatened by the monster" (Wood, 2018). The monster displaces social antagonisms within society to an imagined outside; those that confront the monster become representative of society. The opposition of normality and monstrosity registers a dim awareness of wrongness.

In frozen horror, the narrative hinges on whether the threat is containable. Think of the ending to H.P. Lovecraft's 'At the Mountains of Madness', where the narrator instructs us that

> It is absolutely necessary, for the peace and safety of mankind, that some of earth's dark, dead corners and unplumbed depths be let alone; lest sleeping abnormalities wake to resurgent life, and blasphemously surviving nightmares squirm and splash out of their black lairs to newer and wider conquests (Lovecraft, 2013, p. 283).

Indeed, the advantage of this genre for my analysis is that it tends to make literal what Fredric Jameson calls, appropriately enough, 'strategies of containment': the way that negative feelings must be given an initial expression by a cultural object if they are also to be manipulated, resolved, and contained (Jameson, 1990, p. 39). Horror is singularly apposite for tracking how negative and critical feelings get expressed and managed; and this is true, too, of anxieties about what lurks beneath the ice. Monsters embody social fears and negative attitudes, displaced on to a *thing* that can be contained and killed. In frozen horror, containment tends to be geographical in nature: stay away, keep it out of sight, don't let it reach the surface. Normality is restored when the surfaced threat is returned to the depths.

John W. Campbell, who took up an editorial role at pulp SF magazine *Astounding Stories* a year after it published Lovecraft's 'At the Mountains of Madness', published his own tale, 'Who Goes There?', in 1938. Drawing from the Antarctic Gothic tradition, including references to Coleridge's 'Rime of the Ancient Mariner', his story, like Lovecraft's, describes an Antarctic research station where a mixture of military personnel, scientist, and explorers are slowly driven mad by the intrusion of a shapeshifting alien that has been frozen in ice for millions of years. This short story is the inspiration for Christian Nyby's horror film *The Thing from Another World* (1951) and John Carpenter's *The Thing* (1981).

Campbell's 'Who Goes There?' establishes a generic formula: a combination of scientists and military personnel on a base; scientific experiments lead to thawing ice and a discovery of a monster; tensions mount between scientists and soldiers over what to do; there is a struggle to examine and, ultimately, contain the threat. The scientists represent a Promethean overreach, as they are unable to discern the real threat the discovery poses to civilization. The soldiers, expressing a political realism, must sacrifice themselves, and the base, to prevent the Thing getting back to civilization—including shooting an Albatross that might be a shapeshifting alien. As in Lovecraft's tale, the central fear expressed by Campbell is that of a monster escaping the isolated outpost.

Campbell's story was modelled on real-life Antarctic station 'Little America I', established by military explorer Richard Byrd in 1929 and the location of important documentary *With Byrd at the South Pole* (1930), which won an Oscar in 1930. This is also the era of Herbert Ponting's *The Great White Silence* (1924), and *Nanook of the North* (1922). Campbell's story uses Byrd's *Discovery: The Story of the Second Byrd Expedition* as source material. 'Little America I' was abandoned in 1930, but nearly thirty years later, in the 'International Geophysical Year' of 1958, 'Byrd Station' and 'Little America V' were the first two sites in Antarctica where ice core drilling took place.

Over this period, scientific and military expeditions mapped Antarctica—the 'last frontier' and a 'forbidden world', according to *Byrd at the South Pole*. The southern-most continent became a space of scientific research and geopolitical adventurism, captured for the public by a documentary impulse to record and film the seemingly endless expanse of frozen ice. The social isolation, harsh landscape, and heroic exploration provided a rich symbolic landscape for horror writers. The scientific research and documentary realism provided a useful foil for those whose mental image of Antarctica is steeped in Coleridge and Edgar Allen Poe, as research camps and the surrounding icescapes are recast as Gothic castles and their sinister estates. Both documentary realism and frozen horror operate through a colonial gaze: an ethnographic impulse, of people or monsters, and an imaginative frontier where the line between civilised and savage blurs.

This space took on new importance in the study of climate science. Through interpretation of air bubbles trapped in cylinders of ice drilled from ice sheets and glaciers, glaciologists can measure atmosphere composition and average temperatures over the age range of the ice core, providing data about the deep history of the climate. Glaciers form through the accumulation of layers of snow on top of each other. As the snow compresses, the atmospheric particulates and chemicals dissolved within it are frozen in the ice. These provide a record of the climate conditions, making the cryosphere an important source of information about the history of the atmosphere. Mechanical drills are used to extract cylinders of ice about a metre long, which are then removed from the barrel and stored in ice core facilities. By the 1970s, these ice cores were nearly a kilometre long. The record for deepest ice core is now about three kilometres. According to the National Science Foundation, they are "essentially frozen time capsules that allow scientists to reconstruct climate far into the past" (NSF, 2024). More recently, ice cores have become central to the debate around periodising the Anthropocene. Paul Crutzen, for example, dates it to the late eighteenth century, because "This is the period when data retrieved from glacial ice cores show the beginning of a growth in the atmospheric concentrations of several 'greenhouse gases', in particular CO2, CH4 and N2O. Such a starting date coincides with James Watt's invention of the steam engine in 1782" (Crutzen, 2006, p. 16). As Alessandro Antonello and Mark Carey write, "Ice cores, in short, have been at the heart of late twentieth- and early twenty-first-century developments relating to environmental perceptions and perspectives—and the way people see themselves in this world, not only spatially but temporally" (Antonello & Carey, 2017, p. 184).

As glaciologists began to interpret climate history written in ice, horror films too began to speculate about frozen secrets. Campbell's story involves a shapeshifting, tentacular alien that absorbs all life it encounters. In *The Beast from 20,000 Fathoms,* a nuclear experiment thaws ice in the Arctic, releasing a dinosaur from hibernation that rampages through New York. The horrifying threat of *Alien vs. Predator* is that aliens will escape confinement below the ground in Antarctica. "Don't let it reach the surface", one scientist calls to another. Melting permafrost reveals a woolly mammoth that contains a deadly parasite in *The Thaw*, echoing contemporary fears of 'zombie viruses' trapped in the ice. *The Tomorrow War,* an sf-horror in which humans from the future travel back in time to enlist volunteers to fight a war against aliens who have thawed out of the ice due to warming global temperatures, makes the formula an explicit allegory for climate change. The list goes on, but the formula remains the same, dinosaurs replaced by bears replaced by aliens.

What links these films, I think, is a desire for the known, to form our fear into a shape that can be recognised and rejected. What if the thing in the earth is not, in fact, us? What if it comes from outside of human history, deep time or from beyond the stars? Is there an agency here that we know we can't understand, so need not try? They encounter infrastructure and ecology as horror, and after inspection of this unnerving otherness, turn away.

I am by no means the first to note that horror films are often formulaic and repetitive, successes spawning endless sequels and copycats. Horror tells the same stories over and over, in a familiar formula, minor variations just enough to make it feel new. But the strict constraints of the genre do provide a certain leeway for experimentation. The genre director must satisfy the requirements of the genre—blood, gore, isolation, barren landscapes, scientific discovery, monsters, the cold, and so on—but is free to be innovative within those requirements. And low budget horror often has a financial freedom—and a weaker investment in the status quo—that bigger budget film does not. *The Last Winter* never met with commercial success, although it has retained an important status in the history of climate horror. It is this dual pressure of repetition and autonomy that makes frozen horror a useful barometer for social fears about the cryosphere.

This is because *The Last Winter* doesn't really fit the mould of the subgenre that clearly most influences it. Even though oil does exist as a spectral form, the narrative never really coheres that threat into a particular object or thing but rather disperses through a volatile thawing landscape. The ending refuses a sense of closure at all, as the sole survivor of the base returns to the nearest town find the ground melting under her feet. This is because historical time feels different on the permafrost. While abrupt thaw can trigger rapid landscape deterioration, sinkholes, and thermokarsts, gradual thaw—the gradual decline in near-surface permafrost—takes place over decades, and decomposition of frozen organic material over centuries and millennia (Lenton, 2023). Thaw is not a singular event, but a repetition that will occur for centuries. Permafrost time upends how we organise and understand historical experience; it expands historical time. This finds expression in the fantastical, as ghosts of the past and the future materialise as a disruptive force in the present. *The Last Winter*'s oil curse registers the disorientation that occurs within the ordinary when deep time intrudes, and the fear that what we take as given is due a bloody end. This plays out through the punctuating shocks of violence, which is cut with apocalyptic scenes that draw on visual signifiers of climate disaster: petroleum bubbling straight out of the ground, burning oil fields, floodwaters.

Through its generic discontinuities, the film indexes negative attitudes towards oil and critiques the way that such feelings are managed. What *The Last Winter* shows is that any account of the horror of oil must not only focus on how its temporality introduces a crisis in normality, but how normality is conditioned by oil in ways that we struggle to notice. There is a comfort in representing oil as 'out there' in monstrous form, a vengeful spirit come to enact retributive justice upon those who transgress into its dark spaces; a kind of energy determinism, displacing agency and responsibility on to a substance that has none. But as an evaporative liquid, energy form, petrochemical stock, motive force, and financial abstraction, petroleum is always shapeshifting and ever-returning. It seeps through what Szeman and Boyer describe as "those zones of experience and expectation generated by our energy systems that we take as equivalent to normal life" (Imre Szeman & Boyer, 2017, p. 3). What we take to be normal is a cluster of habits, practices, discourses, affects, and atmospheres enabled by, and creating the demand for, fossil fuel. Graeme Macdonald argues that we should account for the "the horror of oil's banality", ways that oil remains monstrously normal *despite* the ongoing accumulation of environmental disaster—how a culture of delay is sustained through narratives that keep in focus, and promise to stave off, near-term disasters of dependency and depletion (Macdonald, 2016). This requires shifting registers, from the ecological to the political economy of oil.

5.3 Spectres of Dependency

The narrative tension of the film emerges from the conflict between oil company workers and climate scientists. This is expressed most clearly through Pollack, who insists, again and again, that the American public are behind the push to extract petroleum from the Alaskan National Wildlife Refuge, because it is central to securing energy independence. This phrase is repeated as self-evident justification, a normative common sense about energy. The opening corporate video concludes its exposition by describing the new oil prospect as bringing the US "one step closer to energy independence". The phrase was popularised by Richard Nixon, uniting a call for energy development with a hostility to OPEC in the wake of the 1973 oil shock that led to economic crisis, inflation, and a profound anxiety about the future of the American way of life. The desire for 'energy independence' has remained a mainstay of American energy discourse since. ConocoPhillips evoke it as justification for the Willow Project (ConocoPhillips, 2024). In this context, the cultural work of Alaskan oil is to alleviate fears around foreign energy. This is clearly at stake in *The Last Winter*.

Oil was discovered in Prudhoe Bay in 1968, but it was the crisis of 1973 that gave Alaskan oil development a major boost. The Trans-Alaska Pipeline System was approved by Nixon in 1973 and built between 1975–77, which required signing into law the Alaska Natives Claims Settlement Act, terminating Indigenous claims to nearly 400 million acres of land throughout Alaska in exchange for nearly one billion dollars and ownership of 40 million acres (Moeser, 2023). We see the pipeline slicing through empty landscape in the film. Land and logistics were central to the oil boom, as these are activities that "demand great control over space, not only in the regions where the extraction occurs, but also in the constitution and maintenance of logistic corridors" (Silva, 2022). Resources embedded in the soil require that territory and property are made legible, and so land became the object of colonial state governance. Colonial extractive practices are deeply embedded into the economy and infrastructure of the region, as displacement and development produce and promise to resolve social divisions. We see it represented in *The Last Winter*, as a member of the camp watches a corporate video that describes it as "the great Trans-Alaska Pipeline" and shows it slicing through empty landscape.

Szeman notes that pipelines generate zones of spatial and political indifference for consumers separated from extraction frontiers and logistical corridors (Szeman, 2018). Building on top of the colonial myth of the 'empty Arctic', the Trans-Alaska Pipeline System provided a medium for a nationalist discourse of energy independence premised on colonial erasure. No wonder, then, that into this blank space is projected stories about isolation, survival, and unpopulated surfaces (*The Edge, The Grey*). In contrast to more recognisable oil horrors like the *Exxon Valdez* spill of 1989, which occurred at the southern terminus of the pipeline and defined a global visual language of petroleum horror through oil-soaked birds and burning oceans, *The Last Winter* situates its horror in this zone of indifference. The Alaskan oil frontier generates speculative narratives of animate subsurfaces and unpopulated surfaces. In doing so, the oil curse provides a figure for those written out of the landscape: displaced, exploited, and those future worlds that will end because of thaw already set in motion by current temperature rise. It proposes a way of seeing the monstrous normality of infrastructure.

At the same time that ice became a recording medium of geological time, energy futures imagined a reorientation of America's infrastructure from East to North. Landscapes previously associated with heroism and ecological hostility came to signify energy security, infrastructurally maintained and rhetorically available to a nationalist discourse. This is how we should understand Pollack's statement in *The Last Winter* when, confronted with the breakdown of order at the camp and threats to his authority, he insists that "What's needed out here is a pipeline". In a hostile landscape, confronted with unknown threats, he expresses a desire for containment, security, and spatial order. Prospective infrastructures are used to make political claims about land use despite the volatile future that they otherwise index. From the perspective of energy independence, the horror of oil is not ecological but political, its foreignness, its transgression of national boundaries. The idea of energy independence is popular because it articulates fears about energy and promises national resolutions. It plays on important elements of American identity by suggesting that the US has been subordinated to the control of foreign powers, a lasting legacy of 1973 in American petroculture. By making available a narrative of national self-sufficiency, energy independence is an imagined resolution to the social contradiction of a resource invested with national symbolism but mediated by a global energy market.

Like many horror films, *The Last Winter* offers a narrative of communication breakdown, blackout, and resource shortage. Pollack and Hoffman decide to search for help, leaving on a snowmobile towards workers who are building the road to the oil field. By the time they arrive, they discover a fuel leak and are stranded. This is a common horror device, used also in other petroleum-soaked horror films like *Night of the Living Dead* and *The Texas Chainsaw Massacre*. From the perspective of energy critique, it can be viewed as a mediation of depletion and non-renewability. In fact, this narrative device shares coordinates with what infrastructure studies calls 'infrastructural inversion': "infrastructure flickering into visibility and regard—can occur both in the lived experience of infrastructural interruption or failure, and as a methodological shift for scholars thinking infrastructure in a new way" (Wenzel, 2022, p. 159).

What distinguishes horror is the importance the genre places on the infrastructures that create our experience of normality, and what kind of crises emerge as these material systems fall away. It is finely tuned to the fact that our personal feelings, desires, and sensibilities run on the capacities and affordances of fossil fuels. Turning expectations about those systems that are often thought of as "mundane to the point of boredom" into the object of narrative tension and enjoyment, it reveals how we take for granted the massive forces available to us, which usually feel good, or at least normal (Wenzel, 2022, p. 153). But more than a narrative form of infrastructural inversion, in which figure and ground switch places in the paradigmatic critical gesture of infrastructure studies, horror can, I want to argue, inhabit the infrastructural as its normative conditioning recedes. Infrastructures "always serve as the foundation that enables something else to happen" (Boyer, 2018, p. 227). But infrastructure failures also enable alternative and oppositional social relations to convene, converge, and scale. The spaces of horror are breaks in the flow of social time, lingering in moments when the dominant drops away to expose the residual or the emergent. As the present falls apart, what appears are spectres of the past or the unborn future. The lights going out, the phone going dead, or the car engine failing to start: horror's generic fascination with infrastructure failure makes it a rich archive for energy criticism. While it often turns infrastructure failure into a source of fear, the enjoyment derived from horror films suggests a critical ambivalence towards the visibilities, securities, habits, and promises enabled by infrastructure.

When the snowmobile stops, Pollack and Hoffman must traverse the ice on foot, as if to ask what kind of people they are without modern infrastructure. Thus, like polar explorers, they march into the white. Yet rather than infrastructure failure providing the opportunity for a heroic and masculine conquering of Alaskan space (as in *The Edge*), or a suspension of normality in which socially unacceptable feelings can be temporarily expressed and then recontained, both meet their end, first turning on each other, before being killed by the spectral presence. In much horror, the restoration of automobility signals the restoration of normality. This is a formal investment in delay, because it suggests that access to petroleum still makes the difference between life and death. This discourse of delay is no less dominant nearly two decades later, as global emissions continue to rise year on year, and the IEAs most optimistic predictions that, despite fossil fuel usage peaking in 2030, global demand will still be some 55 million barrels per day in 2050 (Millard, 2024). It defines Alaska's role in the coming decades. ConocoPhillips justifies extraction from the Willow Project on the basis that "Willow's projected production will reduce American reliance on foreign supply and support U.S. energy security by producing reliable, low emissions-intensity oil from an existing petroleum reserve"(ConocoPhillips, 2024). The film registers that energy independence operates as a form of foreclosing change; that narrating crisis can become a genre of continuity.

Indeed, read infrastructurally, it can be viewed as a decathexis from a binary of infrastructural normality and the heroic frontier: two fantasies of independence must give way to a force that consumes them. It resists the movement of infrastructure into the background, while recognising how infrastructures hold in place, and indeed determine, particular discourses and aesthetics as more primary matters of political concern and cultural interest.

The fear of oil dependency started when the oil crisis of 1973 led to the gradual unwinding of the energy system that had prevailed in the postwar period, where oil corporations played the primary price-setting role in the global energy market. While OPEC shocked this system into crisis, it would gradually get replaced by a financial system of futures trading based out of New York and London. It was in trading floors and derivatives markets that oil's volatile future would come to be written in the language of risk, uncertainty, and speculation. The market was envisioned as a mechanism for regulating the present through oil futures, and oil exports got pegged to global benchmarks that determined price. In doing so, oil derivatives came to exert a spectral effectivity as claims to future value, as financial barrels get traded many times more than physical barrels. The uncanny effect of this spectral doubling is that oil prices settled in stock exchanges provide the impetus to develop new fields and drill new wells, not the other way around. As the trade and investment of oil has been financialised, oil companies and financial corporations have turned to financial markets, which privilege short-term speculative circulation over long-term productive circulation. The representational dominance that financial exchange has over the commodity itself has led to a blurring of the distinction between present and future, as oil reserves live a spectral life on the commodity exchange long before they extracted, transported, and refined into a market product (Labban, 2010, p. 545).

Rather than solving the situation of dependency, this actually made financial volatility an endemic feature of petroleum life. By the start of the twenty-first century the integration of energy futures into pension funds and commodity indexes connected the 'financialisation of daily life' to hydrocarbon infrastructures. Exposure to oil assets became normal, as markets linked pension funds, portfolios, and pipelines to the permafrost. By simplifying the socio-political complexities of energy to market mechanisms, financialisation reorganised the spatio-temporal form of oil capital *and* the representational forms that generate a sense of energy normality, with volatility an ever-present threat. Oil volatility reverberates through the global economy, producing an infrastructural fear as the background of everyday life becomes a topic invested with worry. The permafrost is part of an expanded oil market setting, as the fear that something might go amiss on the frontier requires not just geographical containment but financial security. It is a space haunted by spectres of depletion, invested with the hope of delay, and rendered as financial value.

In fact, I propose that we can read financial volatility and monstrosity as parallel discourses. The Volatility Index, a measure of the stock market's expectations of future volatility, provides a way of reading market sentiment. Investopedia tells me that high volatility is usually accompanied by 'market fear'(Investopedia, 2024). In her essay on debt and horror, Annie McClanahan says that the Volatility Index, sometimes called the 'fear index', provides a way of making speculative bets "on fear itself" (McClanahan, 2012). This is because, as volatility rises, the rate of change of prices also rises. The inability to determine the value of oil based on market prices erodes the ability to predict and plan, as long-term trends get pulled into the temporal black hole of short-term volatility. As well as being a term for financial fear, volatility is the measure of the deviation of prices from a mean over a given period of time. *Deviation from a mean* is a definition of monsters as much as financial volatility. Or, as energy strategist Kent Moors puts it in a book on oil market volatility, "Volatility is the devil to put into a projection. It never plots well" (Moors, 2011, p. 15). Which means that, as much as *The Last Winter* expresses atmospheric horrors, its climate of fear is shaped by the market mechanisms that became central to the financial mediation of oil after 1973.

Now, financial volatility is not an obvious element of the diegetic level of *The Last Winter*. But nor is it an obvious element of oil's material forms. We may twist and turn an oil barrel as we wish; it remains impossible to grasp it as a thing possessing volatility. Closer to what Marx calls spectral objectivity, its imprint is felt in time. Because volatility describes deviation from a mean, and not a direction of price movement, its temporal signature is the erratic, unpredictable, and non-directional. According to Ackbar Abbas, one figure of volatility's temporal non-directionality in film is chronological inconsistency, or anachronism (Abbas, 2023). And anachronism occurs frequently throughout *The Last Winter*. The diegetic present is spliced with memory-like images and distorted sounds that introduce narrative discontinuity. The setting frequently moves too quickly, as clouds race across the sky at impossible speeds. Landscape shots break the flow of the camp narrative. Wide shots used to establish the space of the film show bones surfacing out of the tundra. Skulls adorn scientific and industry camp sites. Ghosts comingle deep past and distant future. When Hoffman is killed and dragged away by the monster, we get alternating shots of an aerial view of the ice and shaky footage of a small boy running through the snow. I am interested in these coexisting temporalities because they suggest a desire to make the background of this genre into a volatile presence. Less a dynamic of surfacing and containment, *The Last Winter* represents a relation of volatility to security, mediated by the infrastructures that excavate and, ultimately, melt the Alaskan permafrost. This structures the film at the level of setting, narrative, and mood, where permafrost time is caught within the promises, feedback loops, tipping points, and delays of the contemporary oil economy. The tropes of horror—spectrality and splatter—capture how speculative infrastructures entangle the oil frontier with the financial core.

I would not want to suggest that financial volatility is a prominent or deliberate feature of the film. It is instead felt in the way that the horror film colours recognisable settings with dread, a feeling of something about to go wrong. This dread is not directed at any particular object but operates as a kind of anticipatory mood. There is a homology between the mood of horror and the mood of oil markets: each deliberately unsettle a volatile near future, creating opportunities for arbitrage or violence out of the uncertain and the unknown. This is crucial to my reading of *The Last Winter*. Exposure to the curse is contagious, producing a narrative structure suggestive of the circulation of financial exposure to oil assets, literalised through exposure to extreme cold and volatile heat. It circulates through the group, and while each hope to postpone its effects, this desire for delay only intensifies the inevitable violence. There is a wish for containment and safety, but the film recognises that this is a fantasy. Whether out on the ice or in the base camp, no space is separate from this volatile subsurface.

So, the fear emerges from our desire for the delay of what is, after all, entirely predictable: in a horror film, we expect the characters to die. And they do, spectacularly. Horror makes available a narrative in which delay is a kind of desire that ends up in violence. If a discourse of volatility is meant to contain the threat of oil within market mechanisms, and, in fact, this is central to the neoliberal governance of energy and energy transitions, then *The Last Winter* is both an index and a critique of volatility's cultural work—not least because it conjoins that discourse to the infrastructures of delay that ground it. In refusing to give it a fixed image of volatility to be safely identified and banished, we get a powerful account of the transformation of oil from a commodity to a financial asset, and how the accompanying fear of volatility habituates us to delay.

Volatility runs like a faultline through financial petroculture. On the one hand, it is an object of financial governance, on the other, it is a novel kind of historical feeling. *The Last Winter* gives aesthetic form to this financial abstraction through an intensity of alarm at the exhausting, ongoing ordinariness of delay inherent to the petrocultural present. But the difficulty in representing volatility is also a consequence of the divergence of this elusive social form from a predictable narrative logic of crisis and resolution. If plot won't do, then volatility is transmitted through affects and emotions, through the sense of wrongness that haunts the permafrost, and a fascination with timescales that displace standard perception and experience, that pattern and pulse to non-human rhythms.

By breaking with the strategies of containment of its predecessors, *The Last Winter* provides a critical representation of a culture of delay.

This can be most clearly felt in the final scene, in which the sole survivor from the research station returns to find the ground under her feet melting as the ice thaws. At this moment, the film offers not the comfort of a slain monster, the thrill of transgressive destruction, nor the hope of refreeze. It does not quite engage the affective expectations of watching disaster unfold, as we are accustomed to in the horror of oil spills, car-choked highways, or *Mad Max*-style dystopian wastelands—which suggest that oil's horror is something that happens elsewhere or in the future. In fact, as I argued earlier, it makes sense to think of thaw not as an event but as an unfolding disaster across centuries, a glimpse into a different form of time made available by the melting permafrost, as the ground of energy futures erode like thermokarst.

Readily available signifiers of oil horror make it hard to feel delay as a social problem, to convey the fantasy of postponement as monstrous. After all, it's not a powerful denial in need of repression, nor a spectacular event. Delay readily admits the fact of climate change and the need to transition, even as it tempers such acknowledgements through a discourse of political and economic stability. As such, it often feels like a desire for the ordinary to be frozen as it is. It provides a form for mediating the future without forgetting it, where expectations of change have little impact on habits and practices. Against this continuity, permafrost is disjunctive. The causal power of past emissions here rises fastest; the future arrives first and hardest. The permafrost is where delay becomes horror.

References

Abbas, A. (2023). Figuring volatility. *Finance and Society*, *9*(3), 18–36. https://doi.org/10.2218/finsoc.8988

Antonello, A., & Carey, M. (2017). Ice Cores and the Temporalities of the Global Environment. *Environmental Humanities*, *9*(2), 181–203. https://doi.org/10.1215/22011919-4215202

Berlant, L. (2008). Thinking About Feeling Historical. *Emotion, Space and Society*, *1*(1), 4–9. https://doi.org/10.1016/j.emospa.2008.08.006

Boyer, D. (2018). *Infrastructure, Potential Energy*. Duke University Press.

Buell, F. (2012). A Short History of Oil Cultures: Or, the Marriage of Catastrophe and Exuberance. *Journal of American Studies*, *46*(2), 273–293.

ConocoPhillips. (2024). *Willow Project*. ConocoPhillips. Retrieved from https://www.conocophillips.com/operations/alaska/willow-project/

Crutzen, P. J. (2006). The "Anthropocene". In *Earth System Science in the Anthropocene* (pp. 13–18). Springer, Berlin, Heidelberg. https://doi.org/10.1007/3-540-26590-2_3

Imre Szeman, P. D., & Boyer, D. (2017). *Energy Humanities*. Johns Hopkins University Press. https://doi.org/10.56021/9781421421889

Investopedia. (2024). *The Volatility Index: Reading Market Sentiment*. Investopedia. Retrieved from https://www.investopedia.com/articles/optioninvestor/09/implied-volatility-contrary-indicator.asp

Jameson, F. (1990). *Signatures of the Visible*. Routledge.

Jamie, K. (2019). *Surfacing* (Main edition). Sort of Books.

Labban, M. (2010). Oil in Parallax: Scarcity, Markets, and the Financialization of Accumulation. *Geoforum*, *4*(41), 541–552. https://doi.org/10.1016/j.geoforum.2009.12.002

Lamb, W. F., Mattioli, G., Levi, S., Roberts, J. T., Capstick, S., Creutzig, F., Minx, J. C., Müller-Hansen, F., Culhane, T., & Steinberger, J. K. (2020). Discourses of Climate Delay. *Global Sustainability*, *3*, Article e17. https://doi.org/10.1017/sus.2020.13

Lenton, T. (2023). *1: Earth System Tipping Points*. Global Tipping Points. Retrieved from https://report-2023.global-tipping-points.org/section1/1-earth-system-tipping-points/

Lovecraft, H. P. (2013). *The Classic Horror Stories*. Oxford University Press.

Macdonald, G. (2016). *Strange Horizons—Improbability Drives: The Energy of SF*. Retrieved from http://strangehorizons.com/non-fiction/articles/improbability-drives-the-energy-of-sf/

Malm, A. (2017). *The Progress of This Storm*. Verso.
McClanahan, A., & Annie. (2012). Dead Pledges: Debt, Horror, and the Credit Crisis. *Post45: Peer Reviewed*. Retrieved from https://post45.org/2012/05/dead-pledges-debt-horror-and-the-credit-crisis/
Mckie. (2024, January 21). *Arctic Zombie Viruses in Siberia Could Spark Terrifying New Pandemic, Scientists Warn*. The Guardian. Retrieved from https://www.theguardian.com/society/2024/jan/21/arctic-zombie-viruses-in-siberia-could-spark-terrifying-new-pandemic-scientists-warn
Millard, R. (2024, March 1). *Emissions Reach Record High Despite Growth in Clean Energy, IEA Says*. Retrieved from https://www.ft.com/content/d3944463-19a1-4f08-bdfd-f3d69f846ccb
Moeser, E. (2023, February 21). *Decolonization and Arctic Engagement: A Critical Analysis of Resource Development in the US Arctic*. The Arctic Institute - Center for Circumpolar Security Studies. Retrieved from https://www.thearcticinstitute.org/decolonization-arctic-engagement-critical-analysis-resource-development-us-arctic/
Moors, K. (2011). *The Vega Factor: Oil Volatility and the Next Global Crisis (1st edition)*. Wiley.
Neruda, P. (2000). *Canto General, 50th* (Anniversary). University of California Press.
NSF. (2024). *About Ice Cores | NSF Ice Core Facility*. Retrieved from https://icecores.org/about-ice-cores
Pynchon, T. (2013). *Bleeding Edge*. Penguin Press.
Shelley, M. (2012). *Frankenstein*. Norton & Company Inc.
Silva, P. A. M. (2022, October 25). *The Old Colonialisms and the New Ones: The Arctic Resource Boom as a New Wave of Settler-Colonialism*. The Arctic Institute - Center for Circumpolar Security Studies. Retrieved from https://www.thearcticinstitute.org/old-colonialisms-new-ones-arctic-resource-boom-new-wave-settler-colonialism/
STAR, S. L. (1999). The Ethnography of Infrastructure. *American Behavioral Scientist*. https://doi.org/10.1177/00027649921955326
Szeman, I. (2018). *On the Politics of Region*. E-Flux. Retrieved from https://www.e-flux.com/architecture/dimensions-of-citizenship/178284/on-the-politics-of-region/
Wenzel, J. (2022). Forms of Life: Thinking Fossil Infrastructure and Its Narrative Grammar. *Social Text*, *40*(4 (153)), 153–179. https://doi.org/10.1215/01642472-10013360
Wood, R. (2018). *Robin Wood on the Horror Film: Collected Essays and Reviews* (B. K. Grant, Ed.). Wayne State University Press.
Wrigley, C. (2023). *Earth, Ice, Bone, Blood: Permafrost and Extinction in the Russian Arctic*. University of Minnesota Press.

CHAPTER 6

Making Light Work: Genres of Solar Finance

6.1 Solar Pastoral

The aim of this chapter is to read the aesthetic, economic, and political dimensions of solar finance. Solar power often operates as a synecdoche of sustainability. Its exponential growth provides a techno-optimistic, even utopian, economic narrative, in which a market-led revolution in energy generation transforms fossil-fuelled society. Cost of deployment is trending downward, and solar now adds more electricity to grids than any other energy source in the US and Europe. The great success story of green capitalism, the sunlit upland of a solar world promises to leave behind the dirty and exploitative energy forms that have built modernity and plagued its self-image. The first section will turn to photography published by Lightsource bp, a solar energy company and subsidiary of bp (formerly British Petroleum), to analyse the pastoral aesthetic of this novel infrastructure. The second section will show how solar's conceptual abstraction enables narratives of financial accumulation. The third section will look at the discourse deployed by bp when describing their role in the energy transition, and specifically their adoption of a 'Just Transition' framework. I offer a contrasting framework, temporal justice, which aims to supersede the limitations of just transitions as proposed by bp. I have chosen Lightsource bp as my object of analysis for this chapter because of its global success as a financial company (more on that later) and its

H. Pitt Scott, *Financial Petroleum Cultures*, Palgrave Studies in Literature, Culture and Economics,
https://doi.org/10.1007/978-3-031-99661-0_6

representation as the flagship for bp's transition to renewables. The story of Lightsource bp is a story of the market-led transition.

I want to begin by discussing some photographs taken from the media library of Lightsource bp, the largest solar developer in Europe, and a subsidiary company of bp.[1] The first is taken in a photovoltaic power station on a Welsh farm. Two rows of solar panel support structures frame the image. These large, reflective structures run diagonally through the image, a stark grey standing out against the green grass. The panels are striking in form; they slice through the space. Bare trees enclose the setting. The solar panels resemble the colour of the dull grey sky. Against this background, in the centre, are two sheep and three lambs, three stood in the open, and two sheltering underneath the solar panels. They are whiter than the panels, and the sheep are heavy with wool. In the background, other sheep, unaware of the photographer's presence, graze on the grass or rest beneath the panels.

Another. A sheep in centre focus grazes in the foreground, its wool golden in the bright California sunshine. In the background, out of focus, a herd is grazing on vibrant green vegetation, which is uneven, almost wild. Over them is a solar farm; they are underneath it, sheltered. Standing on rectangular posts, these dark blue panels are smooth and neatly wired. As in the previous photograph, the solar panels frame the picture, guiding our observation towards the grazing animals. It must be late in the afternoon, as the sheep and solar panels all cast deep shadows. The surface of the panels directs our attention upward, towards the force and symbol of benevolent sunlight. The wild vegetation and the grazing herbivore evoke both the bounty of natural growth and the order of human cultivation. In this intermingling of solar and agricultural symbols, we turn towards the sun's rays and the future they promise, and towards the earth and the traditions worked into it.

A third. A farm in Texas at sunset. The sun occupies the centre of the picture, a luminous glory. Altocumulus clouds break up its rays as the sky passages from gold to blue. A treeline and a lake enclose farmland, as a solar farm captures the last of the day's warmth. The picture is taken from some elevation, so that the panels make sharp, vertical lines and reflect the sun into the camera. Avoiding this heat, a herd of sheep gather

[1] Around the time this book was going to press bp announced that it was abandoning its green transition objectives and selling many of its renewable assets, potentially including Lightsource, due to pressure from investors. I discuss this problem in the coda.

underneath the panels. They appear to be on the move. Not yet at rest, their alertness contrasts with the coming of darkness. The abstract verticality of the photovoltaics and the disordered milling of the sheep creates a pleasing visual contrast.

An aerial landscape shot in Spain. A photovoltaic power station stretches across the entire image, its straight vertical lines where the panels run parallel to the camera soon become a sea of dark blue. A path runs diagonally through the image, dividing the solar farm, and here a large herd of sheep graze, mostly in the sunlight. Some have entered the solar panel's shade. They are a vibrant white, almost as bright as the brightest of the sun's reflections. But they appear small, directed, even, from this angle, appearing to have a kind of order to their movement. They are overwhelmed by the scale, as the solar farm frames the landscape. Very quickly, a small shift in elevation and perspective, and the natural beauty of the grazing herd is dwarfed by the scale of infrastructures that mediate electromagnetic radiation into electricity. These flat surfaces which, flower-like, follow the sun, make visible and useable what is otherwise invisible and uncaptured: the sun's rays.

A final image, of the largest floating solar panel array in Europe. Another landscape sunset from above, the suns last rays reflecting off the strangely jagged shape of the solar panels on the calm water; sunlight through the trees, and a landscape falling into darkness. The sky, changing from pale pink to orange, takes up more than half the picture. Warm and vibrant colours fading to black in a moment that divides day and night. The floating solar panel array refracts this recognisable scene, inflecting the symbolism of sunset—a moment that captures the sun's absence most keenly—through an infrastructural marvel that invests the sun with an historical destiny: as the technological motor of historical transformation.

What strikes me as significant about these pictures, which are, after all, marketing material for Lightsource bp, is the capacity of solar infrastructure to do aesthetic and affective work in more than one mode, to represent technological progress as ecological harmony. The first pictures I described represent what Myles Lennon has called the 'pastoralization of solar', which "attempts to endow an electricity commodity with the feel of a natural process, the organic liveliness often attributed to the sun's rays" (Lennon, 2023, p. 128). Lightsource bp, undergoing global market expansion, especially in North America, is an inheritor of the Western pastoral tradition, if an unusual one.

This aesthetic emerges quite spontaneously out of the new 'agrivoltaics' industry: dual-use land projects that co-locate photovoltaic power stations and pasture, or solar panels and sheep. This is because one of the major costs to solar power generation is operations and maintenance after construction is complete. Unlike energy stocks like coal, which require constant work and energy to extract, solar power costs are front-loaded in construction. Unlike the unionised utility-scale workers employed by the state, most of the itinerant 'glass throwers' working for private companies in the USA must move across the country in pursuit of lower-skilled construction jobs. These low-paid workers are sometimes expected to pull 10- to 14-hour shifts and work six or seven days a week. Contracting and temp agencies keep the labour force turning over, which prevents the workers from organising and holds labour costs low for investors. (In fact, by no means exempt from the rigours of market competition, contractors and agencies must themselves bid to supply the labour for particular solar projects, which continues to chip away at workers' remuneration and conditions) (Gurley, 2022). In the words of the *New York Times*, the solar farm production process looks "less like the industrial workplace that lifted workers into the middle class in the twentieth century than something more akin to an Amazon warehouse or a fleet of Uber drivers" (Scheiber, 2021). Once installed, solar farms need little maintenance or additional labour, so the largely non-unionised workforce heads for the next installation. Once the solar farm is complete, no more labour is required to convert the sun's rays into electricity. With construction finished, the workers move on to another site, and the solar farm generates revenues as if for free. The only limitation now is daylight which, unlike workers, cannot be sped up, although need not be paid, and the cost of maintaining the site. I have introduced the American labour context, a key region in Lightsource bp's market expansion, because it makes clear the rhythm of solar infrastructural buildout from a labour perspective, dimming some of its utopian shine while providing the landscape setting for its pastoralism.

Solar farms use a lot of land, much more per unit of energy than energy dense fossil fuels, and the booming industry is looking for solutions to keep the costs of maintaining that land low. According to the American Solar Grazing Association, using grazing livestock to manage vegetation growth can often run 30% less than traditional landscape maintenance (sheep are preferred because they are less likely to damage the arrays, like cows, or jump on them, like goats) (Freehill-Maye, 2020).

Vegetation growth, left unchecked, can rapidly outgrow the solar panels, leaving them in the shade. While the strips between support structures are easy enough to mow, the landscaping labour required to keep growth underneath the panels in check is extensive. This poses little problem for sheep, however, who consume the vegetation underneath and converting it, from the perspective of the sheep farmer, into wool and meat. Grazing sheep have become a way of maintaining energy infrastructure, and the solar panels play the role of artificial tree, shading the animals from the heat of the day.

These are obviously working landscapes, solar sitting atop agricultural industries. These pastoral photographs therefore no doubt make absent "the host of industrialised relations that make solar panels possible": silicon extraction, labour exploitation, toxic waste, fossil-fuelled supply chains (Lennon, 2023, p. 128). How could they not? To paraphrase Bertolt Brecht, a photograph of a solar farm tells us next to nothing about these institutions. The social reality of these infrastructures lies elsewhere, beyond the physical installation site. Yet there is a sort of truth to the absence of workers in these photographs. They index economic settings for which the bulk of labour has already taken place and moved on. While capital tends to be associated with productivity and improvement, we can nevertheless see how a certain vision of energy without work is expressed in pastoral feeling. If, from the perspective of capital investment, "the production process appears simply as an unavoidable middle term, a necessary evil for the purpose of money-making", the pastoral might be the most appropriate form for an infrastructure site that converts sunlight into electricity and value without needing the constant input of labour (Marx, 1992b, p. 137).

It is as if Virgil's golden age has been realised, not through the blessing of gods but of technology.

> The plain will slowly turn golden with tender wheat,
> and the ripe clusters hang on the wild briar,
> and the tough oak drip with dew-wet honey.
> The soil will not feel the hoe: nor the vine the pruning hook:
> the strong ploughman too will free his oxen from the yoke (Virgil, 2001).

Virgil's dream-like imagery conjured a world of bounty without intervening human work; a world that gave up its gifts for free. This both reflected natural growth, which only must be cultivated by human hand, and extrapolated that natural proclivity into a utopian image.

> Olives, on the contrary, need no care,
> they don't require curved knife or stubborn hoe,
> once they've clung to the fields, and endured the breeze:
> the earth itself, opened up by the curved ploughshare,
> gives enough moisture and heavy fruit.
> Nurture the rich olive, like this, pleasing to Peace.
> Fruit-trees too race skywards with natural vigour,
> as soon as they sense that their trunks are firmly set,
> and reach full strength, needing no effort from us.
> Meanwhile ever wood's no less heavy with fruit,
> and the wild-bird's haunts redden with crimson berries.
> The clover's grazed: the high wood provides pine torches,
> so the fires of night are fed and pour out their light.
> And do men hesitate to plant and tend the fields?
> Why talk of the greater? Willows and humble broom
> provide grazing for the sheep, shade for the shepherd,
> a hedge for the crops, pastures for the bees.

Linked to this idea of natural vigour is the passing of the seasons, of the passage of time measured in the plants' race towards the sun; yet the joy also derives from a landscape that needs no care. In a cultivated land, the cultivated stands as a reality, yet also a kind of magic of free gifts that spring to life without human input, without work. 'Shade for the shepherd' grounds the poetic voice in a time of rest, a pause in work. Virgil's solar farm—what else could you call it?—does not 'capture' energy like a solar panel, but it does make use of, and mediate, solar power. Virgil's golden days and Lightsource's landscape photography share, if not a dream, then the intimation of solar optimism at the eclipse of human labour. One can only imagine Virgil's delight at the conversion of light into electricity to replace human work.

Do the Lightsource bp photographers have the pastoral mode in mind? I have no idea. They have some affinity for nature photography, to be sure. Beyond intention, what is produced is a pastoral feeling—"the warmth of the sun, the fresh air, and the free perambulation, with purpose temporarily suspended…"—that makes them available to reading as instances of that cultural mode. (Alpers, 1997, p. 6) Lightsource bp's photographs makes use of what Leo Marx calls the psychic root of the simple pastoral dream: "the yearning for a simpler, more harmonious style of life, an existence 'closer to nature'"(L. Marx, 2000, p. 6). They position technology as the driver of a restored harmony: the machine is not so much in the garden as the way back to it. We encounter in these a strange development: a British company, American land-use innovation, and English landscape painting tradition combine unevenly to produce an aesthetic form of renewables as a driver of ecological restoration. It may seem incongruous to move between American and British contexts, but it helps us see the elective affinity between land-use practices and the pastoral as these are pressed into service as an aesthetic form of energy transition.

But it is the presence of sheep I want to return to. There are three primary categories of image available on the website, 'Solar Panels', 'Solar Panels—Aerial', and 'Agriculture, Animals, and Biodiversity'. The first two categories include three hundred and fifty images, the last category four hundred and ninety-three. By far the most photographed animal are sheep. It clearly has an importance to Lightsource's self-image.

Of course, this mild ruminant is more than mere commodity; it is one of the most enduring symbols in the Western tradition. In Christian iconography, the lamb symbolises Agnus Dei, the Lamb of God, who is sacrificed to cleanse the world of sin (as in Fancisco de Zurbarán's *Agnus Dei* (1640)). This has imbued sheep with sacrificial innocence, and the quality of redemption. Sheep are present at the beginning of pastoral art, because of the importance of the shepherd as representative of human experience. In Titian's *Pastoral Concert* (1509), two young men sit with instruments, accompanied by two nude women, potentially nymphs, and in the background a shepherd and a flock of sheep shelter in the shade of a tree. A century later, Nicolas Poussin introduced death to Arcadia (*Et in Arcadia ego*); and in the nineteenth century, Thomas Cole would temporalise it, situating the simple shepherd and his flock before the establishment of an empire leads to decay (in *The Course of Empire*). Indeed, according to Leo Marx, American colonisation was motivated by a pastoral dream: an unspoiled landscape in which mankind might begin anew.

Sheep are also a national symbol in the British tradition, wool once being Britain's most important industry. In William Holman Hunt's *Our English Coasts* (1852), sheep press up against the physical borders of England, the coastline that divides the island from the continent, as if to enclose and therefore define the isles. Samuel Palmer's *The Magic Apple*

Tree (1830) captures the ideal of rural simplicity through the combination of natural wonder and generous bounty, as sheep rest among boughs heaving with fruit and, in the background, fields overflow with wheat.

It is of course this magic, this fantasy that has opened the pastoral to repeated critique, a position that shadows the pastoral across its long history. For example, Williams writes "It is only a short step from a natural delight in the fertility of the earth to this magical invocation of a land which needs no farming... This magical extraction of the curse of labour is in fact achieved by a simple extraction of the existence of labourers" (Raymond Williams, 2011, pp. 17, 32). We have already seen how close the agrivoltaics farm comes to literalising what has historically been the simple pastoral dream. But it is particularly galling for a critic like Williams, for whom the excision of the worker from a working landscape, and the transformation of that landscape into a pleasing prospect for the landowner or the tourist, is ultimately meant to ratify and naturalise an exploitative social order.

It is perhaps the timing of Palmer's *The Magic Apple Tree* that makes it so open to this form of critique, produced as it is at the end of an eighty-year process of enclosure. Building on a slow process begun in the sixteenth century, between 1750 and 1850, approximately 4,000 Parliamentary acts of enclosure were passed, virtually eliminating common land for pasture in England. Enclosure makes the labourer free—of her land, of the means to sustain her own life, making her dependent on the wage. Dispossession, displacement, low wages, long hours, insecure work, and cramped accommodation were the result, as a long tradition of common use in agricultural life was destroyed to transform land into capital. The Enclosure Acts also pushed dispossessed workers into urban areas in search of work, providing the proletarian workforce for an industrialising capitalism (Rosenman, 2012). If Palmer's rural idyll ever existed, it certainly was gone by the time of his painting. This was a "a rupture of the traditional integument of village custom and of right: the social violence of enclosure consisted precisely in the drastic, total imposition upon the village of capitalist property-definitions" (Thompson, 2013). Whatever truth there had been to the simple life of the shepherd and her flock had been made untrue by the violence necessary for establishing capitalist property relations.

Indeed, it is for this reason that humble livestock plays a minor, if not unimportant, role in Marx's narrative of capital's prehistory, of primitive accumulation:

> The prelude to the revolution that laid the foundation of the capitalist mode of production was played out in the last third of the fifteenth century and the first few decades of the sixteenth. A mass of 'free' and unattached proletarians was hurled onto the labour-market by the dissolution of the bands of feudal retainers, who, as Sir James Steuart correctly remarked, 'everywhere uselessly filled house and castle'. Although the royal power, itself a product of bourgeois development, forcibly hastened the dissolution of these bands of retainers in its striving for absolute sovereignty, it was by no means the sole cause of it. It was rather that the great feudal lords, in their defiant opposition to the king and Parliament, created an incomparably larger proletariat by forcibly driving the peasantry from the land, to which the latter had the same feudal title as the lords themselves, and by usurpation of the common lands. The rapid expansion of wool manufacture in Flanders and the corresponding rise in the price of wool in England provided the direct impulse for these evictions. The old nobility had been devoured by the great feudal wars. The new nobility was the child of its time, for which money was the power of all powers. *Transformation of arable land into sheep-walks was therefore its slogan.*(Marx, 1990, pp. 878–879)

Sheep pasture requires large acres of land, far more than that used for subsistence by commoners, leading to the replacement of people by sheep. This then is why Thomas More's *Utopia* opens with a critique of the English enclosures and the violent, bloody establishment of the rule of private property, and describes 'sheep devouring men', which Marx quotes approvingly (Marx, 1990, p. 880). Harry Warwick reads this as a figure of commodity fetishism, arguing that "the image of monstrous sheep thus captures the strangeness of a new world in which livestock, the traditional object of direct human domination, incarnates in its flesh and wool capital's powers of impersonal domination, henceforth to enchain humanity" (Harry Warwick, 2023, pp. 98–99). In turning the symbol of innocence into the personification of nascent capital's primitive accumulation, More and Marx point to the economic mystification inherent in a particular image of the sheep: after all, even if "in the tender annals of political economy, the idyllic reigns from time immemorial [...] the methods of primitive accumulation are anything but idyllic" (Marx, 1990, p. 875). This ecological history is the raw material on which the pastoral mode is forced to work.

The convergence of economic logic and aesthetic form in the figure of the sheep provides a way of seeing the political ecology of agrivoltaics in *longue durée*. A techno-ecological wish-fulfilment, of a break with and transition to a capitalism that has left behind the environmental harm of fossil fuel and the messy labour relations that it entailed. These images index a historical—political-economic and aesthetic—relationship to land, a social being expressed as timeless fact. Economic reality is absorbed into the natural landscape.

These images of sustainability frame the consequences of capital's *longue durée* as natural. They represent the end of ecological history: as if the human-produced environments of yesterday are the most optimal for human flourishing, and so all that is to be done is technological maintenance and management. The goal is set, all the major decisions are settled, all that is left to do is unlock the investment required to arrive at these environments produced by and for capital. They provide a material image of the energy landscape as a landscape without work, a visually pleasing form that suggests easy, even free, energy.

I will later want to return to the utopian core of this fantasy, to recuperate an incipient politics of time I think is intrinsic to the pastoral mode. But before that, I wish to draw attention to the final photograph I have described, which is of the Queen Elizabeth II Reservoir floating solar array, built by Lightsource bp for Thames Water in 2016, because here pastoral feeling rests upon a much more recent history of dispossession. Constructed between 1957 and 63, the reservoir, located in Surrey, provides over 10% of London's raw water (water held prior to treatment), holding over 19 million litres. It was held by the Metropolitan Water board until control was transferred to the Thames Water Authority in 1973, until the 1989 Water Act, when the Thatcher government enabled the privatisation of the English and Welsh water industries.

The scale of financial plunder in British water infrastructure, and the extent of ecological damage caused, is shocking. In transforming infrastructure into an asset class open for private investment, England's water companies have accumulated a debt £60bn, have given out £72bn to shareholders, have seen investment decline by 15% since privatisation, and have led to bills rising by more than 40% in real terms, all while discharging raw sewage into Britain's rivers and seas on average 1,000 times a day (weownit, 2012). Thames Water, owned by China's largest sovereign wealth fund, a private pension fund, a subsidiary of the Abu Dhabi Investment Authority, and other global asset managers, is in particular trouble. It is saddled with debt and infrastructural failures; its reputation is in tatters because it continues to pay out dividends to outside investors.

The British government sold off its energy assets at the same time as it was dismantling its national water companies. Between 1979 and 1987, the UK government sold its shares in bp, ending state ownership. It is no longer a national corporation that moves oil across its commodity chain, but rather owns strategic energy assets, functioning more like a global investor beholden to shareholders than a major state industry or industrial corporation. Instead, the Britishness of what used to be called British Petroleum but now goes by 'bp' is defined by its place on London stock markets. Corporate strategy has shifted to defending its share price and creating profit through engaging in financial trading as much as investments in oil and gas infrastructure. One reason for this business shift is declining profitability in some oil and gas sectors, such as the North Sea, while another is its attempt to rebrand as 'Beyond Petroleum' as an early investor in solar. After the Deepwater Horizon spill, which damaged bp's reputation and market value, its partnership with Lightsource was an important signifier of a new kind of company.

It is conditions such as these—as the stuff that sustains human life gets pulled into the circuit of capital accumulation—that have motivated the emergence of infrastructural critique (Rubenstein et al., 2015, p. 578). The establishment of asset management as a governing infrastructural logic has transformed the stuff of everyday life—or what Rubenstein, Robbins, and Beal call 'the commons' and I would call 'the public'—into financial assets that live a strangely intangible life elsewhere. Brett Christophers writes that, "As increasingly significant owners of housing and infrastructure, asset managers today are directly and intimately implicated—albeit often without most of us even being aware of it—in everyday social existence. They own, and extract income from, things—schools, bridges, wind farms and homes—that are nothing less than foundational to our daily being"(Christophers, 2023).

What links the Enclosure Acts to the 1989 Water Act is a particular relation to capitalist property. Whereas the old enclosure established the capital-relation by dispossessing the commoner of a means of subsistence outside the wage relation, the new enclosure is driven by the capital-relation itself, transforming public goods into investment opportunities to provide new outlets for capital investment (Harry Warwick, 2023, p. 11). In a manner analogous to the way that enclosures made land available to capital investment, so the privatisation of infrastructure makes hitherto public resources available to revenue capture. David Harvey names this 'accumulation by dispossession', turning public utilities into commodity-producing industries, which functions, in the 1980s, as a spatial fix for the overaccumulation of capital with few prospects of profitable endeavour, transforming more of social life into capitalist markets (Harvey, 2005, p. 160). The promise of infrastructure, from the perspective of capital, is financial: it enables not just the flow of water but the flow of claims to future revenue.

In the picture I have been analysing, the surface of the solar panel array directs the gaze upward, in a form that is ultimately less pastoral than sublime. Yet the dazzling awe of the sun is matched by the abstract shape, order, and regularity of the array. The experience of infiniteness of the natural sublime is thereby domesticated by the sublime object of technological reason, the latter becoming a celebration of human engineering. Technology becomes the medium through which the future is embodied; infrastructures locally harmonious yet promise modular scale.

That such infrastructures are literally built atop a history of dispossession confirms the representational prowess of solar fictions. If the solar pastoral positions the solar farm as a return to a deep connection with place, ecology, and community, then the solar sublime makes light work of environmental history in its orientation towards a bright technological future. Here we must return to the overarching argument of this book, to see how Lightsource bp's harmonious integration into capitalist property forms is a way of making solar visible to financial investment.

6.2 Rise and Fall, or, Solar Abstractions

Established in 2010, Lightsource's journey from small renewable energy company to global energy leader is a success story of green capitalism, a trajectory that registers how finance gives form and rationality to solar growth. In the words founder of its, Nick Boyle, Lightsource began "Not a solar company, but a finance company with solar experts. We followed the money first—in the early days of the Feed-in Tariff free-for-all, all the major solar players were walking around Cornwall looking for land, and we were strolling the Square Mile looking for investors". 'Nick's Story' starts with "with six employees and one laptop, to a decade on with close to 500 and offices across the globe". Here the movement from London financial scene to a global landscape provides a spatial scale of economic growth and possibility, of a transition in the making. Its entrepreneurial *bildung* is a multicultural success: "we've built a unique culture of experiences and background" (Boyle, 2022). Two pivotal moments define the decade, analepses that give the narrative its structure: "putting finance first" and "our partnership with bp" (Boyle, 2020). Both establish a financial realism that grounds the narrative logic of their trajectory.

The success of its global growth lies in its financial rendering of solar, its resource aesthetic:

> As an entrepreneur with a background in financial services, I banked on the predictability of solar from the start. Now, a decade later, the simple but logical business case is still the same—solar offers a long-dated, predictable, revenue stream that is attractive to investors. The sun goes up, the sun goes down each day, creating very predictable returns. As long as the sun comes up every morning, you're making money, and if the sun doesn't come up one morning, you've got bigger problems (Boyle, 2020).

If in Lightsource's images, the sun is expressed through a poetics of harmony and wonder, here it is brought down to the quotidian. Bathed in electromagnetic radiation that delivers sufficient energy to create an electric current, the elemental affordances of sunlight striking photovoltaics are now temporalised as a daily rhythm, a financial abstraction. Solar infrastructure becomes a site to make financial claims, configuring a particular kind of financial time.

Interestingly, the "sun rises every day" is the first example that Gerard Genette gives, in *Narrative Discourse,* for the category of 'frequency'; more specifically, the 'iterative narrative', in which repeating phenomena in a story are narrated a single time, to provide an informative frame or background to more singular events (Genette, 1979). 'We were strolling the Square Mile looking for investors' happens against the background of the sun's daily rise. Iterative narrative abstracts from each occurrence everything peculiar to it, to preserve what each occurrence has in common. Variations in generation, due to, e.g., cloud cover, do not trouble the background of daily sunshine and predictable returns.

Such narrative abstractions do important discursive work by framing a predictable, knowable, and investable future of energy. The sun shines everywhere, so the chronotope of the globe evokes the imaginative, endless, scaling of solar power. The global is where capital exerts its flexibility most easily, where it is least trapped in specific sites—which is why it matters to more than just narrative consistency that Lightsource begins its journey in the most global of financial cities, London. But it is the proleptic device that structures this imagined future like fiction that makes the performative recursive to the ideological: "The global energy landscape is rapidly decarbonizing, there's so much opportunity in future innovation, and that's what gets me excited. Not where we are now but the potential of tomorrow" (Boyle, 2020). This offers a temporal orientation to an imaginary future state that *might* be beyond petroleum: the future hinted at but never confirmed. The fact that the global energy landscape is not rapidly decarbonising means that it might be tempting to think of this as fantasy rather than fiction, but I want to suggest that this is not really a lie or delusion so much as a narrative logic of delay: Lightsource imagines a transition *for* finance, in the sense that it envisions an infrastructure as sustainable revenue, to reassure potential investors because its profits—and its energy form—resemble the abstractions assembled from petroleum into a dominant form of work/energy.

For the solar abstraction to enable narratives of financial growth, it must, in turn, rest upon a concept of energy that operates as a "unit of equivalence through which distinct fuels (oil, solar, nuclear) can be compared regardless of space and time, even as what counts as energy changes dramatically" (Daggett, 2019, p. 47). This representation treats energy as "as a material resource squeezed", as Szeman puts it, "into a social form that pre-exists it, rather than the other way around" (Szeman, 2013, p. 146). In other words, it confuses an *effect* of oil's social form with a *condition* of energy as such. Energy appears merely as external input to the real driver of transition, the corporation. Financial discourse is central to relating to energy as an abstraction, as interchangeable inputs drawn from areas relatively distant from, and invisible to, sites of electricity consumption. Because hydrocarbon energy and capital have become bound through various phases of energy intensification, the economic expectations of finance are structured by the levels of productivity and growth of the petroleum age. The search for sources of abstract growth *after oil* means treating future energy forms as equivalent to—and in competition with—current ones. In which case, the energy abstraction is fundamental to financial representation of the future, and of narratives that make use of finance to describe the causes of the coming energy transition. Financial abstraction has metabolised the economic capacities of petroleum and transformed it into a form of value that structures social existence far beyond extraction sites. This brings pressure to bear on what is meant by *after oil* when what comes after oil is a representational dilemma structured as much by oil's economic *form* as its *content.*

Which is why Lightsource's Nick Boyle is so keen to describe the solar chronotope as an abstract rhythm, as regular as the sun rising. His story wavers when he assures us that "I still believe now that there are more investors in the world that want a definite 8–10% return than a "maybe" 15%" (Boyle, 2020) (that 'maybe' is the threat of stranded oil and gas assets). This is often not the case. Investors often shrink from solar investment because the promise, according to the International Renewable Energy Agency, there is "a lack of bankable projects to attract investment and fulfil today's appetite for renewable energy projects" (quoted in Christophers, 2022, p. 151). As bp themselves put it, hydrocarbons "will remain core to bp for decades as an engine of value creation and the enabler of our transformation" (Marshall, 2020). While solar's global boom continues to add gigawatts to the electricity system, it cannot be market-optimised like gas (turned on when prices are high), and it often generates most of its electricity when prices are low in the middle of the day and none at night when prices are high. As renewable energy infrastructure costs decrease and deployment increases, an overcapacity crisis looms, with prices likely to plummet, reducing the capture rate (market prices over time) of solar power (Rystad Energy, 2024). Lightsource is unique in that its global position enables it to begin developments in sites where solar profitability can be found. Its corporate formation implies its narrative of global energy landscapes. The social need for solar likely outstrips its profitability, but this is a social contradiction that Lightsource and bp cannot resolve but only confirm as the frame of their narrated future world.

Yet the story changes when the audience for this light work is the public. Here, bp justifies its subsidiary to the public by material needs: lighting, transport, life and well-being, in short, solar development. As Timothy Mitchell writes, in another context, "Capital seems to arrive after the fact, to enable needs to be met. In creating the effect of a world divided into the real and the financial, infrastructure projects establish the apparent primacy of the real or the material, of physical needs and human wants, and place finance as the servant, the subservient element existing only to help meet such needs" (Mitchell, 2020). Relegating finance to a minor part in the story helps to establish the corporation as a social provider first and foremost. This plays out in the company's public narrative and branding. A 2019 advert titled 'Unpredictable' played on signifiers of Englishness like unpredictable weather, umbrellas, and cobbled London streets and buses, with soothing voiceover that informs viewers "Around here the only predictable thing about the weather is, its unpredictable! That's why we make the most of it when the sun does shine". Part of its public partnership announcement with Lightsource, it positions bp's claims to be an *energy* company with the emphasis on an energy mix: the voiceover tells us that "should the weather change, yet again, our natural gas can step in to keep the power flowing and the light's shining, no matter the forecast", before ending with the Thames and the City of London illuminated at night, the dazzling postindustrial architecture of its financial sector symbolically reinvested with national green renewal (bp, 2019). Making use of the Queen Elizabeth II Reservoir solar farm in its advertising materials and using the same iterative narrative of daily sunshine, although with a twist, bp's rebranding is a representational practice that condenses solar, gas, and transition along a chain of association. Solar *works* in bp's narrative of delay because natural gas does, which is to say that solar is evaluated in conjunction with, and equivalent to, hydrocarbons. The ambiguity of hydrocarbon futures—note the conditional verb in "our natural gas *can* step in to keep the power flowing"—is how bp's narratorial status maintains its resilience against critique, because it is represented as a transitional fuel that enables transformations.

To make use of the Queen Elizabeth II Reservoir is a striking choice, not least because the electricity generated at that site powers water treatment, not London's grid. Its symbolic power as a flagship solar farm is undergirded by an infrastructure turned into assets for global investors. It turns solar power into a saleable input in a capitalist production process. Beside this economic work, it also does a kind of cultural work. By emphasising intermittency, bp positions itself as provider of both solar and gas: it works *through* the knowledge that solar power is inadequate to current needs. Solar infrastructure is what bp can use to claim that, on the one hand, they are contributing to the lower-carbon economy, and on the other, the limits of such a strategy mean that they have little choice to but focus on getting more oil and gas out of the ground. Which is to say that while Lightsource might occupy the foreground of bp's transitional narrative form, petroleum remains internal to the narrative structure—still part of the recounted story, but not part of bp's mimetic representation of a transitioning world.

In a forward-looking statement for its investors called 'Performing while Transforming', with all the usual caveats that alert us we are in a speculative mode, bp described its pivot towards what it calls 'resilient hydrocarbons', rebranding the assets that make up the largest portfolio share (Marshall, 2022). In this communication between an oil company and its shareholders, bp divides oil production and operations from the category of 'low-carbon energy' which includes gas; even so, by 2030 it predicts that oil production and operations investment will double low-carbon energy, and that its revenue from oil and gas will be ten times that of low-carbon energy. Resilient hydrocarbons represent a strategy for negotiating risks: they use new technology to reduce emissions (such as methane), the rigs can easily move, and have much shorter production cycles, making them less vulnerable to stranding and giving frequent posted profits, making them resilient against transition risks (policy, legal, technical, and market changes). This confident, even brazen redescription of the oil world belies a financial anxiety about the value that can be extracted in the time left before oil's undefined endpoint. The conceptual and infrastructural turn towards resilience figures a shift in the global energy landscape towards one that is increasingly volatile, and where long-term oil prospects represent stranding risks, obsolescence, sudden devaluations. The solution is to speed up, extracting at the rate most suitable to the financial landscape of a transitional economy and the long-term horizon of shareholders. Carbon combustion makes the atmosphere into a medium for historical time because it transmits the cumulative effects of anthropogenic CO_2 combustion into the ecologies of human life long into the future—a strange and warping communication that is the uncanny opposite polarity to the financial projections that structure capital's temporal horizon. This temporal dialectic rotates around the real contradiction of fossil finance: the impossibility of sustaining its present future, an impossibility that contours the representational dilemmas of an abstract form beyond abstract energy.

bp CEO Bernard Looney refers to this global energy landscape as the 'backdrop' of bp's energy future no less than three times: "Against an uncertain backdrop we are working hard to provide the energy that customers and economies need" (Marshall, 2022, p. 16). Here, energy surreptitiously becomes metonymic of high- or low-carbon economies, of wealth as such. The world market chronotope is a shaping force on the representation of space and time. It is energy figured through the world market that sustains bp's place in the transitioning world. bp narrates itself into transition at the scale of a financial environment and global energy landscape dominated by petroleum. Indeed, bp sustains its own scale, only becoming "leaner, more agile, digitally-enabled organisation" and in doing so figures the scale of the economy in which transition is imagined (Marshall, 2020, pp. 49–50). No matter its content, the economic form that governs its imagined low-carbon future is a petroleum world.

In a different forward-looking statement, against the 'uncertain backdrop' of the covid-19 pandemic, Looney describes bp's goal to transition from an international oil company to an international energy company; his intention is to give "a coherent story of how this all fits together" (Marshall, 2020, p. 7). The changes required to become an international energy company (streamlining oil and gas, divestment from unprofitable infrastructure, reshaping portfolio to include transitional energy) is "all part of a single coherent plan—all part of the same journey" (Marshall, 2020, p. 8). It is striking that the CEO's communication to the corporation's shareholders hinges on the coherence of its self-narrated journey. Coherence is central to the mode of communication between companies and shareholders describing a net-zero economy.

The financial genre's chronotope is a global atmosphere saturated in uncertainty. Uncertainty is a dominant mood of narrative anticipation. The coherence of bp's self-narration lies in its realistic positioning against this background: there are no alternatives to an energy mix of gas and renewables, with gas as the main player. This narrative form represents a volatile global energy landscape in crisis, and bp poses itself and natural gas as the only realistic option. bp's narrative of transition is shaped by its point of view onto the landscape in which that future is being produced. It does not hide the fact oil remains central to the long-term journey. It can be read, plain as day, in the statistics. bp will have met its net-zero goals by 2050, but it will still be pumping oil out the ground then too. They say that "we see hydrogen & CCUS [carbon capture, utilisation, and storage] as critical to the world delivering net zero and we are accelerating to take early positions" (Marshall, 2020, p. 37). Here, 'world' and 'net zero' are sustained as meaningful political and epistemological visions of transition through reference to two speculative technologies, which enable the economy to continue framing planetary futures. Hydrogen storage represents the great promise of stock energy made from the flow (but so energy inefficient that it requires such an energy abundance as to be fantasy). Unless stored or used, wind and solar are lost, so high-storage batteries and hydrogen power replicates petroleum's spatio-temporal profile. Nick Boyle speculates that "hydrogen could be shipped around the world as an energy source which essentially came from the sun but is captured as a gas, and burned the same way as historic hydrocarbons" (Ambrose & Boyle, 2021). According to the IEA, capturing carbon released by fossil fuels and converting them into hydrogen stock means also the conversion of the fossil energy transmission and distribution infrastructure, retrofitting them for new energy forms so as not to devalue them (IEA, 2021, p. 75). CCUS enables continued petroleum combustion long into the net-zero economy, enabling proven reserves to remain assets rather than liabilities.

This plays out further in the speculative description of avoided emissions. In recent reports, Lightsource bp point out the amount of emissions avoided due to their delivery of utility-scale solar assets, which they estimate to be around two million tonnes of CO_2 (Lightsource bp, 2023, p. 21). Avoided emissions treat CO_2 emissions as pre-standardised and abstract: divisible, measurable units of carbon, with no historical or systemic origins, which are equivalent and exchangeable (Lohmann, 2012). Reducing carbon politics to CO_2 emissions a company or nation produces means all emissions are made equal in such calculations. 'Avoided' emissions in, say, Bolivia, can increase the cap on real emissions in Scotland. With a bit of speculative imagination and the motivation of profit, the possibilities of avoided emissions are endless. Because they are calculations and, in case of carbon offsets, valuations of avoided CO_2 emissions, they rely on counterfactuals: if this forest were cut down, there would be a known number of emissions; because it was not, those emissions are avoided. Through financial instruments, this avoided future can be swapped for a real one, thus relying on seeing a potential that is not happening and then trading it for something that is, extending the value relation into the virtual. Thus, a forest or solar farm can become a quasi-financial object because it enables trading differences between the imagined and real. Like in a science fiction novel, avoided emissions create parallel worlds, in which value in ours depends on the convoluted ghost-like presence of alternative ones which exist only in emissions models. Employing climate and emissions modelling and scenario thinking, governments, regulative agencies, NGOs, economists, scientists, and technicians pursue the carbon flows of industries and natural resources and transform them into commodities in their own right.

These discursive shifts represent strategies to maintain the value of hydrocarbon assets as they risk turning into stranded assets. The fact of unburnable carbon is readily recognised by major oil companies like Shell and bp, even if, "in an era of volatile transitions", the quantity that is unburnable is not (Shell, 2013, p. 1). In a bp publication called 'The New Economics of Oil', fossil fuels are seen as inexhaustible, because the rate of discovery of new reserves and improvements in recovery technology has outstripped consumption over the last fifty years and far exceeds the carbon budget (Dale, 2015, pp. 3–8). As climate becomes a matter of concern, and the carbon budget becomes a limit that can be technologically and politically negotiated, oil resources no longer have an external constraint, and so can be treated as non-exhaustible by industrial actors.

The debate over unburnable carbon is shaped by reference to financial valuation and the price of oil. Yet the question remains as to what extent shifting financial expectations impacts oil extraction at a structural level. It is evident that market changes shape the world of oil within a consistent logic of increased use rates in line with economic growth. But it remains to be seen whether the threat of carbon bubbles and stranded assets exert enough force on oil company share prices to trigger a market-led transition. Crucially, the problem of the end of oil shifts from a geophysical to a political-economic dynamic: the end of oil will be brought about through *making* carbon unburnable. According to bp economist Spencer Dale, this change in the oil market means that carbon capture technologies are of vital importance in subtending the financial value of oil companies, and that there is no longer a reason to think that oil prices will gradually rise over time as shrinking supply meets continued demand (Dale, 2015, p. 6).

Such arguments are readily assimilable to a vision of the future structured by the market: oil will be made uneconomical and so companies will transition to survive. But without the pressure of demand destruction through price increases, *how* it will be made uneconomical is no longer easily identifiable within the market. This dynamic destructuring of the transitional function of energy markets provides oil companies the capacity to manoeuvre in relation to proven reserves and carbon budget targets, as the future is opened to competing representations of petroleum's role in shaping transition. Indeed, carbon capture represents one way that oil may be imagined as remaining economic, because the carbon budget becomes an unstable figure through the projections of different warming targets and carbon futures. The speculative promise of carbon capture does economic and cultural work by sustaining the present future of oil. The positioning of major oil companies in relation to the carbon limit is immediately that of overcoming, or at least deferring it, through technology. Financial abstraction makes the future of capital easier to imagine and harder to contest, even as it fails to figure the scale of the social transformations an energy transition will require.

As fossil fuel reserves far outstrip the carbon budget required to keep the planet within two degrees of warming, we have entered an historical epoch shaped not by finite resources or imminent climate collapse, but an urgent temporality of *too much*. This excess is itself indeterminate, and futures become out of date the moment they are published, even as they seep and spill into our consciousness rapidly expanding to the scale of the planetary. A fiction of limits through natural exhaustion obscures the future, losing clarity through a too-easy imagination of catastrophic depletion. In the absence of a natural depletion, all narratives of transition must locate who makes transition and how they do so.

The voice of bp's transition knows that oil must end but does not admit to knowing how, which implies that what is needed is more information and technology. bp's future is uncertain, but that is to its advantage. This narrative of bp's own lack of knowledge is precisely the representation of space—the global energy landscape—in which the duration of oil is elliptical, shaped by the sense of its ongoingness. If even the net-zero economy remains saturated by petroleum and natural gas, then this financial genre cannot be said to have a sense of an ending to oil, even while it claims to be presenting one. It should be clear that, whatever their technological success, hydrogen, CCUS, and even financialised solar destroy the narrative coherence of a serious transition out of fossil fuels. bp thrives in this contradiction because it sustains its fictitious capital, which is the ground that gives its journey narrative coherence.

This is not to say that bp are deceiving anyone. This is the logical trajectory of a corporation that must transition but, likely, cannot; that must turn energy forms into value-forms that, likely, cannot become them. bp cultivates a transitional realism: to avoid crises—political, financial, ecological—we need natural gas, they assure us, to which there are no credible alternatives. In this mode, decarbonisation is the expansion of alternative forms of carbon deepening. In a financial logic, critique becomes the justification for further rounds of investment, and the prospect of petroleum's end becomes the reason for its pragmatic persistence. In a sense, this is true: we cannot currently do without petroleum, so why not continue to invest in it? That this is a narrative that correlates to the economic logic of avoiding profitless renewables is hardly mentioned. It runs counter to even the optimistic IEA net-zero by 2050 scenario, which states that beyond projects already committed as of 2021, no new oil and gas fields can be approved for development (IEA, 2021, p. 21) . Which means that this energy future is already out of date, even as it confirms the temporality of excess that disorients our sense of the future. bp's narrative is a story whose duration is that of oil's demand over 'the long term', a temporal ambivalence that sustains the resilient promise of hydrocarbons against projects of its foreseeable end.

6.3 bp Beyond Technocentrism: Just Transition in a Marxist Perspective

Using Lightsource bp as a case study, I have been attempting to describe how the problem of transition is, among other things, a problem of representation: what is to be transitioned, who makes transitions, and how they do so—even as a warming world unsettles the conventional subjects and objects of historical change. I have focused on the light work of solar because current trajectories imagine it to replace financialised oil as the primary energy form of modernity (IEA, 2023b). In this energy transition, solar operates as a synecdoche of sustainability. As Dustin Mulvaney argues, often "sustainability and renewable energy advocates see solar energy as sustainable on its surface, without questioning the environmental impacts of production or questioning whether more sustainable alternatives are out there"(Mulvaney, 2018, p. 252). In a Lightsource bp, 2023 Sustainability Report entitled 'Solar Power for our world', they replicate such technocentric thinking, writing that "our primary contribution to global sustainability is through decarbonising the world's energy landscape"(Lightsource bp, 2023, p. 7). Adopting a tripartite sustainability framework of people, environment, and energy, they describe solar as sustainable because it is scalable, economical, and quick to deploy, all of which make it is the ideal technology for re-establishing a sustainable climate while benefitting communities and enabling biodiversity-supporting land-use practices.

Yet, as my historicisation of Lightsource bp's solar poetics makes clear, this new ideology of sustainable capitalism works through a fantasy of a self-evident and harmonious state of environmental sustainability that must be recovered, through the sustaining of a particular set of social relations. 'Sustainability' thus announces a break from the past (fossil fuels), a return to the past (climate before fossil fuels), and a continuation of the present (neoliberal, market-dominated capitalist property-relations), itself the product of capitalism's *longue durée* enclosure and dispossession. As

Allan Stoekl has argued, there is no reason we must sustain our social and ecological world as it is now or was yesterday, and so hidden in (some) descriptions of sustainability is a normative vision wedded to the present (Allan Stoekl, 2021).

If sustainability names what is to be transitioned, who and how it is done so is equally as important to representations of energy transitions. Here it matters that bp and Lightsource bp are early adopters of a Just Transition and energy justice framework, aiming to practice a just approach to their work with governments, businesses, workers, local communities, and stakeholders.(bp, 2023, p. 35) These include advancing human rights, helping workers develop skills for the future energy system, being socially inclusive, and building stronger relationships through responsibility and transparency. All of this, they claim, will contribute to responsible and sustainable development that maximises social benefits.

The just transition evolved out of concerns that the rapid adoption of clean energy would leave behind fossil-fuel workers, deepening inequality and creating political opposition to decarbonisation. It also raises concerns about the potential for negative consequences of clean energy for other communities and consumers, such as the production of toxic waste along the photovoltaic supply chain or unaffordable energy prices in areas dependent on fossil-fuel energy. Developed as a critique of technocentric and market-based solutions to ecological problems, it has become fundamental to contemporary energy transition discourse since it became part of the 2015 Paris Agreement. Lightsource bp describe themselves as "at the forefront of this transition by delivering responsible solar efficiently and effectively, prioritising sustainable materials and practices, and genuine two-way engagement with our local communities and stakeholders" (Lightsource bp, 2023, p. 3).

As frameworks designed to critique capitalist society get incorporated into it and narratives of just transitions are enabled by solar infrastructures, I want to use this as an opportunity to reflect on the keyword justice. Specifically, I am interested in how this framework facilitates a convergence between the concerns of capital and the crisis of climate. While I think it is better that bp commits to a just transition than not, the fact that it can do so points to some significant flaws in the concept, at least from a Marxist perspective. I will now outline the three-tenet approach to just transitions, followed by the critique of distributive justice in the Marxist tradition. I will then connect this to the debate around solar time and enclosure that opened this chapter, to provide a provisional conclusion to the meaning of justice in a moment when the term is being incorporated into capitalist representations of the future.

Just transition is an approach meant to align climate goals with the material needs of workers and marginalised groups. The three-tenet approach to just transitions includes three forms of justice to achieve this. The first, distribution justice, refers to the distribution of harms and benefits within the present and future energy system. It provides a way of seeing the trade-offs between energy practices and looks for mechanisms that reduce the unevenness of this distribution. It focuses attention on how the supply chains and siting of renewable infrastructures produces distributional injustices, such as access to clean, affordable energy, well-paying jobs, or environments unspoiled by extraction or circulation of energy and materials.

The second, recognition justice, is a rights-based approach to justice, emphasising the need to ensure that groups and individuals are recognised when decision-making processes about energy are initiated. This means recognising the specific needs of social groups, ensuring they are free from domination and disrespect, and ensuring wishes and motivations are included and fairly represented.

The third, procedural justice, concerns the decision-making process itself. It focuses on engaging all stakeholders in energy transition processes, including through consultation and representation. It also is meant to ensure that procedures are inclusive, while reflective of the ingrained inequalities of modern society. A central element of procedural justice is ensuring that marginalised groups are represented in the decision-making process, so that historical inequalities are not repeated in the energy transition ('Energy Justice', 2016; 'Just Transition', 2021).

More specifically for the energy sector as laid out by the Council for Inclusive Capitalism, of which bp is a member, this includes universal access to net-zero energy, evolving the energy workforce for a low-carbon energy system, building community resilience, and fostering collaboration and transparency. These pillars, alongside the three-tenet justice framework, are cohering into a socio-political discourse that frames the future of energy (Council for Inclusive Capitalism, 2021).

There is much to be admired in such a framework. Combining an attention to economic benefits, ecology and land use, political process, and cultural equality, it is flexibly adaptable to the specific situations likely to arise in the messy business of energy transitions, while containing principles that, if followed, minimise and prevent structural harm. Producing a more granular picture of the benefits and harms of energy development, it aims to prevent top-down authoritarian decision-making damaging vulnerable communities. Likewise, it should secure at least some democratic input in the form and purpose of new or retrofitted infrastructures. All of which supports what bp call 'sustainable markets' and 'sustainable development' (bp, 2023, p. 55), here meant to mean socially, ecologically, and economically sustainable forms of capitalist production; what asset manager BlackRock call sustainable investing, which aims to use sustainability insights to reduce risks and increase long-term returns (Fink, 2024).

However, the compatibility—or incorporation—of the just transition framework with a corporation, bp, that is at the cutting-edge of green capitalism's infrastructural transformation, should give us pause. Is this a critique of fossil capital, what eco-socialist John Bellamy Foster argues is "the concrete negation of capitalism?"(Bellamy Foster, 2019). Or a discourse meant to secure the working conditions necessary for a transitional capitalist mode of production, asserting the moral right of capitalists to self-regulate their relation to nature? To outline a critique of just transitions from a Marxist perspective requires a detour through Marx's critique of justice, to which we now turn.

This critique—whether or not capitalism is 'unjust' from a Marxist perspective—necessarily and logically arises from the account that Marx gives of exploitation and the wage relation, firstly from the perspective of exchange and secondly from the perspective of production. The wage relation presumes the separation of worker from means of production, a condition of capital accumulation generated through the process of primitive accumulation. In the sphere of circulation, the worker exchanges their labour-power for a wage. The workers sell their sole commodity, the capacity to work, and receive in recompense the value of what they have sold: everything that goes into producing the worker's capacity to work, their subsistence. From the perspective of the sphere of circulation, this is a fair transaction, as the capitalist pays a fair price for the use of the worker's time. This "is a piece of good luck for the buyer, but by no means an injustice towards the seller" (Marx, 1990, p. 301).

The fairness of this exchange looks different, however, from the perspective of the production process. Once we leave the realm of exchange and enter the realm of production, we too leave behind the balance of justice, for labour is a special kind of commodity. It is the sole commodity capable of producing more value than it takes to produce. A worker may produce enough value in six hours to cover the costs of their wage. However, their working day extends for two more hours, value which accrues to the capitalist. The gap between these two values Marx calls surplus-value, the unpaid labour that the capitalist pockets for himself. While capitalist production has the appearance of fair exchange, it is in essence a form of theft, 'the theft of labour time', as he writes in the *Grundrisse* (Marx, 1993, p. 704). The exchange of labour-power for a wage contains the exploitation of the worker by the capitalist, which is the basis of capital's form of appropriation. "There is only an apparent exchange", Marx claims,

> since, firstly, the capital which is exchanged for labour-power is itself merely a portion of the product of the labour of others which has been appropriated without an equivalent; and, secondly, this capital must not only be replaced by its producer, the worker, but replaced together with an added surplus. The relation of exchange between capitalist and worker becomes a mere semblance belonging only to the process of circulation [...] property turns out to be the right, on the part of the capitalist, to appropriate the unpaid labour of others or its product, and the impossibility, on the part of the worker, of appropriating his own product (Marx, 1990, pp. 729–730).

What appears to be a fair exchange turns out to be a form whose content is appropriation. Any programme to remedy social injustices through philanthropy or a fairer distribution of the proceeds of labour cannot challenge the form of injustice inherent to the wage relation. The problem with such distributive justice is that it still presupposes the division that Marx saw as the fundamental injustice of capitalist society. "Any distribution whatever of the means of consumption is only a consequence of the distribution of the conditions of production themselves" (Marx, 1875). A more just distribution of surplus does not, in itself, challenge the distribution of means of production between capitalist and proletarian. Indeed, Marx was critical of the language of justice to the extent that it pertained only to the apparent fairness of the exchange of labour-power for wages (Geras, 1985, pp. 49–54).

Thus, we can see that the first tenet of just transitions, the distribution of harms and benefits, pertains to the material form of infrastructure, not the value-form of infrastructure; to the way that infrastructure is *used*, not the way that infrastructure is *owned*. It thus, in no way, negates the logic of private property. Furthermore, we can see that the second tenet of just transitions, the recognition of the perspectives of users, can only pertain to the material form of infrastructure as the provider of commodities, and need not challenge private ownership. Finally, the third tenet, the integration of a greater diversity of decision-makers throughout the process of infrastructural development, may happily coexist with infrastructure used for capital accumulation. In fact, these decision-makers might strongly desire that, if they have some stake in the profits derived from it. Energy infrastructures *should* distribute benefits and harms fairly; include the perspectives and needs of marginalised groups; and include mechanisms that hold decision-makers to account. But if they do so without challenging the distribution of ownership, then it cannot be said that those infrastructures are just, from a Marxist perspective.

There might be more radical versions of the just transition. It is unlikely that bp supports them. We may thus conclude that whatever else a just transition may mean to bp, it does not mean an end to the form of exploitation specific to capitalism. The just transition may speak to our sense of fairness. But these beliefs must then correspond to capitalist social relations. If that is true, then Foster's claim that the just transition is a negation of capitalism cannot be right. We can therefore see how solar can be positioned as both just and a form of financial abstraction. Financial accumulation is nothing more than a claim to profits, arising from the same source as capital accumulation: the appropriation of surplus-value. Put differently, finance is nothing more than the representation and capture of the expenditure of human labour-power in some future projected out of revenue forecasting. Solar enables narratives of justice and the prospect of financial return to the extent that such novel forms of capturing energy represent a continuity in private property. An restricted focus on the distribution of income, decision-making, and recognition leaves more or less intact the relations of production that generate the inequalities that the just transition is supposed to resolve.

We must look elsewhere for a principle of distribution suitable to infrastructural critique. I thus want to posit the distribution of free time, or temporal justice, as an infrastructural concept meant to support and bridge the three tenets of justice proposed by the just transition framework. Because while Marx saw distribution of consumption as a consequence of the conditions of production, a more just distribution of this latter provides the infrastructural basis of free self-development.

Instead of private property utilised to appropriate the time of workers for the benefit of owners, a collective democratic control over productive resources distributed according to a principle of need would support the flourishing of human freedom (Geras, 1985). Justice, then, is strictly speaking an economic problem that proceeds through a negation of private property, the division of capitalist and worker. To frame justice in terms of the expansion of free time is a way of seeing prospective infrastructures as enabling the conditions of social abundance and human flourishing. We can find evidence of such infrastructural thinking in Marx's writings on freedom and time.

> The realm of freedom really begins only where labour determined by necessity and external expediency ends; it lies by its very nature beyond the sphere of material production proper [...] This realm of natural necessity expands with his development, because his needs do too; but the productive forces to satisfy these expand at the same time. Freedom, in this sphere, can consist only in this, that socialized man, the associated producers, govern the human metabolism with nature in a rational way, bringing it under their collective control instead of being dominated by it as a blind power; accomplishing it with the least expenditure of energy and in conditions most worthy and appropriate for their human nature. But this always remains a realm of necessity. The true realm of freedom, the development of human powers as an end in itself, begins beyond it, though it can only flourish with this realm of necessity as its basis. The reduction of the working day is the basic prerequisite (Marx, 1992a, p. 959).

This passage illuminates how the economic question of infrastructure must be oriented towards supporting human needs, while positing a realm of freedom that supersedes those needs. It therefore clarifies the centrality and limit of infrastructural critique, inasmuch as freedom and self-development require the rearrangement of infrastructural forms to support the distribution of free time, but infrastructural forms cannot give political meaning to the use of that time. Infrastructures are not ends; they are enablers of human projects. While in no way programmatic, temporal justice is an infrastructural concept because it is recursive to the conditions of human freedom. If the role of infrastructure in the distribution of time—waged, free, or otherwise—is unrecognised, justice can scarcely be framed.

It is here that I wish to return to the solar pastoral. The utopian core of Virgil's golden age and its echo in Lightsource's solar dawns are a form of pleasure found in moments of free time; the day's end, when tools are downed, and the shared enjoyment of the produce begins. The poetic voice and later the visual representation of the pastoral arises out of the dialogue of shepherds, shaded from the sun, at rest. What cascades down through the ages is the symbolic economy of solar time—exactly what is at stake in the energy transition—refunctioned for marketing purposes by Lightsource bp but unable to do so without first giving it some fundamental critical expression. This is not the dazzling, even blinding notion of the sun as source of infinite energy, a renewal of the operative and dominant belief in the 'fiction of surplus' relocated from subterranean depth to solar beneficence (Szeman, 2011, p. 324). If the iterative narrative of the rising and setting of the sun enables financial futurity, it also gives figuration to the rhythm of work time and free time, of the time of necessity and the time of freedom. The ineradicable utopian potential of the sun—as aesthetic and energetic force—is not sustainability, the pausing of ecological time, nor the liberation of human life from material, earth, and resource. It is to be found in the fields, environments, and infrastructures that mediate solar power into a social form that justly distributes free time.

References

Alpers, P. (1997). *What Is Pastoral? (New edition)*. University of Chicago Press.

Ambrose, J., & Boyle, N. (2021, September 20). 'The potential for solar is huge': Future looks bright for Lightsource BP. *The Guardian*. Retrieved from https://www.theguardian.com/business/2021/sep/20/the-potential-for-solar-is-huge-future-looks-bright-for-lightsource-bp

Bellamy Foster, J. (2019, June 22). *Ecosocialism and a just transition | MR Online*. Retrieved from https://mronline.org/2019/06/22/ecosocialism-and-a-just-transition/

Boyle, N. (2020). *Making Light Work—10 Years of Solar Success*. Lightsourcebp. Retrieved from www.lightsourcebp.com/stories/making-light-work-10-years-of-solar-success

Boyle, N. (2022). *Shiny Panels and a Sure Thing, Nick's Story*. Lightsourcebp. Retrieved from www.lightsourcebp.com/2022/03/shiny-panels-and-a-sure-thing-nicks-story

bp (Director). (2019). *Unpredictable* [Broadcast]. Retrieved from https://www.ispot.tv/ad/oFi2/bp-unpredictable

bp. (2023). *Bp Sustainability Report 2023.* bp. Retrieved from https://www.bp.com/content/dam/bp/business-sites/en/global/corporate/pdfs/sustainability/group-reports/bp-sustainability-report-2023.pdf

Christophers, B. (2022). Fossilised Capital: Price and Profit in the Energy Transition. *New Political Economy, 27*(1), 146–159. https://doi.org/10.1080/13563467.2021.1926957

Christophers, B. (2023). *Our Lives in Their Portfolios: Why Asset Managers Own the World.* Verso Books.

Council for Inclusive Capitalism. (2021, August 16). *JET Digital Framework | Council for Inclusive Capitalism.* Retrieved from https://www.inclusivecapitalism.com/just-energy-transition-company-framework/

Daggett, C. N. (2019). *The Birth of Energy: Fossil Fuels, Thermodynamics, and the Politics of Work.* Duke University Press Books.

Dale, S. (2015). *New Economics of Oil.* Society of Business Economists Annual Conference, London. Retrieved from https://www.bp.com/content/dam/bp/business-sites/en/global/corporate/pdfs/news-and-insights/speeches/new-economics-of-oil-spencer-dale.pdf

Energy Justice: A Conceptual Review. (2016). *Energy Research & Social Science, 11*, 174–182. https://doi.org/10.1016/j.erss.2015.10.004

Fink, L. (2024). *Larry Fink's 2024 Annual Chairman's Letter to Investors.* BlackRock. Retrieved from https://www.blackrock.com/corporate/investor-relations/larry-fink-annual-chairmans-letter

Freehill-Maye, L. (2020). *Sheep, ag and sun: Agrivoltaics propel significant reductions in solar maintenance costs.* Utility Dive. Retrieved from https://www.utilitydive.com/news/sheep-ag-and-sun-agrivoltaics-propel-significant-reductions-in-solar-main/581879/

Genette, G. (1979). *Narrative Discourse: An Essay in Method* (J. Culler, Ed.; J. E. Lewin, Trans.). Cornell University Press.

Geras, N. (1985). The Controversy About Marx and Justice. *New Left Review, I*(150), 47–85.

Gurley, L. K. (2022, June 27). Shifting America to Solar Power Is a Grueling, Low-Paid Job. *VICE.* Retrieved from https://www.vice.com/en/article/shifting-america-to-solar-power-is-a-grueling-low-paid-job/

Warwick, H. (2023). *Dystopia and Dispossession in the Hollywood Science Fiction Film, 1979–2017.* Liverpool University Press.

Harvey, D. (2005). A Brief History of Neoliberalism. *Oxford University Press.* https://doi.org/10.1093/oso/9780199283262.001.0001

IEA. (2021). *Net Zero by 2050.* IEA. Retrieved from https://www.iea.org/reports/net-zero-by-2050

IEA. (2023, September 26). *The Path to Limiting Global Warming to 1.5 °C has Narrowed, but Clean Energy Growth is Keeping it Open—News.*

IEA. Retrieved from https://www.iea.org/news/the-path-to-limiting-global-warming-to-1-5-c-has-narrowed-but-clean-energy-growth-is-keeping-it-open
Just Transition: A Conceptual Review. (2021). *Energy Research & Social Science, 82*, 102291. https://doi.org/10.1016/j.erss.2021.102291
Lennon, M. (2023). Affective Energy. In C. Howe, J. Diamanti, & A. Moore (Eds.), *Solarities: Elemental Encounters and Refractions* (1st ed.). Punctum books. https://doi.org/10.53288/0404.1.00
Lightsource bp. (2023). *Solar Power for Our World: 2023 Sustainability Report.* Retrieved from https://assets.lightsourcebp.com/app/uploads/2024/06/19152736/Lightsource-bp-Sustainability-Report-2023.pdf
Lohmann, L. (2012). Financialization, Commodification and Carbon: The Contradictions of Neoliberal Climate Policy. *Socialist Register, 48.* https://socialistregister.com/index.php/srv/article/view/15647
Marshall, C. (2020). *From IOC to IEC: Second Quarter 2020 Financial Results and Strategy Presentation.* bp. Retrieved from https://www.bp.com/content/dam/bp/business-sites/en/global/corporate/pdfs/investors/bp-second-quarter-2020-results-presentation-slides-and-script.pdf
Marshall, C. (2022). *Performing While Transforming: Bp First quarter 2022 Financial Results.* bp. Retrieved from https://www.bp.com/content/dam/bp/business-sites/en/global/corporate/pdfs/investors/bp-first-quarter-2022-results-presentation-slides-and-script.pdf
Marx, K. (1875). *Critique of the Gotha Programme.* Retrieved from https://www.marxists.org/archive/marx/works/1875/gotha/
Marx, K. (1990). *Capital: Critique of Political Economy v. 1* (B. Fowkes, Trans.; Illustrated edition). Penguin Classics.
Marx, K. (1992a). *Capital: A Critique of Political Economy, Volume 3.* Penguin Classics.
Marx, K. (1992b). *Capital: Volume II: 2* (D. Fernbach, Trans.; 2nd edition). Penguin Classics.
Marx, K. (1993). *Grundrisse: Foundations of the Critique of Political Economy.* Penguin Classics.
Marx, L. (2000). *The Machine in the Garden: Technology and the Pastoral Ideal in America* (Anniversary). Oxford University Press.
Mitchell, T. (2020). Infrastructures Work on Time. *E-Flux, New Silk Roads.* Retrieved from https://www.e-flux.com/architecture/new-silk-roads/312596/infrastructures-work-on-time/
Mulvaney, D. (2018). *Solar Power.* University of California Press.
Raymond Williams. (2011). *The Country and the City.* Spokesman.
Rubenstein, M., Robbins, B., & Beal, S. (2015). Infrastructuralism: An Introduction. *Modern Fiction Studies, 61*(4), 575–586.

Rystad Energy. (2024). *Renewable Energy's Rise Creates Challenges for Traditional Power Utilities*. OilPrice.Com. Retrieved from https://oilprice.com/Energy/Energy-General/Renewable-Energys-Rise-Creates-Challenges-for-Traditional-Power-Utilities.html

Scheiber, N. (2021). Building Solar Farms May Not Build the Middle Class. *NY Times*. Retrieved from https://www.nytimes.com/2021/07/16/business/economy/green-energy-jobs-economy.html

Shell. (2013). *New Lens Scenarios: A Shift in perspective for a World in Transition*. Shell. Retrieved from https://www.shell.com/news-and-insights/scenarios/what-are-the-previous-shell-scenarios.html

Stoekl, A. (2021). *The Three Sustainabilities: Energy, Economy*. University of Minnesota Press.

Szeman, I. (2011). Literature and Energy Futures. *PMLA*, *126*(2). https://www.jstor.org/stable/41414106

Szeman, I. (2013). How to Know about Oil: Energy Epistemologies and Political Futures. *Journal of Canadian Studies/revue D'études Canadiennes*, *47*(3), 145–168.

Thompson, E. P. (2013). *The Making of the English Working Class*. Penguin Classics.

Virgil. (2001). *Virgil (70 BC–19 BC)—The Eclogues* (A. S. Kline, Trans.). Retrieved from https://www.poetryintranslation.com/PITBR/Latin/VirgilEclogues.php

weownit. (2012, August 6). *It's time to take back our water*. We Own It. Retrieved from https://weownit.org.uk/public-ownership/water

CHAPTER 7

Transitional Utopias: Financial Representation and Utopian Negation

7.1 Thinking the Break

Utopias are neither the blueprints of a future perfect state, nor the naïve fancy of idle dreamers. They are the diagnostic tools of social tinkerers, narratively organised around the removal of a particular cause of suffering and exploitation. Hence the debasement of gold in Thomas More, the evils of money in Edward Bellamy, industrial labour in William Morris, and so on: these utopian narratives must be read negatively, as worlds accomplished through destructive removals that remake worlds. As such, utopias are always forms of both negation and reconstruction, critical diagnostic and form-building. Yet that strange exercise we call utopian thinking, in which we erect systems in the mind, is impossible in our own time, as the infrastructures upon which we might rest such future societies crumble under the weight of planetary history. Fantasy and dystopia are everywhere, the former representing an ideological suspension of the determining crises of the Anthropocene; the latter, the return of the repressed of that temporality of newness practically eliminated in postmodernity, in which space becomes a social dominant and time

H. Pitt Scott, *Financial Petroleum Cultures*, Palgrave Studies in Literature, Culture and Economics,
https://doi.org/10.1007/978-3-031-99661-0_7

compresses to the movement of markets.[1] To represent that totality, or its negation in utopian form, depends upon the representability of a fundamental problem around which a social analysis and aesthetic form can be organised: "The view that opens out onto history from a particular social situation must encourage such oversimplifications; the miseries and injustices thus visible must seem to shape and organize themselves around one specific ill or wrong" (Jameson, 2005, p. 12). The emergent feeling of planetary history, of the causal power of cumulative emissions and the ecological crisis, pushes us back towards the system of the social totality, to see the complex whole. Yet, for all the suffering of the Anthropocene, it is highly uneven, variegated, dispersed: it is nigh-on impossible to identify a single cause. Not even fossil fuels lend themselves to utopian negation, as their absence too readily begets declinist or apocalyptic narratives. Likewise, the absence of ecological destruction appears as fantasy given how much climate change is already locked in. Class, too, hardly presents a unifying social bond.

> The problem, of course, is that the collective in which the new labour question, that is, self-protection in the context of climate change, is being developed, looks nothing, or almost nothing, like a class understood in its classic socioeconomic sense. People living near dangerous installations, victims of extractive devices, alternative land users, commoners, scientists and educators, and many others whose experiences are still diffracted by gender and race, compose, with the Earth, a collective hardly comparable to a dominated class, quite simply because they are united neither by the experience of exploitation nor by collective identification with a common condition or identity, or even simply by the fact of being victims. (Charbonnier, 2021, p. 256)

This climate realism—a volatile maelstrom that unites through disintegration, the wreckage ever-growing—works its way through utopian totalisation and dissolves it from the inside; every attempt to think the break with the current system only reinforces its smothering weight. Partial, piecemeal, reformist, ineffective: these political diagnoses of climate action

[1] Jameson suggests that the vision of a coming time of troubles are a return of the historicity of Utopianism, only passing the censor of the postmodern end of temporality through an inversion into the more tolerable—because rejected—form of the nightmare; utopia, of course, never really being about an alternative space or future time, but a method for awakening a new form of perception of time and historicity.

sediment into an atmosphere of belatedness, a political feeling of too late, as the grind and churn turns hope to dust. Such modifications that exist fail to represent the systemic closure necessary for the utopian form.

It is striking, then, when two novels I am tempted to call utopian appear as a breath of fresh air amid the dystopian gloom; whose reach for alternatives illuminates the oppressive atmosphere suffocating historicity. Stephen Markley's *The Deluge* (2023) and Kim Stanley Robinson's *Ministry for the Future* (2020) have significant similarities. These are novels of crisis, ecological breakdown, war, political repression of the most extreme kind, personal agony, and the feeling of accelerating into a volatile future. The first is a political novel of the climate crisis in the USA, told through a related cast of characters, from activists and bankers to politicians and outcasts. The second focuses on the eponymous 'Ministry for the Future', a transnational organisation established in the wake of a wet-bulb heatwave in India (a combination of high temperature and humidity in which the body can no longer regulate temperature through sweat). Both represent attempts to think the break with fossil capital, to identify forces of negation and transition.

These novels are not reducible to that faint echo of difference named the utopian wish, even if do not they have the solidity of the utopian form proper, in which the alternative society has been discovered or achieved, but at any rate certainly exists. They necessitate the invention of a new term, the transitional utopia, to describe narratives of the passage towards the alternative society, in that ominous 'time of change' (as named by Morris in *News From Nowhere*, to distinguish his own utopian society from the peaceful evolution into industrial utopia in Bellamy's *Looking Backward: 2000–1887*). If the utopian romances of the nineteenth century turned their presents into the history of a distant future, and the critical utopias of the twentieth projected their alternative systems into contrasting worlds, then the transitional utopias of the twenty-first century narrate the beginnings of a transition towards a different kind of system located in their own near future, for which 2050 stands as historical marker. This is perhaps symptomatic of an inability to think beyond the cascading climate tipping points that dissolve the future into a convoluted series. But it also functions as narrative closure, or what Robinson calls 'proleptic realism' bound to the temporality of climate scenarios and projections. For this reason, these novels are more extrapolative than speculative. While the speculative more easily introduces alterity into the alternative society, extrapolation is more obviously social, as it tracks the causal mechanisms by which a future might arise out of the present.

The transitional utopia is therefore a near future history. Yet the near future affords neither the speculative freedom of the far future nor the givenness of the present. Future history is usually associated with science fiction, but as climate shifts the ground of individual life and national destiny—the conventional terrain of realism—a combination of the two modes occurs (science fiction has always borrowed its reality-effect from realism anyway). Realism is pulled into the future, while the speculative dimension of science fiction becomes evidence of its mimetic dimension. This generic combination has a determining effect on the novel. Science fiction is a mode that, according to Darko Suvin, evinces a novel perspective on the present through the contrast between the alterity of its setting and the historical present of the reader (Suvin, 2016). Realism, however, has often been understood as the attempt to bring common experience into aesthetic form, a new way of seeing and imagining a historical reality through empathy with ordinary, if fictional, individuals. Indeed, according to Anna Kornbluh, this attention to the social in realism is a method for drafting and building social worlds, a way of thinking the constructive work of forms (Kornbluh, 2019, p. 16). As these two distinct modes converge in the climate realism of the near future, we are forced to shift between two often contradictory dispositions: one critical and estranging, the other constructive and form-building. One mode must be convincingly different from our reality, the other must be convincingly of it (in however complex a fashion).

We can therefore see that transitional utopias are engaged with narrating the transition's actants and objects—those who do the transitioning and the things they transition. But this pressure of generic combination means that they must make change convincing. Their problematic is, strictly speaking, historical difference in a realist mode.

In previous chapters, we have seen how finance turns imagined transitions into economic narratives. Finance is both problem and solution in a way that simplifies both: investment in dirty fuels makes transition harder, but investment in clean fuels makes transition happen at all. This is because, I have been arguing, finance has reorganised the spatio-temporal forms of fossil capital and is determining the form of the renewables boom, while, in the era of financialisation, "the leading stock market indices act as a kind of barometer for the economy as a whole" (Krippner, 2005, p. 174). Finance represents and is representative of the economy, and as such is understood as a cause of and reflection on historical change. Because of the structural centrality of finance to late fossil capitalism, its negation folds back into the representability of social totality and historical difference: peculiarly, the transitional utopian form is enabled by finance's representational hegemony, which it critically refunctions and negates in the description of forms of transition.

The Ministry opens in 2025 in the middle of a wet-bulb heatwave in an unnamed town in the state of Uttar Pradesh, India.

> It was getting hotter [...] All over town the stressed hum of windowbox air conditioner fans buzzed like giant mosquitoes. And then the sun cracked the eastern horizon. It blazed like an atomic bomb, which of course it was. The fields and buildings underneath that brilliant chip of light went dark, then darker still as the chip flowed to the sides in a burning line that then bulged to a crescent he couldn't look at. The heat coming from it was palpable, a slap to the face. Solar radiation heating the skin of his face, making him blink. Stinging eyes flowing, he couldn't see much. Everything was tan and beige and a brilliant, unbearable white. Ordinary town in Uttar Pradesh, 6 AM. He looked at his phone: 38 degrees. In Fahrenheit that was—he tapped—103 degrees. Humidity about 35 percent. The combination was the thing. A few years ago it would have been among the hottest wet-bulb temperatures ever recorded. Now just a Wednesday morning. (Robinson, 2021, pp. 1–2)

Surging energy demand for air conditioning causes a regional infrastructure failure and a dramatic energy shortage. With no air conditioning, human bodies are incapable of cooling at wet-bulb humidity and temperature. The heatwave causes the death of many in the town, and millions of others in the region. Frank May, a young American NGO worker helping to provide medical assistance, barely survives the heatwave.

When this novel was published, this opening passage was set in the near future, with an event that had not taken place. But the likelihood of wet-bulb heatwaves tends towards the inevitable as the climate heats up. If emission trends continue then at some point this event, or something much like it, will take place. The major climate catastrophe is the catalyst for India to begin a unilateral geoengineering programme. Meanwhile, Frank, overwhelmed with survivors' guilt and unable to find work, drifts through Europe and murders a wealthy man working for a fossil-fuel company. Later, in Zurich, he breaks into the apartment of Mary Murphy, the head of the eponymous Ministry for the Future.

The encounter between Frank and Mary is disturbing. Wielding a gun, he accuses her of not doing enough to reduce carbon emissions.

> She said, "The ministry was set up after the Paris meeting of 2024. They thought it would be a good idea to create an agency tasked with representing the interests of the generations to come. And the interests of those entities that can never speak for themselves, like animals and watersheds."
> The young man gestured dismissively. This was boilerplate, known to him already. "And so? How do you do that, how do you defend those interests?"
> "We've made divisions that focus on various aspects of the problem. Legal, financial, physical, and so forth. We prioritize what we do to portion out the budget we're given, and we do what we can."
> He stared at her. "What if that's not enough?"
> "What do you mean, not enough?"
> "It's not enough. Your efforts aren't slowing the damage fast enough. They aren't creating fixes fast enough. You can see that, because everyone can see it. Things don't change, we're still on track for a mass extinction event, we're in the extinctions already. That's what I mean by not enough. So why don't you do something more?"

This scene is focalised through Mary, so the accusations put to her are put to the reader too.

> "You're not doing everything you can, and what you are doing isn't going to be enough." He leaned toward her again and captured her gaze, his eyes bloodshot and bugging out, pale tortured blue eyes scarcely held in by his sweating red face—transfixing her—"Admit it!". (96)

The encounter between this volatile young man and the head of the ministry, which it is tempting to identify as an allegory for the encounter between radical and centrist politics, breaks through institutional inertia because, shaken, Mary becomes willing to facilitate more radical responses to a changing climate, from science and technological solutions to social, political, and financial revolutions. This feeling of urgency is the novel's dominant affect, a way of perceiving the present and what is happening to direct its temporality, as well as expressing a subjunctive mood that seeks the political feelings that might animate a transition. Through interrelated subplots, the novel narrates how each of these change under the pressures of climate and transition. The story ends thirty years later, around an imagined COP58 meeting, with the retirement of Mary and the relative success of her ministry.

Bill McKibben, a liberal figurehead of the climate movement, wrote a review of the novel entitled 'It's Not Science Fiction': it "is not utopian, it's anti-dystopian, realist to its core" because, "in taking on heat and glacial melt and fire, Robinson is writing more realistic fiction than most contemporary novelists, for whom the physical world remains a backdrop for more interior stories" (McKibben, 2020). For Marxist Andreas Malm the novel "is a utopia more than a dystopia" because "humanity manages to rid itself of fossil fuels and begin to undo the damage they have already done and restore a liveable climate" (Malm, 2020b). Nick Robins, co-founder of Carbon Tracker, suggests "the book can be read as a vast scenario exercise showing how the transformation of finance becomes part of the solution to the climate crisis" (Robins, 2021). Gerry Canavan, a literary critic and expert on Robinson and science fiction, offers no categorisation at all, simply calling it his "grimmest book to date" (Canavan, 2020). For his own part, Robinson thinks his writing is what he calls 'proleptic realism': in his words, "trying to cast realism into the future" (Galvin, 2020).

These different categorisations intimate the politics of genre in the energy transition. I am going to offer my own categorisation of *The Ministry* by suggesting that, while it seems continuous with older forms, it really is offering something new. In the transitional utopia, components of the present, imperfect as they are for an alternative future, are assessed to see how they might function as transitional forms. Alongside locating transitional forms, the genre identifies antagonistic impediments to a desirable transition and narrates how they are overcome: from states to markets, petrodollars to pipelines, the ways of life and the sedimented habits, feelings, and comforts of petroculture. The alternative society remains an essential temporal orientation, but the utopian form has been adapted to a new historical situation by placing the most narrative weight on the social potentials of the present.

What I want to argue for here is the critical estrangement of the extrapolations we call imagined transitions. It is because a transitional society is, of necessity, a speculative one, that utopia finds its function in the modifications to financial extrapolations that regulate the present. Another way to put this is that, to do its critical work, utopian thinking must internalise and modify the speculations that govern a transitional society. It registers the historicity of speculative financial temporality. It does this through three interconnected narrative stands: one to do with scientific development, another to do with a financial revolution, the third to do with political activism. A revolution in the social form of energy requires an emergent transitional culture building alternative relations to energy systems. The transitional utopia is a literary form that engages this temporal horizon.

The Ministry narrates a single generation, 2020–2050. It is the story of Mary's career as head of the ministry, in a transitional period that lays the groundwork for a different world. Mary's main role in the novel is to attend a lot of meetings: with scientists, bankers, government officials, military personnel, activists, economists, and, it is suggested, clandestine actors. As a central figure, Mary, and the ministry she works in, is a useful device for the novel's presentation of the social totality. To follow Lukács, this is "a central figure in whose life all the important extremes in the world of the novel converge and around whom a complete world with all its vital contradictions can be organized" (Lukacs, 1991, p. 142). An Irish woman, middle-aged, a former lawyer and politician, capable of emotional and political sensitivity, is an ordinary hero. A mediating figure at the head of a mediating institution, she facilitates connections between characters dispersed throughout the world-system; characters who, in turn, bring conflicting social and historical forces into a singular planetary narrative.

The Ministry is a descriptive future history that conjoins two modes of narrative organisation: the history of institutions and the history of individuals, as two perspectives on planetary history. This alternation of the reader's position between a historical chronicle of events and close narrative focus on the relationships between people is highly significant. The endless meetings—with their recordings, minutes, scientific reports, economic theories, discussion of political events, and catalogues of historical data—provide a representational solution to these incommensurable formal structures, allowing historical description to develop within the representation of definite social relationships. These two narratological axes enable *The Ministry* to sustain a narrative of institutions and individuals over an imagined transition.

The first social character Mary regularly encounters is the scientist. Scientists are prominent figures throughout Robinson's novels, and science—both real and fictional—provides a useful narrative function, as a collective discourse in which social contradiction, antagonism, and, ultimately, compromise is mooted. The way science gets used is repeatedly shown to be a *political* issue—as one scientist remarks to another, "a scientist gets into geoengineering, they're not a scientist anymore, they're a politician" (83).

After the heat wave, India breaks the 2024 Paris Agreement and make the unilateral decision to begin geoengineering. Called 'solar radiation management' (SRM), it involves depositing reflective particles in the stratosphere, reflecting heat away from the earth, slowing global warming. It is controversial in the climate science community, in reality and in the novel. Its justification, however, is compelling. As the head of the Indian delegation to the Paris Agreement says to Mary,

> But no one is fulfilling commitments, no one is paying the developing nations, and now we have this heat wave. And another one could happen next week [...] Everyone knows, but no one acts. So we are taking matters into our own hands. We'll lower global temperatures for a few years, everyone will benefit. And perhaps we'll dodge another massacre like this one. (20)

In the novel, science drives the narrative into boardrooms and institutions and out into the atmosphere and the earth system, connecting policy discussions with atmospheric shifts. Geoengineering, a hypothetical in our world, is a technology that can function as a narrative vehicle for a reflection on the politics and ethics of climate response. Through it, humanity becomes atmospheric, and the atmosphere becomes humanised. But it is not an abstract humanity that drives this transformation, but the political situation of climate delay. In this case, geoengineering provides an acute contradiction between a national tragedy and a planetary force, because the unilateral decision to deploy solar radiation management cannot be contained to the territorial borders of India, but rather is dispersed through weather currents into the climate. The fictional geoengineering has a limited effect on the climate: enough to slow heating, perhaps, but not to stop it. It is a way of buying time. But more importantly, it is about how particular a political feeling generated by climate delay might, in fact, precipitate a solution to the crisis that only deepens the crisis. If SRM interventions have a rapid effect in reducing global warming but is not sustained while cumulative emissions continue to rise, it might produce a termination shock, with more severe consequences.

One episode of the larger narrative is that of glaciologists in Antarctica trying to work out how to slow its melting to stop sea level rise. The first plan, to pump seawater directly onto the Antarctic sheet, is a completely unfeasible dead-end. The second is more promising. As icesheets melt, water builds up where glacier meets rock and the friction that holds glaciers in place decreases, slowing their slide into the ocean. The glaciologists decide to try using pipes to pump water from the bottom of the icesheet to the top, where it would melt on the frozen surface, increasing the friction between glacier and bedrock, slowing the slide of the icesheet into the ocean. Much like the solar radiation management, however, there is no delusion about its function.

> Hey, someone else said, geoengineering isn't always just a fantasy. The Indians did that sulfur dioxide thing and that worked. Temperatures dropped for years after that.
> Big deal, someone else replied.
> It was a big deal!
> But it didn't do anything to solve the bigger problem.
> Of course not, but it wasn't meant to do that! It was a fix!
> That's why we're here, I pointed out. This is a different fix (122).

Named 'Project Slowdown', it takes years to come to fruition. The length of the novel contributes to this sense of time, drawing together long strands of separate but interconnected subplots in one hundred and six chapters—when the plot is planetary history, all stories are episodes in that vast tapestry. Geoengineering is perhaps the novel's greatest speculative indulgence, but even at this project's most effective, it is, as the name implies, merely a slowdown to give more time to decarbonise.

In suggesting and testing such climate science fictions, *The Ministry* undermines the cathexis so central to the modernist faith in technology. The temporality is crucial. Long, exhaustive lists of glaciers make the science seem solid, realistic, considered: more realism than science fiction.

> Still, a lot of water to pump, but that's for all of Antarctica. Around the circle of the continent, about fifty glaciers dump the majority of the ice now rushing into the sea, with a few being the major contributors. Starting from McMurdo and running clockwise, you need to stick the Skelton, the Mulock, the Beardmore, [...] the David, the Mawson, and the Mackay... (263–4)

Its costs, funding, and technological implementation are all described, too. Repurposing technology and expertise from the oil industry, who are used to drilling in extreme environments, the novel suggests a transitional role for the industry. The work sounds dull, iterative, the renumeration more academic than financial. It takes place in unpleasant conditions, but not Romantic ones: the scientists are not echoes of the heroic explorers of the nineteenth century. Project Slowdown meets with disaster, as the lead scientist dies in an accident, as well as scientific difficulties, setbacks, and misdirections.

> So; ten years in Antarctica, with good work to do, and no more grant applications either. Papers got written, science got done, but mostly it was engineering the drills and pumps and dispersion technologies. There were papers to be had there too, even if it wasn't exactly what we had gone down there for. Actually the glaciologists were getting data like never before, especially structures of ice and flow histories, and most of all, bottom studies. (472)

Geoengineering is not described for the frisson of the technological sublime or climate anxiety relief, but to afford it some specific role in a total social transformation. The reading duration and the gaps between the episodes of the subplot mean that it is neither valorised as a heroic moment, nor assumed and forgotten; it is not reified into a solution—after all, reading the process is exhausting—nor allowed to become the dominant process, the master narrative of the transition. It is not caustically denied nor joyfully affirmed, but slowly, almost unconsciously, worked through and neutralised.

Drawn out of the ideological gravity well of the techno-fix, applied science is represented as a mode of politics. This is an operation repeated throughout *The Ministry*, approaching institutions that are considered non-political (usually by themselves), describing their resistance to inclusion within the transition project before they are incorporated within it. I have highlighted how the novel does this because something similar happens with finance and central banking. The similarities between how the novel treats science and finance shows how the novel conceptualises finance in the transition: as a tool subordinated to political goals.

The Ministry synthesises climate and financial knowledge, suggesting ways that finance can be employed to assist in decarbonisation, such as funding for geoengineering and investing in climate-resilient infrastructure and agriculture. Mary holds regular meetings with Dick, the economic advisor to the ministry. An early chapter explains how a discount rate—that is, how much the future value of money is discounted relative to its value in the present through interest—produces difficulties for intergenerational politics, because value in the present is worth more than in the future (129–131). Alongside offering lessons in economics and cautions against faith in its solutions, this character system enables the novel to test economic theories against "the next world system. New metrics, new kinds of value creation" (317). The novel calls these "speculative fictions" (344), making it an economic thought-experiment, asking what financial concepts, instruments, and tools could be employed towards transition.

The most ambiguous of these economic speculative fictions is the 'carbon coin', meant to address the tragedy of the time horizon and the economic discounting of the future. *The Ministry*'s carbon coin is a currency issued in exchange for *not* burning carbon, or sequestering carbon over a long time period. A carbon coin's value is made through storing CO_2 in the ground. The novel offers a (literal) ground of value beyond hydrocarbons, imparting it with a climatic character that is abstract but, crucially, not dependent on extraction. The carbon coin is meant to guarantee the value of money across time but in a way that detaches this temporality from the abstract materiality of hydrocarbons.

Carbon sequestration is an emblematic transitional technology. It is capitalist, a privately-owned means of production whose value is derived from the labour time and infrastructure required to sequester carbon. But if used at scale, most of the stored carbon cannot be sold as a commodity. Its means are in contradiction with its ends. It remains extraordinarily expensive, and totally insufficient to meet current needs for a carbon-negative or -neutral world-economy. Holly Jean Buck suggests that carbon sequestration might be little more than greenwash, whose ultimate effect is reassuring fossil finance investors about the long-term viability of oil production, while deferring and never delivering on the promise of negative emissions (Buck, 2019, p. 127), The problem is scalar. While some sequestered carbon can be used for other purposes, to make it climate-significant requires that most (as much as ninety-nine per cent) remains unused and placed in storage. As Malm points out, this directly contravenes the logic of the commodity-form: why produce something for it *not* to be consumed? (Malm, 2020a, p. 141). There is little financial incentive to invest in this infrastructure at climate-significant scales because it destroys value rather than creates it.

The carbon coin resolves this impasse by turning a sequestered or unused carbon and unextracted fossil fuel into long-term bonds. It is a financial form with a different scale of financial time, connecting value to socio-ecological projects. It provides an alternative to the dominance of the petrodollar, a socio-technical assemblage whose power derives from the structural necessity to purchase dollar-denominated oil in energy markets.

> Petrodollars had first been real pre-existing money, paid for a commodity turned into electricity or physical movement, thus turned into economic activity; carbon coins, on the other hand, were created by the actual removal of that same electricity and transport potential from the world [...] They were functionally opposite. (343)

The institutional basis of the fictional carbon coin connects currency to politics. Mary and Dick decide the only way to guarantee the value of the currency is through central banks. Why central banks? Well, "when things fall apart, something from the old system has to be used to hang the new system on, hopefully something big and solid" (410).

Historically, the mandate of central banks has been to ensure financial stability. Because the stability of the financial system is a longer time horizon than election cycles, central banks have been insulated from the political process (Riles, 2018, p. 10). This is the basis for much of the populist ire directed at them: central bankers make important decisions about social value—what gets protected in a crisis—which crystallise new political and cultural movements and moods. Their mandate targets citizens, because the purpose of controlling inflation is to protect consumer wealth and the financial security of modern publics. This functions best when there is a separation between experts and citizen-consumers.

A changing monetary environment from one in which central banks' primary responsibility was governing the distant future through regulating monetary supply, to one where unconventional monetary instruments like quantitative easing become a central representative mechanism for governing the present, has shaped the financial environment of transition. In essence, quantitative easing (QE) is a financial tool that increases the liquidity of financial markets. Central banks purchase huge quantities of government bonds, which drives down their yields (their interest rates). Falling bond yields reduces revenue investment bank revenue, which incentivises them to move out of safe bonds into higher-risk, higher-yield stocks, thereby boosting the stock market. By inflating asset prices, QE indirectly boosts higher-risk businesses and makes stock owners wealthier, incentivising them to consume, all while increasing inequality and polarising populations through their social positioning by stock markets (Tooze, 2018, p. 367).

Historically low interest rates and cheap credit caused by quantitative easing and the need for growth provided the perfect financial environment for a boom in fossil-fuel developments, including high-risk shale oil and bitumen, articulating progressively greater quantities of financial promises and claims on future fossil fuel profitability. The Federal Reserve's QE program made cheap credit available to the shale oil industry. Such 'junk bonds', as they are called, are not circulated as a consequence of sound economic judgement, but because of the exuberance of medium-term returns as they are telescoped into view by the quantities of state-backed public debt reducing long-term interest rates, creating a boom and bust tied to the financialised dynamics of state central banks. Oscillating within this structural double bind, oil volatility became increasingly regulated not by expectations of price trajectories in relation to so-called economic fundamentals but the policies and prognostications of central banks, and their capacity to shape the future with cheap credit (Thompson, 2018, pp. 47–92).

Central banks are central institutions for sustaining belief in market liquidity. Yet *The Ministry* seeks to refunction them as transitional institutions. So, while in reality QE welds markets to states, creating fictitious capital by drawing on the promise of growth, *The Ministry* suggests that central banks can be retrofitted for a different purpose: carbon quantitative easing. This is a form of quantitative easing, but "targeted, directed. Meaning the creation, the first spending of the new money, would have been specifically aimed at carbon reduction" (174). Which means that the novel is engaging in the cognitive estrangement of financial forms. As Sherryl Vint argues, "in its role as a genre that defamiliarises the present by exaggerating it into an imagined future, science fiction can serve a vital role in reminding us that money is a social technology, not a thing" (Vint, 2018, p. 63). Contrasting petrodollars and carbon coins shows how currencies are socio-technical, ecological, and class technologies. Whether or not the carbon coin would be a successful currency is beside the point. The objections are obvious: abstract wealth at the expense of material wealth is the opposite of socialist visions of abundance; premising financial value on competitive sequestration through human labour-power would likely proletarianise those doing it (although waged work for sequestering carbon might be necessary labour); commodity production, and so social reproduction in capitalism, is premised on fossil-fuel energy, which means that without alternative means of producing life, carbon coins would drive up energy prices and increase poverty, producing political backlash, and so on. I am more interested in how plotting carbon coins is meant to highlight the way finance is regulated by petroleum extraction and how finance shapes social reproduction, to cultivate a newly shared perception of finance as a dominant social form. What makes this critical representation available is the actual dominance of central banks, whose representational prowess enables this refunctioning from tool of capital to form of negation. Whether or not the carbon coins works is less important than changing assumptions about financial forms. With this in mind, the novel's proposals no longer look like solutions, but the sort of response one would expect to be common in democratic decision-making over the future of energy systems, problems of public consideration, not private investment.

But finance must be changed before it can be democratised. This involves Mary attempting to persuade the major central banks to adopt the proposal for CQE. The objections, however, from the US Federal Reserve, the BoE, the Bundesbank, the ECB, the People's Bank of China, are predictable: supporting an alternative currency undermines their mandate, which is stabilising their national currencies. The meeting compresses the geopolitical antagonism of national currencies.

> This was not just a meeting of two women and three men, but of five teams, five institutions, five nation-states at the heart of the global nation-state system. The Paris Agreement's Ministry for the Future was small and impoverished, these central banks were big and rich. Just because the need was urgent and her case was good, that didn't mean anything would change. You couldn't change things with just an idea, no matter how good it was. (189)

This initial journey leads to despair. But social chaos and upheaval dramatically change the situation. This is one of the novel's strengths: the sense of interconnection and interdependency across the world-system, emphasising the historical embeddedness of institutions and ideas. Economic stagnation, unemployment, and social upheaval; escalating extreme weather such as seawater rises, heatwaves, floods; species extinction; sabotage, warfare, and violence targeted at the centres of fossil finance—each exerts pressure on the central bankers.

As a result of "all these converging factors [...] The specific principal tasks that central banks were charged with could no longer be fulfilled if the climate emergency got out of hand. Central banks would fail in their principal tasks if they did not save the civilization that had charged them with those tasks" (293). The major central banks agree to support the carbon coin as part of the mandate of central banks. There is detailed description of carbon coin economics. This realism is not, however, to be read as a concrete proposal, but rather is found in exploring what conditions and pressures make the adoption of a new currency not only possible but necessary, and it does so by describing the relationships between institutions, ideas, and a whole way of life undergoing dramatic social and ecological change. It aims to establish a convincing possible reality, extrapolated from several realistic assumptions to suggest that money must change in a low-carbon economy. In fact, making central bankers into unlikely heroes both highlights their real institutional power in the present and just how unimaginative they are in addressing climate change.

The Ministry is at its most realist when the story is contained to the work of Mary and her associates in the Ministry, and the various characters within its orbit. It switches into a different style when describing historical changes: more historical, abstract, and distant, while fossil fuel and climate become characters in the financial plot.

> The new carbon coin had stimulated many short-term investments in carbon sequestration projects, and many longer-term investments in the coin itself. It had caused some of the biggest carbon owners to cash out and keep fossil carbon in the ground, or use it for plastics if they could. Coal had become just a black rock you could turn into money by leaving it alone. (421)

The novel imagines the social forces required for a radical break with the logic of finance capitalism, and the responses that attempt to prevent this change. Financial attacks against the carbon coin begin in earnest, attempting to devalue it. But with trust in money necessary to avert climate catastrophe, the unified central banks are mandated to defend the currency and enact regulation that prevents such counterattacks. These measures include currency controls, limiting tax havens, taxation on high-frequency trading, so that money sloshing around in dark pools is brought into the light. Financial changes make new economic arrangements such as land reform and employee ownership of business possible. The novel narrates finance as a transitional form. Previously an impediment, the central banks and financial institutions are transformed into instruments that fulfil a necessary function in getting from one world-system to another. The carbon coin is an object lesson in thinking transitional forms at the conjuncture of energy and financial temporality.

7.2 Transitional Forms

Utopian literary form provides the occasion for the drafting of critical negation and reconstruction. But the preconditions for such formal projections are to be found in the objective forms of social life. In this way, Robinson recuperates and expresses an argument made by Marx about the transitional role of finance that emerges out of the objective form of money-capital itself. For this reason we must open the third volume of Capital, where Marx addresses credit.

Credit, or interest-bearing capital, is useful because it smooths the production process, making sure that there are sufficient quantities of means of production and labour-power, raw material, transport, storage, etc. so that the value invested in the production process can be valorised in the form of produced commodities. It can be alienated, exchanged, priced, and traded, making it into a source of income for its owner and a source of profit for its borrower. Likewise, credit equalises profit rates, reduces circulation costs, reliance on money reserves, and reduces barriers to productive activity. To the financial capitalist, money-capital possesses the "capacity to represent and increase value" (Marx, 1992, p. 473). Because money can be used to initiate the productive process, it appears to set in motion in the entire productive process. While interest is, ultimately, nothing more than the share of surplus-value that accrues to the finance capitalist, from their perspective, money appears as "self-valorizing value, money breeding money, and in this form is no longer bears any mark of its origin" (Marx, 1992, p. 516). As a result of this "misrepresentation and objectification of the relations of production", we encounter "a form in which all capital's determinations are dissolved and its real elements are invisible" (Marx, 1992, pp. 515, 516). While from the perspective of the borrower, the money form of capital is only temporary, on the money market capital is always in this form. Hence its representational prowess, shorn of determinations, appearing to set all other activity in motion. All the world-making powers of human labour, transforming and transformed by its metabolism with the earth, is arrogated to finance.

Yet a strange inversion of this complete fetish comes about as a result of the consolidation and concentration of money-capital in the credit and banking system. As the borrowing and lending develops into a special business in the capitalist mode of production, banks coordinate and concentrate this function. Idle money is put to work by the banks, which enables larger loans and the further development of the scale of industrial operations. Small sums combine into great masses, forming into monetary power. This form of capital therefore contains, if only potentially, the abolition of capital.

> In joint-stock companies, the function is separated from capital ownership, so labour is also completely separated from ownership of the means of production and of surplus labour. This result of capitalist production in its highest development is a necessary point of transition towards the transformation of capital back into the property of the producers, though no longer as the private property of individual producers, but rather as their property as associated producers, as directly social property. It is furthermore a point of transition towards the transformation of all functions formerly bound up with capital ownership in the reproduction process into simple functions of the associated producers, into social functions. (Marx, 1992, pp. 568, 571)

Comparing joint-stock companies to cooperative factories, he writes

> The cooperative factories run by workers themselves are, within the old form, the first examples of the emergence of a new form, even though they naturally reproduce in all cases, in their present organization, all the defects of the existing system, and must reproduce them. [...] Capitalist joint-stock companies as much as cooperative factories should be viewed as transition forms from the capitalist mode of production to the associated one. (Marx, 1992, pp. 570–571)

These are emergent forms that revolutionise life even if they also reproduce the existing system. A transitional form is therefore the mixing of historical temporalities, one dominant and one latent. Further,

> The social character of capital is mediated and completely realized only by the full development of the credit and banking system ... It places all available and even potential capital that is not already actively committed at the disposal of the industrial and commercial capitalists, so that neither the lender nor the user of this capital are its owners or producers. It thereby

abolishes the private character of capital and thus inherently bears within it, though only inherently, the abolition of capital itself. (Marx, 1992, p. 742)

Beverly Best, glossing these passages in an interesting discussion of this topic, describes these transitional forms as "unrealized but objective portals beyond capital itself" (Best, 2024). What Marx seeks to capture is the forms that might undo capital from within, that contain the negative immanently, if only potentially. I have pursued this brief digression because, it seems to me, in capturing the dual character immanent to finance—representational fetish and transitional form—Marx delineates precisely the narrative dilemma and solution of the transitional utopia: negation of finance is the means to the abolition of capital, but this occurs through finance itself.[2]

A comparable diagnostic exercise occurs in *The Deluge*. Beginning in 2013 and ending some three decades later, Markley's is a novel of the near future. Indeed, by the end of the novel, it is revealed that the diegetic narrator is an AI software which has assembled a narrative from the data surveillance records of the characters. This formal conceit therefore cultivates a sense of the present as historical, by turning it into the past of that fictional future. In the fictional 2030s of the novel, surveillance capitalism and the rise of AI have massively expanded the repressive powers of the carceral state, political polarisation is driven by culture wars and conspiracy theories, and the crisis and collapse of financial markets is an ongoing reality. The narrative focuses on the political struggle over decarbonisation in the USA. Focalising this future is a series of characters that intend to capture a broad spectrum of the nation. Climate scientist, climate activist, policymaker, data analyst, hedge fund manager, saboteur (or 'ecoterrorist'), an addict: blown forward by the storm of history, these characters brought into alliance or antagonism against the rising affective intensity of ongoing crises in the reproduction of capitalist society.

This is a novel interested in the social mediation of global warming, of planetary history collapsing into human history. It opens in 2013 with a climate scientist named Tony Pietrus working on the phase transition of methane hydrates having difficulties getting grand funding for

[2] Lenin too saw something of the unrealised potential of banks, writing that "a single State Bank, the biggest of the big, with branches in every rural district, in every factory, will constitute as much as nine-tenths of the socialist apparatus [...] the skeleton of socialist society" (Lenin, 1917).

his research. The novel establishes a concern with the narrative problem of translating scientific research into public knowledge and action: "To him, the obviousness of studying deep-sea methane molecules felt like a bright red elephant walking down La Jolla Shores Drive, but explaining it to the layperson required a convoluted story, especially as to why hydrates deserved to take money from vanishing schools of tuna or adorable chirping dolphins" (Markley, 2023, p. 3). A detailed explanation follows (deep-sea methane hydrates are a trapped greenhouse gas that could be released very rapidly by ocean circulation changes caused by warming global temperatures, leading to catastrophic temperature increases), and much of the novel is concerned with providing this kind of scientific detail, to find ways of convincingly rendering the climate, and the difficulties communicating it, in narrative form. Methane hydrates strain epistemological and historical sensibility, ascribing historical causality to something no one will ever see, through the study of atmospheric data of previous global warming events. It is tempting to read this as a metaphor of the climate unconscious, the return of the repressed leaking out of the ocean depths, "gurgling from invisible pores in the sediment of the ocean floor, beading up, clinging momentarily, and then writhing free of a soft sand carpet. Zipping back and forth, they climbed through frigid water. A mad poetry scrawled in the unseen corners of the oceans' expanse" (Markley, 2023, p. 14). Yet the narrative force of this opening is not the discovery of a new and horrifying climate tipping point, but the fact that Tony receives a letter that, potentially, contains anthrax, sent by a climate conspiracist with a warning that he will be "CHARGED WITH THE GREATEST FRAUD EVER PERPETRATED" (Markley, 2023, p. 9). This shift in focus captures a central concern of the novel, which is that climate change is mediated through a politics of climate denial and delay that defines our historical present.

This will be the novel's greatest concern, as climate action is repeatedly thwarted by the fossil-fuel lobby, the White House, the US Congress, the FBI, right-wing militias, and markets, even as a warming world comes to inflect and condition all politics. An Evangelical Right see climate action as a threat to an American way of life, a hoax meant to introduce socialism to America. Powerful fossil-fuel lobbyists push back against any regulation or carbon pricing, whipping up pro-American free-market sentiment as justification. Climate activists throw their organising weight behind an alternative Republican candidate to undermine the deadlock of centrist Democrats unable or unwilling to take meaningful legislative action; her victory is short-lived and she is brushed aside, replaced by an openly homosexual ex-military veteran Democrat who, threatened on the right by an Evangelical that makes Trump look moderate, runs on a policy of climate security that really means stopping the boats. He is responsible for the most violent crackdown in American history, causing the deaths of hundreds of climate protestors: a consequence of his personal psychology, his predisposition to violence and will to dominate, as much as vast historical forces. His resignation leads to a constitutional crisis, the attempted secession of several states, and a march of climate fascists on the White House whose promise to execute all political enemies is matched by right-wing militias lynching those they identify as socialists.

Yet amidst the chaos the novel narrates the establishment of transitional forms, as in the Outposts set up climate activist group A Fierce Blue Fire:

> This is how the idea of the Outposts began: taking the values of climate justice into communities abandoned as ecological or economic sacrifice zones. Staff, money, and volunteers began to flood into places like Flint, Michigan; Kemmerer, Wyoming; and Zanesville, Ohio. Amid decay they've built jewels of renewable energy, open green space, concert venues, addiction services, and small farms. Out of thin air, they create a vocal stakeholder, with roots in the community, waging a perpetual influence campaign on the district's congressperson and the state's public utility commission—a board of influential decision-makers in each state who have their hands on the levers of enormous amounts of carbon energy. (Markley, 2023, p. 127)

They thus link the politics of the protest to the economics of cooperative societies, a form of socialist organisation with a long history (indeed, Engels describes Robert Owen's similar organisations as "transition measures to the complete communistic organization of society" in *Socialism: Utopian and Scientific*) (Engels, 1880). The establishment of these organisations become utopian enclaves, zones of historical difference within the space of late-capitalist society.

While much of the narrative is driven by the actions of climate activists, eco-terrorists, and policy makers, one strand concerns hedge fund partners Jacquelyn and Fred. Pioneering an ESG (Environmental, Social, and Governance) fund, they claim to represent ethical investment while pushing for investment opportunities in the Arctic. This financial discourse of ethical investment is coming to be a cornerstone of green financial hegemony. Markley is keen to demonstrate how often this is just a veneer to cover exploitation.

> Fred had sent me the report, and I opened it on my tablet. Despite the title, it was dry reading and described much of what I expected. Strong positions in Arctic oil, gas, uranium, minerals, and the companies best positioned to access those riches. Huge bets on Norman Nate's Solar Solutions with high confidence that the next COP would produce an agreement to begin albedo management of the planet. I searched the document for ANøNosiki. The only mention of it read:
>
> Natural disasters, freshwater scarcity, and desertification trends will continue to lead to denationalization. While maintaining long positions in security and detention, it will be advantageous to invest in services providing transcontinental transportation, as well as future employment, for stateless migrants. Now that migrant paths are moving out of the gray market and falling under the purview of publicly traded companies, these firms are routinizing previously dangerous journeys. Not only has ANøNosiki reduced migrant fatalities but they've provided workers with opportunities to pay off the costs of their transportation with pollination labor in China or sugarcane harvesting in Brazil.
>
> A frustrating bit of research on ANøNosiki revealed it was owned by several international conglomerates, including a Spanish construction firm, a Dutch-based chemical conglomerate, a US private equity firm, and the Qatar Investment Authority, the country's sovereign wealth fund. (Markley, 2023, p. 591)

Later, they will fight over this strategy. Jacquelyn, guilt-ridden over the obvious hypocrisy of investing in companies profiting from climate crisis, and Fred, who believes that private investment and geoengineering are sufficient remedies.

> "Socially responsible," I said plainly. "Fred, you were long on a company that's institutionalized human trafficking as its core business model. That moves dispossessed people into slavery."
>
> He shook his head. "That's bullshit, Jackie. You've been reading all the propaganda, so now you have that stupid, ignorant frame on it."
>
> "Then what do you call it?"
>
> "Nosiki helps people find work and a home! If you didn't notice the world is swarming with people who don't have either."
>
> "And prison companies to house the ones who either won't or can't indenture themselves. And security companies to guard them. And walls to

keep them out—yeah, in the future, they'll really be singing songs around the campfire about Tara Fund's noble work, I'm sure." (Markley, 2023, p. 706)

Fred embodies a market and technocentric ethos towards climate catastrophe, trusting in algorithms, technology, and progressive profitability to keep alive the promise of modernity, even as that promise comes to be sustained by economic practices such as indentured servitude that contradict a liberal, progressive telos of history. These two characters, who achieve remarkable financial success, therefore represent a genre of the good life enabled by the most oppressive of economic practices, a kind of life that might once have been a promise, if not a reality, for all.

7.3 Financial Historicity

I am interested in this as a way into framing our own historical present, as a moment in which the promise of capitalism breaks apart under the pressures of climate catastrophe, the upward distribution of wealth (here represented through finance), and the increasing visibility of forms of labour that were meant to be banished to a less enlightened past. Harry Harootunian writes that "a historical present filled with mixed temporalities has always been a condition of capitalist modernisation, even as its copresent uncanniness was suppressed by both the authority of the future perfect and the expectations of progress that vowed to raise all societies to the same level" (Harootunian, 2007, p. 486). The hedge fund becomes a meditation on the waning of the promise that has historically organised and legitimised capitalist temporality, even at its most cutting-edge. Markley thereby dramatises a structure of feeling in which the present is released from playing the role of a prehistory of that progressive future, as the financial ethos and technological conventions of that temporal genre are increasingly volatilised by increasingly destructive heatwaves, including one that devastates Los Angeles, the threat of rising sea levels, and a global food shortage.

If the novel is, in part, animated by the breakdown in the efficacy of historical time organised around finance, it is concerned with the affective structures that crystallise around the reality that climate change deprives us of time, in a quantitative and qualitative sense. We are running out of time, and so the time we have left feels different, every moment of delay raising the intensity of what remains. This is felt most powerfully in narratives of what seems possible and what blocks change. *The Deluge* captures this feeling of blocked historical agency through delay, state repression, and extrajudicial violence, on the one hand, and a pervasive atmosphere of unpredictability. Tony Pietrus is arrested and imprisoned for eighteenth months without being charged with a crime. In 2036, flooding triggers a financial crisis in insurance markets, which ripples through the economy and leads to a collapse that, with echoes of 2008, no one in that moment can properly grasp, let alone manage. Kate Morris, an important figurehead of the climate movement and leader of the group A Fierce Blue Fire, is, after a major climate action that shuts down most of Washington D.C., killed by a lone gunman, whose motive seems to be that of a stalker. A fictional *The New Yorker* article written by a journalist who breaks the story of the hedge fund's illegal activities reads "There are years that simply rock the world, when events collide to produce unrest and dislocation on scales outside the imagination of those living at the time. Nineteen fourteen, 1968, and 2020 all come to mind. In 2036, two years of the highest food prices since World War II triggered famines in nine countries, the worst downturn since Covid-19, and at least three documented genocides" (Markley, 2023, p. 639). A fictional document titled 'A Contemporaneous Account of the Eco-Economic Crisis of 2037', written by policy maker and data modeller Ashir Al-Hasan, recounts explaining to important politicians that "We are talking about an ensemble of processes of enormous complexity. In all my work on social and economic consequences of warming, not one system dynamics model spat out The Pastor's electoral victory or Victor Love's abdication or the political crisis that ensued. We can only do our best with the information we have available" (Markley, 2023, p. 727). It comes through clearest in the life of the former addict, Keeper, who spends time in prison having been made a fall guy for the eco-terrorists, and is tasked with retrieving bodies from climate disaster zones as part of his sentence: "What was revealed to you years ago when you were picking through the ashen wreckage of the megafire or the soggy detritus of the floods was the simplicity with which everything unravels [...] Now everyone was getting a glimpse of what you long knew: the fragility of all those things that seem so permanent and steadfast" (Markley, 2023, p. 765).

I recount these moments from the novel (there are many more like it) because I want to draw attention to a formal problem that shapes the near future history and the transitional utopia: namely, how it is to represent contingency, or the unpredictability of historical change, and the need to think through historical outcomes, including future ones, as dependent upon prior conditions, in a complex interconnected tapestry. This is reflected in the novel's composition, in which the various characters all turn out to be connected, and the character system comes to function as a cognitive map of this time of change. The eco-terrorist is a former lover of the activist, Kate, and Kate later in life works with Jacquelyn after she leaves the hedge fund; the hedge fund models were built by Al-Hasan before he went into politics, who in turn works with Tony Pietrus, the climate scientist; while the addict, Keeper, is made into a fall guy for the eco-terrorist's most dramatic act of violent sabotage. This, I want to claim, is motivated by the realist impulse—narrating contingency is a way of transcoding volatility into a historical register, because, as the character of Ashir Al-Hasan explains to us, it describes what falls outside extrapolative models and scenarios. In much the same way that, in previous chapters, we identified volatility as a narrative problem, in the novel contingency is a reality principle, because the one thing that we can predict about climate change is that its consequences are likely to be, emphatically, unpredictable. I am claiming, then, that this historical feeling of volatility is here expressed through the semantic figure of the unpredictable and the contingent, and this occurs where the capitalist genre of temporal progress loses its grip on our sense of the historical present.

But, at the same time, if the novel is to engage in utopian negation, it must make a systemic diagnosis of the conditions for a break in the dominant form of social reproduction, rather than relay a series of singular, non-repeatable events. Which returns us to finance, which acts as both climate barometer and form of historical time.

> The housing panic chewed up and down the Eastern Seaboard, the Gulf Coast, and California. Banks had spent years off-loading risky mortgages to Fannie Mae and Freddie Mac, which now owned so many that the two were effectively insolvent, and government rescues would be necessary. Yet the crisis extended well beyond the coasts. Owners like my brother were scrambling to get rid of property as far as twenty miles inland. People were walking away from their mortgages in droves, not willing to put another red cent into a property that was uninsurable and, they assumed, doomed to be washed away by the next hard rain. The foreclosure rate had hit 1.53 percent, its highest since 2010. (Markley, 2023, p. 699)

The measures to address this are extensive and severe, but do not pass easily. Still libertarian politicians block the necessary change. But after a process of extensive negotiations, threats, and even assassinations, a series of reforms are put in place, a combination of taxation on carbon, geoengineering, carbon removal, and a National Green Infrastructure Bank. But the more radical and transformative dimension includes the establishment of a Civilian Climate Corps, a national workforce trained to provide climate relief services, and a policy of buying out all property within range of sea level rise, a total restructuring of the American shorelines to increase its resilience and to stabilise financial markets, preventing the collapse of the American economy through the devaluation of uninsurable property. Fiscal power becomes almost Promethean, remaking the very geography of the US.

Led by the federal government, finance becomes a mechanism to transform American society, not towards a greater dominance of private finance, but towards a public project of negation, rebuilding, and construction. Like *The Ministry,* this is a novel that is educational in intent, communicating and narrating alternative financial forms emerging out of the crisis of the present. Importantly, it represents finance as capable of de-commodifying zones of social life. What makes these novels utopian, I have been arguing, is their commitment to negation and refunction.

But institutions such as the Ministry, the central banks, and scientific research institutes, all have limits. Outside of these formal organisations, with definitive political projects and aims, lies the entire realm of social experience that must equally adapt to transition, but without the structure of organisational goals. Frank, not quite a major character but not a minor one either, is a sort of narrative underworker, filling in the gaps in the narrative structure that Mary's central position cannot reach, and attuned to social frequencies resonating beyond the institutions. This character system lets the novel stage moral and strategic arguments through dialogue in a different mode of address to the politics of geoengineering and high finance.

> So, if your organization represents the people who will be born after us, well, that's a heavy burden! It's a real responsibility! You have to think like them! You have to do what they would do if they were here."
> "I don't think they would countenance murder."
> "Of course they would!" he shouted, causing her to flinch. (101)

Earlier, Frank, unable to hold a job because of his PTSD, travels to India to try to join the Children of Kali, a radical group formed after the wet-bulb heatwave who have declared war on fossil fuel companies and those supporting them, such as investors, military contractors, and arms manufactures. They reject him and tell him instead to do what they do, back home, where they cannot operate. So, now in Zurich, he breaks into Mary's apartment, before fleeing from the police and going into hiding. Frank's formal function is clear. Frank is a character who is exposed to the climate volatility of the periphery, but, unlike those most at risk, travels freely into the secured enclaves of the core, thanks to his American passport. The character of Frank resolves the narratological problems of the differentiated geography of fossil capital, mediating the peripheral extremes to institutions that are typically insulated from climate effects.

Mary consults with Badim, her chief of staff, to establish a black wing of the ministry, able to operate outside of legal and institutional constraint. It turns out the black wing is already in operation. Badim hints that acts of sabotage have been perpetrated against Indian coal factories and the financial backers have been 'persuaded' to invest in solar instead. Recounted obliquely, and almost entirely through dialogue, the novel does not narrate the events but offer them in the form of discussion: is this necessary? To what extent? How far will it go? Who will get hurt?

There is nothing unusual about the representation of violence in post-oil worlds: dystopias and apocalypses are rife with it, and these are dominant modes of imagining the future of our own present. Violence in *The Ministry* cognitively maps the interconnected fossil financial system, showing a world-system premised upon atmospheric violence in which the deaths of millions does not summon the political will to change—and it speculates as to what would happen if, as a result, an equivalence was made between climate violence and conventional violence, and punishment issued accordingly.

Revolutionary violence targeted at energy infrastructure is certainly not speculative. Anticolonial struggle has consistently targeted the energy systems of colonial regimes, seeing the disruption of energy flows as the basis for revolutionary change. In fact, Malm sees the absence of violence in the contemporary climate movement as a denial of political reality. The question, he argues, is "not if sabotage from a militant wing of the climate movement will solve the crisis on its own—clearly a pipe dream—but if the disruptive commotion necessary for shaking business-as-usual out of the ruts *can come about without it*" (Malm, 2021, p. 69). Malm claims that a dialectic of militant and mainstream wings of the climate movement is necessary to force states into decarbonisation, not too dissimilar from the relation between Badim and Mary in *The Ministry*.

This, in effect, is Badim's justification.

> "So you terrorize them!"
> "Well, but terrorism means killing innocent people to scare other innocent people into doing what you want. That's what it means today, right? It isn't just boo in the dark."
> "No, I suppose not. But you scare people. You use intimidation."
> "If we had, it might be a good thing. It might be doing the needful". (114)

Several chapters later it is put more bluntly, in yet more dialogue addressed to the reader, by an anonymous member of the Children of Kali: "They killed us so we killed them" (135). Almost no information is provided, other than that they are a group formed by those who experienced the heatwave first-hand and who, like Frank, feel the need to punish those responsible. They are an organisation that works in the text's background, showing that, in Frantz Fanon's words, "that violence is in the atmosphere" (Fanon, 2001, p. 55). It permeates the fossil-fuel regime, and the violence of atmospheric volatility is experienced most by those who contribute to carbon emissions least. In retaliation, they declare a 'War for the Earth'. But they do not kill innocents. The novel displays an alertness to accusations of terrorism and pares violence down to a single function: the development of a structure of force that prevents carbon emissions. Later, once this is achieved, Badim will persuade the Children of Kali to stop, because such violence has only a temporary, transitional role. Reducing violence to this function strips away its symbolic resonances, as well as preventing the novel from transforming into *ressentiment* fantasy. By reducing it to sheer necessity, the content and meaning of violence changes in the long shadow of anthropogenic climate change: a direct equivalence is established between climate catastrophe and human violence.

The violence is gruesome work, as a member of the Children of Kali recounts after breaking into the compound of an arms manufacturer and murdering him. "Now to spread the headset photos, spread the story. The guilty need to know: even in their locked compounds, in their beds asleep at night, the Children of Kali will descend on you and kill you. There is no hiding, there is no escape" (136–7). The ministry, whose black wing are providing information about the location of these figures, also helps circulate the sabotage, to change the financial investment climate and scare investors. In contrast, the carbon coin represents physical and financial safety. The attacks continue, at greater scales, on what future historians call 'Crash Day', in which, simultaneously, attacks are made against flights, shipping, and transport. This combination creates an economic crisis, a stock market collapse, and huge damage to international trade. The Children of Kali issue a manifesto, threatening violence against any use of fossil fuel burning transport. The violence is imagined as a response to a fundamental imbalance of power that insulates the carbon-emitting industrial nations from the political claims of those at the coalface of a warming world. It is still mediated through finance, whose volatility transmits direct action into contagious fear and political change.

Speculative military technology is commonplace in science fiction, and *The Ministry* is no exception. But rather than engage in the technological sublime of powerful weaponry, it speculates on what force could disable the petroleum-fuelled military powers that dominated the twentieth and twenty-first century. Petroleum and nuclear power fundamentally changed warfare, cheapening the means of destruction, fuelling armature, vehicles, artillery, and air forces, ending the reliance on large numbers of citizen-soldiers, and replacing them with a technologically advanced, professional militaries. By changing armies from mass proletarian forces to small, professional ones, this neutralised their revolutionary potential, and entrenched fossil capitalist states from threats within and without.

This is perhaps one of the great strategic difficulties posed by the secured and militarised landscapes of fossil capital. The problem is shown when an assassination attempt is made against Mary, forcing her to move to a secret military base, in the Alps. She looks upon the fighter jets of our own era, "obviously outdated and old-fashioned, like weapons from the set of a James Bond movie", useless in a newer kind of warfare, which was "invisible and online for the most part, but also including the possibility of drones, and of fast targeted missiles" (313).

The new military technology is called a pebble-mob missile, an extremely fast, undetectable drone that cannot be stopped by conventional missile defence or tracked on radar, and can target individuals with extreme precision.

> Aircraft carriers? Sunk. Bombers? Blown out of the sky. An oil tanker, boom, sunk in ten minutes. One of America's eight hundred military bases around the world, shattered. Death and chaos, and no one findable to blame. (347)

They might "even be a force for good, because now war was rendered impossible. It was mutual assured destruction, not of civilian populations, but of war machinery" (348). The Swiss bankers Mary meets are scared because the structures of force developed in the petroleum era are nullified and the integration of warfare and the industrial system disabled. Banks and offshore havens are under financial attack and physical threat. Mary uses this as an opportunity to persuade them into backing the carbon coin: the only way, she claims, to preserve them.

Suddenly, the US Navy, the enforcer of fossil capital's ocean routes, is useless. The novel suggests, in ways that echo Markley's Civilian Climate Corps, coastal relief and other climate resilience work. This would mean an energy transition in the US Navy, no longer reliant on the logistical chains that connect aircraft carriers and fighters to a fuel source, and effectively ending American imperialism in the world-ocean. Although the novel does not mention it, without the protection provided to fossil capital's sea lanes, and under extreme threat of sabotage, the financial value of such routes is likely to collapse. It is difficult to think of a new intercontinental drone as utopian, but under its shadow is found the imperative to imagine alternative political arrangements and to refunction the wasted military resources and labour. The novel encourages such speculations. It foregrounds the possibility for new kinds of relationships that had previously been impossible under the sway of petroleum-fuelled militarism.

But what distinguishes *The Ministry* as a transitional utopia is how the novum is introduced, its strange novelty brought before the reader through certain focalising characters who are instruments that scan this new reality and mediate it to the reader, as if in conversation.

> The news often disturbed him. Heat waves, terrorist attacks [...] And to Frank it seemed different than it had when he was a child, when terrorists were universally abhorred. Now it felt different. Many attacks now were on carbon burners, especially those rich enough to burn it conspicuously. Car races and private jets. Yachts and container ships. So now the terrorists involved were perhaps saboteurs, or even resistance warriors, fighting for the Earth itself. Gaia's Shock Troops, Children of Kali, Defenders of

> Mother Earth, Earth First, and so on. People read about their violent acts and the frequent resulting deaths, and shrugged. What did people expect? Who owned private jets anymore? (368)

Between the conventional realist style of free indirect speech and Frank as a registering device, the reader is invited to assess these events as if they are as real as geoengineering and financial instruments, without the distorting weight of an authorial voice shaping our judgement.

Meanwhile, Frank spends years evading the police, while volunteering at a refugee aid centre: serving meals, cleaning, washing up: the sort of tasks that are missed in the ministry's boardrooms. This simple, necessary work connects him to the victims of climate-related social upheaval, and he is allowed to continue it even after he is arrested and imprisoned for breaking into Mary's apartment, years before. He returns to the aid centre because "he could work, put his shoulder to the wheel, help turn the world" (198). Away from the airy abstractions of economics and finance, the strategies and tactics of revolutionary change, Mary's meetings and negotiations, rousing speeches and thinly-veiled threats, Frank's struggle to cope with guilt is the emotional heart of the novel. He finds the civic hall in which free dinners are distributed "simple and calming, and there was time to sit or kneel by some of their guests and ask how they were doing, without getting involved in their lives beyond that" (199). He meets others, like himself, who have suffered directly from climate change, situations of violence, war, and terror; "all had made desperate journeys to get here, sleeping on the ground, hungry. Now they were in a new place where possibly new things could happen, different things, good things" (368).

These narrative moments are temporary pauses within transitional spaces. Refugee aid centres are, ideally if not always in reality, places of immediate relief from terror, and a point of connection between one life and another. But, as in the real European refugee crisis, they are also spaces of stasis and internment, and sites of nationalist rage. In one chapter, the refugees are violently attacked by far-right thugs. But they are also, in the novel, spaces of care and civic community. Focalised through Frank, whose need for meaningful activity is matched by the difficulties he faces connecting with others, there remains a curious distancing effect which gives everything a strange clarity, as if the reader is caught somewhere between participant and observer. These spaces, so emblematic of the modern world-system, seem, in the eyes of Frank, to contain two different worlds: the promise of an alternative future and the violent exclusion of the present.

Frank observes and feels change around him, without necessarily acclimatising to the transition, as if permanently arrested somewhere near the 2024 heatwave. This means that he is a visitor to a different society, not through a voyage in time or space, as in the classical utopia, or between two different worlds, as in the critical utopia. He simply continues to exist, able to help turn the world but unable to adapt to it, while his failures and minor successes become an instrument through which change is detected, a stable point against which history can be seen to move. This contrasts strongly with Mary's own personal and political development, an agent of transition; and with Badim, who must bear responsibility for the violence and death caused by the clandestine operations he helped direct. But these figures all disappear before any new world is complete. This itself becomes a caution for utopian thinking. It does not impose theories on what a future consciousness might look like, and its narrative energy should rather be invested in the desire to change the present—a ministry *for*, not *of*, the future.

In the novel, at the 58th COP meeting in 2053, the world-system is well underway to full decarbonisation, with most energy generated cleanly, while the various problems of energy storage and the perennial worry of energy flow are channelled into local and regional necessities, such as desalination, carbon capture, and water pumping. Taking place over two days, the COP Meeting dedicates the first to summarising successes, the second to outstanding problems, a convenient formal device for a retrospective on our energy present as a future history, and a prospective view of what might problems remain, generations later. The latter include Arctic ice, nuclear weapons, poverty, American imperialism, plastics and waste, gender inequality, water supplies, ocean health, and so on (483).

Around this time, Frank discovers he has a terminal illness and is moved into palliative care. Mary visits him, which allows her to reflect on the changes since their first meeting back in 2025, as well as their relationship; his feverish dreams and confused questions force her to reflect on her own death, which "obtruded as if out of another dimension" (486). Frank's illness begins to take the shape of a narrative closure, as both reflect on what will happen after not only his but her death, too.

> Another time he woke and stared at her, then knew her, and where he was. He said quietly, "I'll be sorry not to see what happens next. It sounds like things are getting interesting."
> "I think so. But, you know. No one will live long enough to see an end to it."
> "More trouble coming?"
> "For sure." She looked at her in-box; she would have to scroll down for a couple of minutes to get to the bottom of it. "Something this big is going to go on for years and years."
> "Centuries." (494)

Mary retires soon after, after thirty years running the ministry. A lifetime of work, but a lifetime is not long enough to observe the long transition from petroculture to whatever comes next. The novel ends with Mary contemplating

> That there is no other home for us than here [...] That the only catastrophe that can't be undone is extinction. That we can make a good place. That people can take their fate in their hands [...] we will keep going, we will keep going, because there is no such thing as fate. Because we never really come to the end. (563)

It turns out that Mary and Frank are themselves transitional figures: her retirement, and his death, signal the closure of the narrative. Both put their shoulders to the world to make "a good place", but one they will never see—an ongoing, long transition that is the deliberate creation of historical difference.

Scattered among this narrative are dozens of shorter chapters that stage abstract debates on political economy, science, and technological determinism, describe social movements and economic systems—such as the Paris Commune *redux* and the farmers who integrate carbon sequestration into their agricultural rotation—and include riddles, chronicles, and interviews. Bursting with ideas and concepts, *The Ministry* is a vast utopian warehouse to wander through and peruse. But this is not just a repository of information. The formal combination of such material establishes vital connections across a wide range of activities that, when seen through the lens of the novel, suddenly come into view as part of a shared, although weakly articulated, tradition. This is a strong vision of a transitional utopia which also encompasses within it many forms of transition that bloom around us, if only we can be made to look. The strength of its representation lies in how it generates recognisable correspondences across ideas, institutions, and organisations. *The Ministry* encourages us to grasp them as transitional forms, of great significance until, used and worn, they can be laid aside as testament to the strangeness of that moment of planetary history called the present.

If *The Ministry* is synthetic and totalising, then *The Deluge* is a messier composition, more closely concerned with relationality, and about the impediments of contingent historical events to disrupt any smooth transition to a society beyond fossil fuels. Both are composite forms, seeking and testing articulations between divergent social forces. I have argued that the transitional utopia describes how the transition towards a better world is actively created and lived in the present. So, I want to propose that the vocation of this genre is to demonstrate our capacity, individually and collectively, to build transitional forms. In other words, the object of this genre is the economic forms that inherently bear within them their own abolition. That being said, the transitional utopia is not a blueprint for a future society. Instead, it restores to the problem of transition the historical sense that energy is not something passively received, but collectively chosen, made, and lived. It is a literary form concerned with probing the conceptual and affective dimensions of energy democracy, which reframes energy systems as sites of political, economic, and cultural contestation, and insists that energy systems are constitutive of wider social patterns. From this perspective, energy transition is not a question of substituting one input for another, but a consideration of how transitions proceed. Neither novel wishes to commit to a positive vision, a future blueprint; but neither is satisfied with the given, whose givenness is a powerfully sustained fiction. So, they communicate this not through direct representation, but a kind of feeling and thinking about the future I understand to be an investment in transition, in change. In these novels, where finance is both symptom and mechanism, object of critique and narrative infrastructure, this is answered by the potential capacity of financial institutions to recalibrate ownership and property at a systemic scale. If this feels unsatisfactory compared to the genre's predecessors, whose utopias were more complete and revolutionising, it is at least a way of feeling dissatisfaction as an emergent historical sense—a utopian feeling indeed.

References

Best, B. (2024). *The Automatic Fetish: The Law of Value in Marx's Capital*. Verso Books.

Buck, H. J. (2019). *After Geoengineering: Climate Tragedy, Repair, and Restoration*. Verso Books.

Canavan, G. (2020, October 27). *Of Course They Would: On Kim Stanley Robinson's "The Ministry for the Future"*. Los Angeles Review of Books. Retrieved from https://lareviewofbooks.org/article/of-course-they-would-on-kim-stanley-robinsons-the-ministry-for-the-future

Charbonnier, P. (2021). *Affluence and Freedom: An Environmental History of Political Ideas*. John Wiley & Sons.

Engels, F. (1880). *Socialism: Utopian and Scientific*. Retrieved from https://www.marxists.org/archive/marx/works/1880/soc-utop/

Fanon, F. (2001). *The Wretched of the Earth* (C. Farrington, Trans.; 1st edition). Penguin Classics.

Galvin, A. (2020, September 23). The Realism of Our Times: Kim Stanley Robinson on How Science Fiction Works. *Public Books*. Retrieved from https://www.publicbooks.org/the-realism-of-our-times-kim-stanley-robinson-on-how-science-fiction-works/

Harootunian, H. (2007). Remembering the Historical Present. *Critical Inquiry*. https://doi.org/10.1086/513523

Jameson, F. (2005). *Archaeologies of the Future*. Verso.

Kornbluh, A. (2019). *The Order of Forms*. Chicago University Press.

Krippner, G. R. (2005). The Financialization of the American Economy. *Socio-Economic Review, 3*(2), 173–208. https://doi.org/10.1093/SER/mwi008

Lenin, V. (1917). *Can the Bolsheviks Retain State Power?* Marxists.Org. Retrieved from https://www.marxists.org/archive/lenin/works/1917/oct/01.htm

Lukacs, G. (1991). *Writer and Critic* (A. Kahn, Ed.; A. Kahn, Trans.). The Merlin Press Ltd.

Malm, A. (2020a). *Corona*. War Communism in the Twenty-First Century. Verso Books.

Malm, A. (2020b). *When Does the Fightback Begin?* Verso. Retrieved from https://www.versobooks.com/en-gb/blogs/news/5061-when-does-the-fightback-begin

Malm, A. (2021). *How to Blow Up a Pipeline: Learning to Fight in a World on Fire (1st edition)*. Verso.

Markley, S. (2023). *The Deluge*. Simon & Schuster.

Marx, K. (1992). *Capital: A Critique of Political Economy, Volume 3*. Penguin Classics.

McKibben, B. (2020). *It's Not Science Fiction*. The New York Review of Books. Retrieved from https://www.nybooks.com/articles/2020/12/17/kim-stanley-robinson-not-science-fiction/

Riles, A. (2018). *Financial Citizenship: Experts, Publics, and the Politics of Central Banking* (Illustrated edition). Cornell Global Perspectives.

Robins, N. (2021). *Coming Back from a Time of Illness: How Finance can Learn from Climate Change Fiction*. Grantham Research Institute on Climate Change and the Environment. Retrieved from https://www.lse.ac.uk/granthaminstitute/news/coming-back-from-a-time-of-illness-how-finance-can-learn-from-climate-change-fiction/

Robinson, K. S. (2021). *The Ministry for the Future*. Orbit.

Suvin, D. (2016). *Metamorphoses of Science Fiction* (G. Canavan, Ed.). Peter Lang UK. Retrieved from https://www.peterlang.com/view/title/36664

Thompson, H. (2018). *Oil and the Western Economic Crisis* (Softcover reprint of the original 1st ed. 2017 edition). Palgrave Macmillan.

Tooze, A. (2018). *Crashed: How a Decade of Financial Crisis Changed the World*. Viking Pr.

Vint, S. (2018). Currencies of Social Organisation: The Future of Money. In W. Davies (Ed.), *Economic Science Fictions*. Goldsmiths Press.

CHAPTER 8

Coda: Energy Futures

In Thomas Pynchon's financial thriller, *Bleeding Edge* (2013), a shady investor describes a new infrastructural mediation of global warming and finance.

> More and more servers together in the same place putting out levels of heat that quickly become problematic unless you spend the budget on A/C. Thing to do," Ice proclaims, "is to go north, set up server farms where heat dissipation won't be so much of a problem, take your power from renewables like hydro or sunlight, use surplus heat to help sustain whatever communities grow up around the data centers. Domed communities across the Arctic tundra [...] but the future is out there on the permafrost, a new geopolitical imperative—gain control of the supply of cold as a natural resource of incomputable worth, with global warming, even more crucial... (Pynchon, 2013)

What this character recognises is the centrality of the material and the thermodynamic to the future of finance. The energy fantasy that this character articulates is a closed loop between energy source, infrastructure, financial data, and the 'surplus heat' necessary to sustain human communities; a kind of delirium in which money becomes more money, energy becomes finance, autonomous and insulated with no externality. In reality, no one is setting up data centres on the hydrological frontier

H. Pitt Scott, *Financial Petroleum Cultures*, Palgrave Studies in Literature, Culture and Economics,
https://doi.org/10.1007/978-3-031-99661-0_8

of a warming climate. Instead, this critical infrastructure is maintained by computer room air conditioning powered by electrical energy. Cold is supplied by an infrastructure that remains wedded to thermal combustion but might ultimately be replaced by renewable energy. But perhaps the point to be taken from this dream is that the materiality of finance has come to matter in an entirely new way under the pressure of its infrastructuralisation. Where finance might once have appeared to abstract wealth from nature—once described by Raymond Williams as a 'world made out of paper and money'—it has been sunk much more deeply into it.

Since the time that I began this work, a major shift has occurred in the conceptualisation of the financial economy in relation to the climate and to energy. At the 2021 United Nations Climate Change Conference (COP26), hosted in Glasgow in the middle of the covid-19 pandemic crisis, finance was a major focus. Alongside securing net zero, protecting natural habits, and establishing international governance, the conference aimed to map how to 'Mobilise Finance': "To achieve our climate goals, every company, every financial firm, every bank, insurer and investor will need to change" (Sharma, 2021, p. 22), the COP26 President, Alok Sharma, announced. Major financial institutions have become cognisant of the need to transform (at least in appearance). For the participants at COP26, finance was given an agency within a narrative about how an energy transition will play out: currently an impediment, but, with the right accounting practices and social values, ultimately an economic enabler. While the transition theorists of the 1970s thought that the market would be sufficient to make a transition from cheap exhaustible to expensive unlimited energy, there is now a recognition that finance must be helped, even if there is little questioning of the need for private finance to be the primary driver. There is a sense of urgency, and the scale of the task, but also a kind of optimism of the future tense that I take to be the narrative function of finance in an energy transition.

What slips out of view in this story is the performative claim that holds a financial future in place. If it turns out to be true, much will change, and much will stay the same. Fossil fuels will recede in importance, replaced by renewables and a new economic geography of solar, wind, and nuclear production and infrastructure. But the kinds of property relations that sustain the financial dominance of infrastructures will continue, making transition in the image of a carbon economy that has never been subject to democratic control (Diamanti & Szeman, 2020, p. 149).

The argument of this book has been guided by Etienne Balibar's description of transition as a rupture in the economic form of a society *and* a social structure with its own logic. "The forms of transition", he writes, "are in fact necessarily modes of production in themselves" (Balibar et al., 2016, p. 473). They must be directional and self-sustaining, otherwise they would not be able to transform a mode of life. I have been tracking the forces that are seeking to become the regnant logic of transition, historicising its ideological dimension through cultural representations. My contribution to the critical studies of energy, ecology, and finance, has been to specify the determination of energy by this strangely elusive value-form at the level of discourse, narrative, and representation.

In much of the energy and environmental humanities, energy is richly investigated in its material, infrastructural, ecological, and thermodynamic dimensions. In this book, I have attempted to relocate the cultural position of energy to sites of financial mediation; to identify technologies that produce a discursive, visual, and narrative form of energy; and that make sense of energy's sensuous forms through representational abstractions. My aim has been to develop a cognitive map of energy transition through an archive that is attempting to make sense of the determination of energy by finance, and finance by energy. By reading reflexively between narrative and infrastructure, I have argued for the importance of financial representations to the cultural and economic modes of petroleum, and of the capacity of financial technologies, from petrodollars to derivatives, to frame and orient a social being saturated in petroleum. I have also been attentive to the forms and feelings of historicity in financial petroculture, as volatility becomes an object of, and force destabilising, narrative. This has been tracked across a moment of disjunction, as a financial petroculture recomposes itself in, and through the knowledge of, the ecological crisis.

Despite the simple graphs of energy forecasters, the transition to a decarbonised world will not be smooth and linear. In early 2025, bp announced its intention to divest from Lightsource, the renewable energy subsidiary that was the focus of chapter six. Subject to a stricter financial environment in an economic downturn and needing to signal to its shareholders its capacity to grow, the company that positioned itself as transitioning from oil to energy undercut its own narrative. "Our optimism for a fast transition was misplaced and we went too far, too fast", wrote the new chief executive. "Oil and gas will be needed for decades to come" (Moore & Wilson, 2025). Abstracted from the messy reality of transition targets, carbon emissions, and the petrocultural forms of modern life, oil and gas are rewritten as safe financial assets in energy futures intended to reassurance investors. This is the narrative form of financial abstraction, written as value into a volatile future cascading into ecological crisis.

These reversals and delays are to be expected when the narrative of energy transition is constantly positioned as a market problem of weathering volatility. Even as narratives change, the financial imperatives determining the limits of what is possible remain. Despite limits, possibilities abound. In 2023 Larry Fink, CEO of the world's largest asset manager BlackRock, pioneered a strategic shift away from ESG (Environmental, Social, Governance) investing towards a more expansive 'transition investing' framework, which involves tracking the massive reallocation of capital necessary to rewire energy systems, from sustainable energy to lithium mining. This leviathan of finance has been broadcasting a simple message: the demand for clean energy is an opportunity to make money. In his 2024 'Annual Chairman's Letter to Investors', he promises investors that there "will be better opportunities for our clients to invest in the infrastructure that keeps our lights on, planes flying, trains moving, and our cell service at the maximum number of bars" (Fink, 2024). The financial future is infrastructure indeed.

References

Balibar, É., Althusser, L., Establet, R., Macherey, P., & Rancière, J. (2016). *Reading Capital: The Complete Edition* (Unabridged Edition). Verso Books.

Diamanti, J., & Szeman, I. (2020). Nine Principles for a Critical Theory of Energy. In *Polygraph: An International Journal of Culture & Politics* (pp. 137–159). Duke University Press.

Fink, L. (2024). *Larry Fink's 2024 Annual Chairman's Letter to Investors*. BlackRock. Retrieved from https://www.blackrock.com/corporate/investor-relations/larry-fink-annual-chairmans-letter

Moore, M., & Wilson, T. (2025, February 26). BP pivots back to oil and gas after 'misplaced' faith in green energy. *Financial Times*. Retrieved from https://www.ft.com/content/8bcf131f-c820-493f-8ea6-6a35440facd3

Pynchon, T. (2013). *Bleeding Edge*. Penguin Press.

Sharma, A. (2021). *COP26 EXPLAINED*. UN Climate Change Conference. Retrieved from https://webarchive.nationalarchives.gov.uk/ukgwa/20230401054904/https://ukcop26.org/wp-content/uploads/2021/07/COP26-Explained.pdf

Index

H. Pitt Scott, *Financial Petroleum Cultures*, Palgrave Studies in Literature, Culture and Economics,
https://doi.org/10.1007/978-3-031-99661-0

The manufacturer's authorised representative in the EU is Springer Nature Customer Service Centre GmbH, Europaplatz 3, 69115 Heidelberg, Germany. If you have any concerns regarding our products, please contact ProductSafety@springernature.com

Printed and bound by CPI Group (UK) Ltd, Croydon, CR0 4YY

30/09/2026

02225591-0002